Current Issues in
Islamic Banking
and Finance
Resilience and Stability in the Present System

Current Issues in Islami☾ Banking and Finance

Resilience and Stability in the Present System

Editor

Angelo M Venardos

Heritage Trust Group, Singapore

 **World Scientific**

NEW JERSEY · LONDON · SINGAPORE · BEIJING · SHANGHAI · HONG KONG · TAIPEI · CHENNAI

Published by

World Scientific Publishing Co. Pte. Ltd.
5 Toh Tuck Link, Singapore 596224
USA office: 27 Warren Street, Suite 401-402, Hackensack, NJ 07601
UK office: 57 Shelton Street, Covent Garden, London WC2H 9HE

Library of Congress Cataloging-in-Publication Data
Current issues in Islamic banking and finance : resilience and stability in the present system / edited
by Angelo M. Venardos.
   p. cm.
   ISBN-13: 978-981-283-392-1
   ISBN-10: 981-283-392-7
   1. Banks and banking--Islamic countries. 2. Banks and banking--Religious aspects--Islam.
3. Banking law (Islamic law) 4. Finance--Islamic countries. 5. Finance--Religious aspects--Islam.
6. Finance (Islamic law) I. Venardos, Angelo M.
   HG3368.A6C87 2010
   332.10917'67--dc22

                               2009052120

British Library Cataloguing-in-Publication Data
A catalogue record for this book is available from the British Library.

Editor: Juliet Lee Ley Chin

Typeset by Stallion Press
Email: enquiries@stallionpress.com

Printed in Singapore.

DISCLAIMER

The views and opinions expressed in this whole book are the authors' and do not necessarily represent those of their affiliations.

FOREWORD

Southeast Asia is the powerhouse of skills and innovation in Islamic finance as the GCC is the pool of liquidity. Recently, there have been many issues of concern in the sector, with some recalled certifications and Shariah incompatibility concerns. The sector is young and growing rapidly, thereby demanding close monitoring to enable the establishment of a robust and sustainable alternative to conventional finance.

This is a timely book as it addresses the issues facing the momentum that Islamic finance has taken in the world. The sub-prime crisis and the credit crunch have focused considerable attention on the sector: its viability and sustainability. The challenges are many and not insurmountable. The market place is constantly evolving and expanding beyond the Muslim clientele and regions. The expected growth of the Islamic finance sector worldwide is estimated at about 15% by the year 2020, but if it exceeds that it should come as no surprise.

Standardisation and harmonisation are issues raised consistently at many fora and being addressed and dealt with by many of the active members and institutions involved in the Islamic finance sector. It takes time but the start has been made and many intelligent minds have committed to establishing this means of finance.

Dr. Angelo Venardos has provided a valuable service in the publication of this book with contributions from some of the legends in the Islamic finance industry who have considerable knowledge of their subject and are active practitioners. The leading lawyers, bankers, regulators, and accountants in the sector are among the contributors and some of them are personal friends. They are talking the talk and walking the walk on a daily basis and are at the cutting edge of development in the industry. There is not much available in the form of literature on the current issues in the sector and this is a fine addition that will prove useful to academics, practitioners, students, and others who would be interested in this sector — where it has been, where it is, and where it is going. All extremely relevant.

Majid Dawood
CEO, Yasaar Limited
Dubai, UAE

CONTENTS

RESILIENCE AND STABILITY: SOCIOECONOMIC RESPONSE IN SOUTHEAST ASIA

Angelo M. Venardos

Islamic Banking and Finance (IB&F) is recognised by both Muslims and non-Muslims as an ethical alternative, protecting against the worst excesses of leverage whilst reinstating values, such as trust, which have been lost in conventional finance. Figures cited show that Islamic finance is growing in popularity as a result of the current crisis and there is scope for it to move into the financial mainstream with the sector estimated to reach US$4,000 billion in the next 5 years.

However, the first defaults of Sukuk are set to expose the vulnerabilities of Islamic finance, with most investors expected to have no better legal redress than conventional bondholders as underlying assets have not been truly transferred to them.

Dr. Zeti Akhtar Aziz, the Governor of Bank Negara Malaysia, has drawn attention to the issue of the resilience of IB&F in confronting the financial crisis. The resilience of IB&F can be tested only if it is exposed to the current turmoil in the financial markets. Dr. Zeti has

1

stated that IB&F had proven to be resilient during the Asian financial crisis. These statements drew attention to the issue that whilst
IB&F was able to withstand the Asian crisis, the Asian crisis was only
confined to a certain region and, hence, the resilience of IB&F
remained to be tested in the light of the present crisis, which is of a
greater magnitude and wider geographical scope.[1] Undoubtedly,
compared to the Asian crisis, the magnitude and scope of the current financial crisis is substantially greater owing to the processes of
financial globalisation and liberalisation which have reinforced the
global inter-linkages across the financial markets. Given that the
Islamic financial system has evolved to become part of the global
financial system, it is therefore timely and appropriate to deliberate
the issues relating to the question: Is the Islamic financial system
truly strong enough to weather the current economic and financial
crisis?

The current financial crisis essentially emanated from the operations of the originate-to-distribute business model, in which large
international banks originated loans (or underwrote loans originated by brokers) in the US sub-prime mortgage market, and then
securitised the loans thus taking the credit exposure off their
balance sheets. In contrast to conventional finance, in Islamic
finance, lending on the basis of interest is prohibited by the
Shariah. The Islamic financial system is driven by trade and
production and is intimately linked to the real sector ('Main Street'
and not 'Wall Street'). Islamic banks do not act as pure lenders; they
have to be directly involved in trade and investment operations and
assume direct ownership of real assets. This activity pre-empts un-
backed expansion of credit and restricts speculation. Although
Islamic banks have debt receivables on their balance sheets arising
from credit sale transactions, they cannot securitise and offload
these debt receivables, as the majority of Shariah scholars prohibit

---

[1] Zeti, Dr. Akhtar Aziz, Governor, Bank Negara, Malaysia at IFSB and IIFC Conference,
KL, November 2008.

the trading of debt except at par value. Even in the Malaysian case, where debt receivables are currently allowed to be securitised and traded, the securitisation process is limited to only a single-tier transaction. Shariah also prevents Islamic banks from purchasing instruments that carry debt-based credit risks.[2]

In addition, Shariah prohibits selling or leasing something which one does not own, and hence excludes the practice of speculative short selling from the Islamic financial system. In essence, the IB&F system derives its fundamental strength from the Shariah principles, which assure discipline and responsibility in financial activities that are necessary requirements for financial stability.

However, even with the strong fundamental Shariah underpinnings, the Islamic financial system is not immune to risks and can be susceptible to financial crises due to a number of reasons. First, as Islamic finance is closely linked to the real sector, unexpected adverse developments in the real sector may adversely affect the business activities and performance of Islamic banks in the absence of robust and effective risk management practices. Risks in the real sector have been declining consistently in the past decades, as shown by recent studies, while risks in the financial sector have been consistently increasing.[3] This suggests that financial institutions face less risks and instability than those that are not. Nevertheless real economic shocks of large magnitude may create systemic risks in the Islamic financial sector.

Second, Islamic banks may be influenced to pursue aggressive speculative investment strategies with higher risk and higher expected returns, particularly during economic upturns, without a concomitant adherence to fundamental and sound risk management standards. A key cause of the current crisis was the fundamental combination of aggressive lending and inadequate

---

[2] Krichene, N. and Mirakhor, A. *Resilience and Stability of the Islamic Financial System — An Overview*, p. 47.
[3] Ibid.

risk management leading to a breakdown in confidence between counterparties.

These basic considerations confirmed the need for rigorous and consistently applied global standards of prudent risk management and other supporting infrastructure for safeguarding financial stability in the Islamic financial system. To date, the Islamic Financial Services Board (IFSB) has issued a whole spectrum of prudential and supervisory standards — covering risk management, capital adequacy, corporate governance, and transparency and market discipline — which together constitute the equivalent of Basel II in IB&F. These standards take into account international prudential standards across the banking, investment and securities market sectors and simultaneously cater effectively for the specificities of Islamic financial business, its risks and Shariah compliance.

Examples of these safeguards of the Islamic financial business model include the following: (a) the universal banking model that integrates commercial banking, investment banking and asset management activities that are carried out without clear and established legal, financial or administrative separation; (b) the transformation of risks in Islamic financial instruments; (c) direct investment in real estate activities for the objective of financing real economic activities, rather than speculative trading; and (d) the management of investment accounts which contractually share in the overall risks of assets funded by these accounts and managed by the bank. The management of investment account holders' funds also raises specific governance, transparency, depositor protection and investor protection issues, which have been addressed in the standards. The IFSB standards also deal with the unique operational risk aspects of Islamic banks arising from Shariah non-compliance risk and fiduciary risk towards current account and investment account holders, which may expose Islamic banks to reputation risk and thus adversely affect their market position, profitability, solvency and liquidity.[4]

---

[4] Op. cit. in 1.

In October 2008, the IFSB Council approved the issuance of two additional standards, one on the governance of Islamic investment funds and the other on capital adequacy standards for Sukuk securitisations and real estate investments. In Sukuk structures, the discipline that Islam introduces theoretically prevents events such as the current credit crunch. For example, some of the Shariah rules and principles to be observed include: (a) the asset which is being sold or leased must be real, and not notional; (b) the seller must own and possess the goods being sold or leased; and (c) the transaction must be a genuine trade transaction with full intention of giving and taking delivery. The current credit crunch revealed that significant failures in risk management have been inherent in the way the originate-to-distribute business model has been implemented. The capital adequacy standard issued by the IFSB for Sukuk securitisations sets out different minimum capital adequacy requirements to address the specificities of risks underlying the different Sukuk structures. The standard also deals with issues surrounding the securitisation process, in particular as regards compliance with Shariah rules and principles. For example, Islamic asset-backed securities (ABS) must involve effective legal or beneficial transfer of ownership rights to the underlying assets, in virtue of which the Sukuk holders have an effective right of recourse to the assets in case of default. This is in contrast to conventional finance, where bond holders have the right to collateral over such assets, but no ownership rights.[5]

Another criterion which led to the current turmoil, according to Professor Karim, the Secretary-General of the IFSB was the surge in the global demand for US sub-prime mortgage debt, fed by unrealistically positive rating designations by the credit agencies. In the context of IB&F, the IFSB has issued a Guidance Note in Connection with the Capital Adequacy Standard.[6]

---

[5] Karim, Professor Rifaat Ahmed Abdel, Enhancing the resilience and stability of the Islamic financial system, *IFSB and IIFC Conference KL*, November 2008.
[6] Ibid.

Recognition of Ratings by External Credit Assessment Institutions (ECAI) on Shariah-compliant financial instruments, which is intended to assist supervisory authorities in recognising external rating agencies as being competent for the purpose of allocating risk weighting to the assets held by the institutions offering Islamic financial services (IIFS). The Guidance Note emphasised the need to acknowledge Shariah-compliant financing assets as a distinct set of asset classes, for which ECAIs should develop a dedicated rating methodology. This should contribute to ensuring that the rating of Islamic financial instruments would realistically reflect the specific features and risks of such instruments in a manner that would assist investors more appropriately to apply necessary market discipline.

Apart from the standards that have been mentioned above, work was also in progress for the preparation of 4 new standards, namely, on Corporate Governance for Takaful (Islamic insurance) Undertakings, the Solvency of Takaful Operations, Conduct of Business and Shariah Governance. The standard currently being developed by the IFSB on the conduct of business of institutions in IB&F addresses issues with respect to their treatment of clients, namely, customers, policyholders and investors. For these institutions, the code of ethical business conduct is derived from the principles of the Shariah. The observance of principles of good business conduct by Islamic institutions is both a religious obligation and in some cases, for example Islamic securitisation, a requirement in order for the transaction to be valid or for a contract to be enforceable. Indeed, the ethical crisis, which lies at the heart of the present crisis in the conventional financial system, involves issues of bad faith, corruption, concerns of fairness and lack of confidence.[7]

The IFSB was also developing a standard on the *Guiding Principles on* Shariah *Governance*, which complements the other IFSB

---

[7] Akerlof, G. A. and Shriller, R. J., *Animal Spirits — How Human Psychology Drives the Economy and Why It Matters for Global Capitalism*, Princeton University Press, NJ, 2009.

prudential standards. The IFSB standard on Shariah Governance outlines the necessary structures and procedures that should be put in place for effective Shariah-compliance on both an *ex ante* and an *ex post* basis. This standard is crucial, as non-compliance with Shariah principles would erode confidence in IB&F and undermine the stability of IB&F. In addition, in order for the Shariah injunctions to function effectively as an in-built mechanism that promotes financial stability in the Islamic financial system, the Shariah principles must be upheld in their true essence.

Given that IB&F currently operates in a global environment that in most cases caters for conventional financial practices, financial innovation in Islamic finance at times involves emulating conventional financing techniques and products, for example multiple SPVs. This may expose IB&F to similar destabilising forces inherent in the conventional financial system. In this regard, the work of the IFSB is intended to create an enabling environment for Islamic financial practices to comply with Shariah principles in economic substance and not just in a legal form.

Further, the current financial turmoil has highlighted the significant and unexpected tensions in the major (uncollateralised) interbank money markets. Situations of massive illiquidity occurred in certain financial market segments such as those for complex structured products. The turmoil also underlined the importance of effective liquidity risk management for cross-border and foreign currency operations, owing to the increasing integration of financial markets and cross-border flows.[8] The development of a robust systemic liquidity management infrastructure for the IFSI is indeed an area that needs to be accorded priority. The IFSB has issued a *Technical Note on Issues in Strengthening Liquidity Management of Institutions Offering Islamic Financial Services*, which outlines a

---

[8] 'Weaknesses revealed by the market turmoil: Where do we go from here?' Keynote address by Mr. Malcolm D. Knight, General Manager of the BIS, at the Chatham House event: 'The new financial frontiers', London, 29 April 2008.

comprehensive strategy for developing Shariah-compliant and tradable money market instruments and Islamic money markets, so as to ensure effective monetary management and foster financial stability in IB&F. The implementation of the above strategy involves extensive work and significant commitment at both national and international levels of the Islamic banking global community of all stakeholders.

Another equally important characteristic of the global financial system exposed by the sub-prime crisis is the high correlation and interconnectivity between the banking, insurance, investment and securities market sectors, where vulnerability in the securities market sector had a contagion effect on the banking and insurance sectors and as a result posed a threat to global financial stability. In essence, the turmoil accentuated the fact that enhancing the resilience of financial institutions and markets cuts across the financial sectors and even transcended national borders and hence required close cooperation among policymakers and financial supervisors with different mandates and in different jurisdictions. In the context of IB&F, the IFSB has emphasised the need for the adoption of a cross-sectoral approach to the regulation and supervision of IB&F that encompasses, in particular, the banking sector and the investment and securities market sector, and possibly also the regulation of non-financial activities of financial conglomerates. The design of the IFSB standards for IB&F takes into account the standards on banking issued by the Basel Committee, the standards issued by the IOSCO for the investment and securities market sector and the recommendations of the Joint Forum for financial conglomerates before adapting these standards to address the specificities of IB&F. For example, in designing the disclosure regime for IB&F, the IFSB drew on the disclosure standards for collective investment schemes — developed in accordance with IOSCO criteria — to complement the risk disclosures in IB&F in support of banking supervision as envisaged in Pillars 2 and 3 of Basel II.

The current 'subprime' period of major global financial distress has also revealed, among other things, significant weaknesses in risk management, as highlighted in the "Final Report of the IIF Committee on Market Best Practices: Principles of Conduct and Best Practice Recommendations — Financial Services Industry Response to the Market Turmoil of 2007–2008", issued by the International Institute of Finance. The banking and financial crises in the past 2 decades have also been triggered by fundamental inadequacies in risk management by financial institutions, especially in times of financial innovation.[9]

Given that IB&F is rapidly expanding globally with an increasing number of countries aspiring to become international Islamic financial centres, coupled with the fact that IB&F is not immune to risks, the Secretary-General of the IFSB believes that it is of the utmost importance to ensure that all the IFSB standards are promptly and properly implemented and effectively enforced in jurisdictions, where Islamic financial services are being offered. This would have the great benefit of enhancing the understanding by the stakeholders of IB&F, of the idiocentricities of Islamic financial business and its risks, thus strengthening their ability to manage these risks effectively in order to achieve the desired outcome of financial stability in IB&F.

The Malaysian Response

In response to this challenge, Malaysia, as a 'first to market mover' in IB&F which has a highly developed and regulated domestic market, has considered these issues.

To consider these issues in the context of the Islamic financial system, in particular whether Islamic finance as a form of financial intermediation could be vulnerable to such risks of instability. Dr. Zeti,

---

[9] Opt. cit. 1.

the Governor of Bank Negara, Malaysia reviewed what were the possible steps that might be taken to strengthen the resilience and stability of the Islamic financial system, at least from the Malaysian perspective, as market leader in Southeast Asia.

Her position focused on the implications for the strategic direction of the Islamic financial industry taking into consideration the lessons learned from such past financial turbulences, and including the current crisis. As Islamic finance becomes an integral part of the international financial system, Dr. Zeti believes that it will be increasingly tested by such developments. History has shown that the world will continue to be plagued by such crises. The key for the Islamic financial industry is therefore to ensure that it would not be a source of such financial instability and be able to achieve a level of resilience that would ensure its sustainability.[10]

Financial Crisis and Islamic Finance

In the midst of the unfolding of the global financial crisis, Dr. Zeti noted that it would be useful to review the foundation and structures of IB&F to assess its resilience in withstanding the impact of the current and future crises. In taking into account the dynamics of the crisis and the potential implications for Islamic finance, 2 important dimensions were key in undertaking the assessment.

The first key dimension highlights the inherent ability of the Islamic financial system to deal with the test of such a crisis. As previously stated, Islamic finance is well supported by 2 essential features, which serve as pillars to Islamic financial transactions. Firstly, Islamic finance encourages business and trade activities that generate legitimate profits, subject to an explicit requirement of materiality and validity of the transaction.

---

[10] Op. cit. 1.

This requirement ensures that the funds are channelled into real financial business activities, reinforcing a close link between financial and productive flows. This reduces the Islamic financial system from overexposure to risks associated with excessive leveraging and imprudent risk taking. In Islamic financial transactions, money is not a commodity but a medium of exchange, a store of value and a unit of measurement. Money represents purchasing power and cannot be utilised to increase the purchasing power without any productive activity.

Secondly, it needs to be highlighted that Islamic finance encourages business transactions on a mutual risk sharing basis. The practice of risk sharing provides the impetus for the Islamic financial institutions to conduct the appropriate due diligence and maintain the explicit requirements for disclosure and transparency. These requirements thus serve to promote the adoption of sound risk management practices by the Islamic financial institutions.

By embracing these essential features and the objectives of Shariah in its entirety and by exemplifying the true practice of Islamic finance as required by the principles of Shariah, the resilience of the Islamic financial system is strengthened. It is therefore paramount that Islamic financial professionals, practitioners, scholars and regulators fully understand the inherent requirements of Islamic finance, which are in fact consistent with the international best practices and standards in the conventional financial services industry. It is the very elements of Islamic finance that provides an additional in-built mechanism that enhances its prospects for soundness and stability.

The second key dimension relates to potential risks for Islamic finance in a crisis environment. This could arise when the economic environment and the conditions in the financial markets turn adverse. The increased globalisation of Islamic finance and its greater integration with the international financial system increases the exposure of the system to a contagion effect from such developments.

In the dynamics of the financial crisis in the conventional financial system, this is referred to as the second round effects. The first round effects occur when developments within the financial system trigger (Wall Street) the financial crisis which in turn impacts the real economy (Main Street). The second round effects are when the resulting slower growth causes further strains to the financial sector.

The experience has shown that when such a crisis is not contained, the consequent deterioration in economic conditions results in a worsening of the financial crisis. For this reason, resolution had to take place quickly. For Malaysia, in the 1997–1998 crisis, every effort was taken to give attention to financial sector resolution so as to prevent the spiral that could have set in as economic activity became affected by the financial crisis.

In this indirect manner, Islamic finance can also be affected by such financial turmoil. Slower economic growth and the reduction in the global liquidity will affect those institutions that are heavily reliant on a business model that focuses on real estate and asset finance. Islamic financial institutions can also be exposed to increased inventory risk due to the increased volatility and the reduction in asset prices. Islamic financial institutions with a high proportion of their businesses in profit-sharing business (Mudaraba and Musharaka) may be exposed to losses due to equity investment risk, possibly by the inability of the enterprises in generating the expected returns. The absence of an Islamic money market infrastructure would also expose the Islamic financial system to higher liquidity risks.

Strategies to Strengthen the Resilience of the Islamic Financial System

As innovation of Islamic financial products and services intensifies and as Islamic finance becomes more integrated with the international financial system, it becomes imperative that the foundations upon which Islamic finance has been built remain intact. Dr. Zeti believes that this will be the key to sustaining the resilience of the Islamic financial system in this current and more challenging international financial environment.

The key to this is to embrace Shariah innovation in the development of Islamic financial products. In a highly globalised financial market, innovation has been a key differentiating factor to remain competitive. The current turmoil has, however, highlighted that highly complex, unbridled innovation can become highly destabilising resulting in major disruptions in a financial system. It is therefore important for financial innovation to have clear Shariah objectives and adhere to the requisite principles of Shariah. In this manner, Shariah-based innovation would contribute towards Islamic financial products that have distinct value propositions with in-built strengths arising from the essential features of Shariah.

To achieve this objective, it was important, according to Dr. Zeti, to have strong initiatives that promote Shariah-based innovation in Islamic finance. In Malaysia, several steps have been taken. The establishment of the International Shariah Research Academy for Islamic Finance (ISRA) aims to engage in applied research on dynamic Shariah-centric innovation. ISRA can provide a global platform for greater global engagement and research with the focus on innovation.

In addition, the central bank also embarked on the initiative to develop the Shariah Parameters to promote more consistent application of Islamic financial contracts. This initiative aims to determine the essential features of Islamic financial products derived from underlying key Shariah contracts. These features will serve as a guide for the application of the Shariah contracts for the Islamic financial products.

The second strategy has been to raise the bar in the status of the Islamic financial infrastructure that supports the risk management and governance of Islamic financial institutions. To ensure sustainability of the resilience of Islamic finance, it is important to have the comprehensive enabling infrastructure that allows for the management of the risks peculiar to Islamic finance. There is a need for IB&F to have the capital requirements, effective risk management and strong governance that are fully equipped to manage the risks specific to Islamic financial transactions. It is also important for the institutions to spread the risks by having prudent asset allocation based on different Islamic contracts so as to ensure a sustainable revenue stream and to ensure the institutions that are in a position to absorb the extreme circumstances that occur during a crisis.

In the case of Malaysia, an additional capital requirement is required to cushion inventory risks of underlying assets and to cover the potential equity position risks that are embedded within the partnership contracts. This is also reinforced by the requirement on the appointment of board representatives in the invested entities under the partnership contracts so as to serve as a safeguard for the interest of the Islamic financial institution, thereby allowing for continuous monitoring and surveillance. Islamic financial institutions are also allowed to transfer the risk to investment account holders under Mudaraba, that is, profit-sharing and loss-bearing contract, if the institution can demonstrate the appropriate disclosure and governance practices that would ensure an effective risk transfer. Islamic banks are also permitted to set aside a portion of income derived from assets funded by Mudaraba contracts, in the form of profit equalisation reserves (PER) to sustain stable and competitive returns. Several of these requirements are based on the international standards that have been issued by IB&F. The implementation of IFSB standards across jurisdictions will be key in the continued robust expansion of Islamic finance.

While the above measures facilitate the managing of risks peculiar to Islamic finance, the legal, regulatory and supervisory infrastructure also needs to keep abreast with the evolution and rapid transformation taking place in the industry. As part of this infrastructure, there needs to be an integrated crisis management framework to ensure that any emerging crisis in the Islamic financial system will be promptly managed. Such efforts, among others, need to involve 3 basic aspects. This includes having the mechanism and vehicle to preserve short-term liquidity, to remove troubled assets from the balance sheets of financial institutions and to recapitalise the Islamic financial institutions.

In the case of Malaysia, this infrastructure has been put in place. The central bank has a range of Islamic financial instruments to manage liquidity in the financial system. This is supported by a well-developed Islamic money market. In addition, the financial safety net framework in Malaysia encompasses the lender of last resort facility and a comprehensive deposit insurance system that provides coverage for both conventional and Islamic deposits. The Deposit Insurance Corporation has also been given sufficient statutory powers to ensure a prompt, effective and least cost resolution to safeguard the stability of the Islamic financial system. This entails, among others, the regulatory powers and mandate to ensure expedient resolution of financial institutions in distress. The supervisory oversight also subjects the Islamic financial institutions to periodical stress testing to assess whether the institutions would be able to cope in extreme conditions.

Global ramifications of the crisis also call for more concerted efforts at the international level to avert an escalation of the scale of a crisis. Central to this is to have coordinated initiatives, by having in place on-going assessments of any vulnerabilities in the Islamic financial system so as to avoid a crisis. As part of this, the close cooperation of the central banks would enable a swift response if it is required.

The infrastructure also has to assimilate the Shariah values in the realisation of benefit (Masalih) to the relevant stakeholders. Islamic finance industry may, by according attention to the preservation of good relationship with the customers and relevant stakeholders, avoid extreme solutions when severe deterioration has taken place. Consistent with this is the principle in Islamic finance to promote justice, fairness and shared responsibility. The focus of Islamic finance thus transcends beyond just the pursuit of growth and monetary performance by emphasising ethical market conduct practices. Central to this is the adoption of a comprehensive consumer protection framework.

Conclusion

These developments by the leading regulatory authorities IFSB and Bank Negara hold significance for Islamic banking and finance in Southeast Asia, if it is to position itself as offering an alternative, and not just a religious product. They may even hold the key to its long-term sustainability.

LEGAL AND REGULATORY CHANGES TO PROMOTE THE DEVELOPMENT OF ISLAMIC BANKING AND FINANCE IN SINGAPORE

Arfat Selvam

Singapore took centre stage in Islamic banking when it launched its first global Sukuk programme — a sovereign-rated Sukuk facility in January 2009. As a non-Muslim majority country, Singapore first expressed interest in Islamic banking and finance in 2005. As a major international financial centre, Singapore regards Islamic finance as a component part of the suite of financial services that could be offered from the country.

Singapore has a unique set of five pillars:

- its robust and transparent regulatory environment;
- its responsive regulatory approach to the needs of the Islamic finance industry;
- its well-developed financial markets;

17

- its broad base of financial talent; and
- its strong legal and judicial system.

With them, Singapore has the resilience and stability to leverage itself as an internationally recognised Islamic finance centre, despite the current global financial turmoil.

The Legal and Regulatory Framework

Singapore is a common law jurisdiction. As a Republic, it also enacts its own statutes. The common law applies only to the extent that it does not conflict with the Singapore statutory laws. In the application of laws, the principles of judicial precedent are observed. The Singapore courts will take into cognisance judgements passed by the courts of other common law jurisdictions when the law and facts are similar. To this extent, in the application of laws, there is uniformity with the laws of other Commonwealth jurisdictions, such as England.

Banking

Banking is regulated by the Banking Act (Cap. 19) and its subsidiary legislations. Singapore does not have an Islamic Banking Act. The rationale for this is as outlined by the Monetary Authority of Singapore (MAS), the central bank and regulator for banking and financial institutions in Singapore:

> As the prudential objectives of adequate capitalisation and liquidity, appropriate management of risks and concentration, corporate governance and controls are largely similar between Islamic financial services and conventional financial services, our existing regulatory framework, with suitable requirements, can facilitate the development of Islamic finance in Singapore.[1]

---

[1] See the address by Mr. Heng Swee Keat, Managing Director of MAS, on 12 June 2006.

Islamic banks seeking to do business in Singapore are subject to the same processing requirements under the Banking Act. As at 2008, there were 10 Middle East banks.[2] In addition, Islamic banking services are offered by international banks with Islamic windows. The first Islamic bank in Singapore with the full banking licence from MAS — The Islamic Bank of Asia (IB Asia) — was established in 2007.[3]

Financial Services

Singapore's Securities and Futures Act (Cap. 289) (SFA) regulates the business of financial services outside banking and insurance. The MAS has systematically reviewed this Act to ensure that there is adequate balance between the need to promote Singapore as an international financial centre and the need to protect the unsophisticated investing public.

The securities regulations are relaxed for sophisticated investors. Offers for the sale of shares, debentures and units in business trusts and collective investment schemes may be made in Singapore to institutional investors and accredited investors[4] without having to issue a prospectus.[5]

---

[2] As at 31 December 2008, Arab Bank PLC, National Bank of Kuwait SAK and Qatar National Bank S.A.Q. have branches, while Arab Banking Corporation (BSC), Doha Bank, Emirates Bank International PJSC, The International Banking Corporation B.S.C. (C), The National Commercial Bank of Saudi Arabia, Riyad Bank and RBC Bank have representative offices in Singapore.

[3] The Islamic Bank of Asia is a 51% subsidiary of The Development Bank of Singapore Ltd., with the remaining 49% held by 34 investors from the GCC countries.

[4] An 'accredited investor' is defined under the SFA as including:

(a) an individual (1) whose net personal assets exceed S$2 million, or its equivalent in any foreign currency, or (2) whose income in the preceding 12 months is not less than S$300,000, or its equivalent in any foreign currency;

(b) a corporation with net assets exceeding S$10 million, or its equivalent in any foreign currency, within the preceding 12 months and

(c) an entity (other than a corporation) with net assets exceeding $10 million, or its equivalent in any foreign currency.

[5] Sections 274, 275, 282Y, 282Z, 304 and 305 of the SFA.

Capital market services providers[6] have, as a general rule, to be licensed under the Act. There are exemptions, for instance, for fund managers managing assets of up to 30 accredited investors.[7]

With the secure regulatory regime for asset management, several Middle East finance houses have established operations in Singapore. Islamic funds under management in Singapore stood at S$28 billion in 2007.[8]

The Regulatory Changes to Promote Islamic Banking and Finance

Singapore has a well-developed conventional banking and finance industry. In formulating the regulatory changes for the growth of Islamic banking and finance, Singapore adopts a conscious policy of ensuring that there is level playing field.

Islamic finance should not be disadvantaged *vis-á-vis* conventional finance. Changes have been made where existing regulations impose specific risks or impediments to the development of Islamic banking and finance.

The regulatory changes have been made to meet the following objectives:

- first, to enhance the capability of banks operating in Singapore to undertake Islamic finance transactions;
- second, to increase the capacity of the Islamic banking system in managing the liquidity and investment risks;

---

[6] Capital market services providers carry on one or more of the following regulated activities under the SFA; (1) dealing in securities, (2) trading in futures contracts, (3) leveraged foreign exchange trading, (4) advising on corporate finance, (5) fund management, (6) securities financing, (7) providing custodial services for securities. See Second Schedule of the SFA.

[7] Paragraph 5 of the Second Schedule to the Securities and Futures (Licensing and Conduct of Business) Regulations 2002.

[8] See the speech by Senior Minister Goh Chok Tong at the opening ceremony of the Singapore International WAQF Conference on 6 March 2007.

- third, to facilitate the creation of Islamic finance products for banks and other investors to have access to a wide range of Shariah-compliant investment opportunities; and
- fourth, to incentivise financial institutions to undertake Shariah-compliant financial activities and to provide for a competitive tax regime for investors.

Enhancing the Capability of Banks

The Banking Act (Cap. 19) prohibits banks from dealing in non-finance assets.[9]

In 2005, new banking regulations[10] were introduced to allow banks operating in Singapore to purchase and sell non-financial assets (including commodities) in connection with Murabaha financing — such arrangement is recognised as fundamentally a financial product.

As a further enhancement in 2006, banks were permitted to carry on reverse Murabaha financing arrangements.[11] Reverse Murabaha financing forms the basis of a Shariah-compliant fixed deposit product.

In reverse Murabaha financing, the fixed return on the customer's funds placed with the bank is achieved through the following structure:

- the customer purchases and pays for existing specified assets;
- the customer sells them to the bank at a marked-up price;
- the bank immediately re-sells them at the same original price paid by the customer; and

---

[9] Section 30(1)(d) of Banking Act (Cap. 19).
[10] Regulation 22 introduced by the Banking (Amendment) Regulations 2005, which came into effect on 29 September 2005.
[11] Regulation 23 introduced by the Banking (Amendment No. 2) Regulations 2006, which came into operation on 12 June 2006.

- the difference between the marked-up price and the lower original price represents the return to the customer for making funds available to the bank — and it is returned by the bank after it has sold the product, either in one lump or on a deferred payment basis.

In January 2009, banks operating in Singapore were also allowed to enter into Murabaha placements and offer Ijara Wa Iqtina financing[12] to further widen the range of instruments for the management of liquidity and their matching of assets and liabilities.

The MAS regulatory framework applies to both local and foreign banks operating in Singapore. They are applicable to both conventional and Islamic banking.

MAS has specific regulations that are applicable only to banks incorporated in Singapore on the calculation of the minimum capital adequacy ratio (CAR). They are set out in MAS Notice 637. In May 2009, MAS issued new guidelines clarifying its policy on the application of the minimum CAR requirements in relation to Islamic financial products.[13]

These new guidelines apply to specific Islamic funding and financing structures. The bank is required to assess the economic risk of the structure and to decide whether it should be regarded as a credit risk or an equity exposure. The following Islamic structures were addressed under the guidelines:

- Murabaha Deposit;
- Murabaha Financing;
- Murabaha Interbank Placements;
- Ijara Wa Iqtina;
- Diminishing Musharaka;

---

[12] Regulations 23A and 23B introduced by the Banking (Amendment) Regulations 2009.
[13] Guidelines on the Application of Banking Regulations to Islamic banking issued on 7 May 2009.

- Spot Murabaha; and
- Sukuk.

The guidelines set out the specific requirements for each structure and give an analysis for their treatment for CAR purposes.

Increasing Liquidity in the Islamic Banking System

One of the impediments to the growth of the Islamic finance industry is the lack of high-quality Shariah-compliant products that can be used to manage the liquidity risks.

In 2008, the MAS announced its intention to develop a facility to make available sovereign-rated Sukuk. MAS distinguished this facility from traditional issuances as follows:[14]

> First, the issuance will be on a reverse enquiry basis, which means we will issue according to the needs of financial institutions in Singapore conducting Islamic finance.
>
> Second, at the initial stage we plan to price these against the liquid Singapore Government securities market. As the S$ Sukuk market grows and deepen in time, it can then develop its own pricing benchmarks. The design of our Sukuk issuance facility reflects efforts to harness the price discovery potential of existing liquid instruments while adhering carefully to Shariah principles.

MAS, an 'AAA'-rated sovereign announced the launch of the S$200 million Sukuk issuance facility in January 2009. The Sukuk qualifies as a Tier 1 asset in the computation of the liquidity requirements under the Banking Regulations. It serves to strengthen the ability of financial institutions to meet their capital and liquidity requirements when they conduct Shariah-compliant activities in Singapore.

---

[14] See the speech by Mr. Heng Swee Keat, Managing Director of MAS at 5th IFSB Summit on 13 May 2008.

The Sukuk facility gives MAS the flexibility to issue Sukuk on an on-going reverse enquiry basis. The size, price and maturity of each Sukuk issue will depend on the needs of the investor and the prevailing market conditions. The Shariah-approved facility is based on the Ijara sale and leaseback of units in the MAS Building, a first-class real estate asset in Singapore. The Islamic Bank of Asia has expressed its interest to be the first investor to tap the Sukuk facility.[15] This Sukuk facility will give added resilience and stability to the current Islamic banking and finance system.

Creation of Islamic Finance Products

The Singapore approach in facilitating the creation of Islamic finance products is to align the tax treatment for the products with conventional financing contracts that they are economically equivalent to. This is intended to give the industry maximum flexibility for innovation whilst preventing any unintended tax treatment that would place the Islamic finance product at a disadvantage.

Four Islamic products were identified for specific tax treatment:

(1) Sukuk;
(2) Ijara Wa Iqtina;
(3) Murabaha; and
(4) Mudaraba.

Sukuk

Sukuk has been aligned with conventional bonds for tax treatment purposes. There is of course a fundamental difference between Sukuk and the conventional bond structure. It is not a debt transaction. It is asset based, where the holder of the trust certificates issued under a

---

[15] See the remarks of Mr. Vince Cook, CEO of The Islamic Bank of Asia on 19 January 2009.

Shariah-compliant investment scheme is entitled to the undivided proportionate ownership interest in the underlying asset. The return on the investment is based not on interest, but on the recurring income stream from the asset.

Stamp Duty

The change effected under the Stamp Duties Act (Cap. 312) gives recognition to this fundamental difference. Under Singapore law, stamp duty is chargeable on the transfer of Singapore real estate at the rate of approximately 3% of its current market value.

A Sukuk arrangement with real estate as the underlying asset is structured based on an Al-Ijara contract (sale and leaseback):

- the original owner sells real estate to a special purpose vehicle (SPV);
- the SPV pays for the asset through the sale of trust certificates to investors;
- the SPV leases the asset to the original owner or its affiliate and receives periodic rental payments under the Shariah-compliant lease (which has a re-purchase option (Ijara Wa Iqtina)); and
- at the end of the lease term (which would coincide with the maturity of the trust certificates), SPV sells the asset to the original owner at the same price and returns the proceeds to the investors.

Ordinarily, stamp duty at the full rate would be payable on (i) the purchase of the real estate situated in Singapore by the SPV; (ii) the lease by SPV; and (iii) the sale back to the original owner.

In aligning the stamp duty treatment with conventional debt securities, a remission will be granted on application, for any stamp duty payable in excess of that chargeable for the equivalent conventional debt securities.

With this remission, only S$500 stamp duty will be payable on the instruments effecting the purchase, lease and sale-back transactions.[16]

---

[16] MAS Circular dated 27 July 2006 (Circular FDD Cir 11/2006).

The Sukuk structure must be endorsed as a Shariah-compliant Sukuk by the Shariah Board.

In the case of Sukuk which qualifies as qualifying debt securities,[17] in addition the originator or its related party must not at any time hold any beneficial interest or fund (directly or indirectly) 50% or more of the Sukuk.

There is no Singapore stamp duty payable for the acquisition, lease or sale-back of underlying assets other than real estate to support a Sukuk structure.

Income Tax

Singapore does not have any capital gains tax. Interest is subject to income tax if it is derived from Singapore. It is deemed to be derived from Singapore if:[18]

- the payments are made by a resident or permanent resident in Singapore;
- deductible from any income derived in Singapore; or
- if the principal funds are brought into or used in Singapore.

In order to promote the development of an active bond market, several tax incentives have been in place since 1998. These include:

- tax exemption on interest income received from debt securities; and
- tax concession on fee income derived by financial institutions from arranging debt securities in Singapore.

---

[17] See 7 under the section 'Income Tax' paragraph for definition of qualifying debt securities.
[18] Section 12(6) of Income Tax Act.

With effect from 2005, the tax exemptions were extended to Islamic debt securities.[19]

Islamic debt securities means debt securities and trust certificates:

> which are endorsed by any Shariah Council or body, or by any Committee formed for the purpose of providing guidance on compliance with Shariah laws (Shariah Board); and the amounts payable from such securities and trust certificates are periodic and supported by a regular stream of receipts from underlying assets.[20]

While the word 'debt' has been used, this exemption clearly extends to the periodic distributions under a Sukuk paid not as interest but out of receipts from the underlying assets.

In the tax treatment of the periodic distributions, there is a distinction between Sukuk that are qualifying debt securities (QDS) and those that do not fall within the QDS Scheme.

Qualifying Debt Securities are bonds, notes, commercial papers and certificates of deposits (other than Singapore Government Securities) issued by any financial institution or financial sector incentive (bond market) company licensed or approved by MAS.[21] They include Islamic debt securities but, unless approved by the Minister, such Islamic debt securities will not be regarded as qualifying debt securities if during the primary launch, they are issued to less than 4 persons and 50% or more of the issue is beneficially held or funded (directly or indirectly) by related parties of the issuer.[22]

---

[19] MAS Circular dated 31 March 2005 (Circular No. FDD Cir 04/2005).

[20] Section 43(N)(4) of Income Tax Act.

[21] See also the requirements under Regulation 4(1A) of the Income Tax (Qualifying Debt Securities) Regulations 2005 for the need in certain situations for staff based in Singapore to have a leading role in the origination, structuring and distribution of the Islamic debt securities.

[22] Paragraph (c) in the definition of QDS in Section 13(16) of Income Tax Act.

All amounts payable whether to residents or non-residents of Singapore on Islamic debt securities that are qualifying debt securities are exempted from income tax if:[23]

- the QDS are issued not later than 31 December 2013;
- any amount payable by the issuer to the investors is not deductible against any income of the issuer accruing in or derived from Singapore; and
- all other conditions under the QDS Scheme are met.[24]

Where the issuer is not a financial institution and the Sukuk does not qualify as QDS, the amounts payable to investors who are individuals (residents and non-residents) are still exempted from income tax.[25]

As in the case for conventional debt securities, payments made to non-individual investors under the Sukuk structure will be subject to income tax, unless exemption is granted by the Minister.[26]

---

[23] MAS Circular FDD Cir 2/2008 dated 30 May 2008.

[24] The other conditions under the QDS Scheme are:

  (i) the amount should not be payable to a permanent establishment in Singapore;
  (ii) the QDS are not acquired using funds from a Singapore operation by a non-resident person, who carries on any operation through a permanent establishment in Singapore;
  (iii) all offering documents must include a statement in terms of (ii) above;
  (iv) where a Singapore resident company issues the QDS to a non-resident SPV which in turn issues QDS to investors, all offering documents must include statements restricting (1) acquisition by any investor, who is resident or has permanent establishment in Singapore and (2) acquisition by using funds from its Singapore operations; and
  (v) the issuer must submit a Return in the prescribed form to MAS and Comptroller of Income Tax within 10 days of the issue of the securities.

[25] Section 13(1) of Income Tax Act. The exemption does not apply to amounts derived by the individual through a partnership in Singapore or from a sole-proprietorship business.

[26] The Minister has power under Section 13(4) of the Income Tax Act to exempt the payment from tax where he is of the opinion that the payment will enhance the economic or technical development of Singapore. Interest payments under conventional bond issues by non-financial institutions to non-residents have been exempted from tax under this provision in selected cases.

The withholding tax obligations under the Income Tax Act do not apply to Islamic debt securities, which are qualifying debt securities.[27]

Ijara Wa Iqtina

Ijara, the Islamic financing arrangement involving the sale and leaseback of assets, is the typical arrangement used for the financing of purchase of real estate. The tax treatment accorded to it in Singapore is aligned to that for conventional mortgage financing.

Stamp Duty

Under conventional mortgage financing, where real estate in Singapore is mortgaged to secure bank borrowings, S$500 stamp duty is payable on the mortgage instrument.

The Islamic finance equivalent is based on leasing with option to purchase (Ijara Wa Iqtina) concept under which:

- the bank purchases the property on instructions from customer;
- the bank leases the property to the customer with an option for the customer to purchase at the end of the lease period; and
- the difference between the total lease payments received and the original cost to the bank represents the return to the bank for providing the financing.

The end result is the same but the stamp duty payable is considerably enhanced — each sale transaction attracts 3% duty based on

---

[27] Section 45A(2A) of Income Tax Act. The issuer must, however, include in all offering documents a statement requiring any person who receives payments not known to be tax exempt to file a return of income under the Income Tax Act (Regulation 5(2) of 2005 Regulations).

the market value of the property and *ad valorem* duty is payable on the lease based on the rental payable.

In 2005, the Stamp Duties (Qualifying Islamic Financing Arrangements) (Remission) Rules[28] were passed to align the stamp duty treatment with that of conventional mortgage financing. Pursuant to these Rules, where an arrangement is entered into between a financial institution[29] (the capital provider) and its customer under which the capital provider purchases real estate in Singapore and then leases it to the purchaser with an option for the purchaser to purchase the same (Ijarah Wa Iqtina), the stamp duty is capped at S$500 on each of the documents relating to the lease and the sale to the purchaser at the end of the lease term.

There is no remission of stamp duty on the initial purchase by the capital provider, as in conventional mortgage financing, such initial purchase would attract full stamp duty.

The arrangement must be endorsed by the Shariah Board of the financial institution.

Income Tax

The effective return received by the financial institution[30] in lieu of interest will be accorded the same treatment for income tax purposes as interest under a conventional mortgage financing arrangement.[31] It will be regarded as income subject to Singapore tax if it is derived from Singapore.

---

[28] No. 5/733 of 2005 dated 17 November 2005.
[29] 'Financial institution' is defined in the Stamp Duties (Qualifying Islamic Financing Arrangement Remission) Rules as an institution licensed or approved by MAS or exempted from such licensing or approval.
[30] For income tax purposes, 'financial institution' has been defined in Section 34B(6) of the Income Tax Act to also include any institution outside Singapore that is 'licensed or approved, or exempted from such licensing or approval, under any written law administered by its financial supervisory authority for the carrying on of financial activities'.
[31] MAS Circular dated 27 July 2006.

Goods and Services Tax

While Singapore does not have capital gains tax, it does have a Goods and Services Tax (GST). Currently at the rate of 7%, GST is imposed on the cost of supply of goods and services in Singapore and on the importation of goods into Singapore.[32] GST does not apply to the sale of residential real estate, but is levied for the acquisition of any interest in non-residential real estate, such as commercial and industrial properties.

Under the Ijara Wa Iqtina arrangement, the leasing of the non-residential property has GST implications. It attracts GST based on the total lease payments, which include the effective return to the financial institution. To rectify the situation, GST is exempted in respect of the effective return earned by the financial institution.[33] This is in line with conventional financing as interest is exempted from GST.

Murabaha

The Murabaha concept is regarded as an Islamic financial arrangement equivalent to conventional financing. The financial institution acquires an asset and immediately sells to its customer at a marked-up price. The customer pays the higher price for the product either in one lump sum or by instalments after the date of sale. The mark-up is the effective return to the financial institution.

Similarly in a reverse Murabaha transaction outlined in paragraph 3 of Section "Enhancing the Capability of Banks", the mark-up is the effective return to the customer for placing funds on deposit with the financial institution. It is equivalent to a conventional deposit product.

---

[32] Section 16(c) of the Goods and Services Tax Act (Cap. 117A).
[33] The effective return is treated as 'Exempt Supplies' under Section 22 read with para. 1(r) of the Fourth Schedule of the GST Act.

Income Tax

The effective return to the financial institution in the Murabaha transaction is accorded the same tax treatment as interest for income tax purposes.[34] Accordingly, the mark-up paid by the customer in a Murabaha transaction is available as a tax deduction as if it were interest paid on capital employed in acquiring the income.

Similarly, in a reverse Murabaha transaction, the effective return received by the customer will be treated as interest for income tax purposes. Accordingly, no income tax is payable on such effective return received by any individual from an approved bank in Singapore.[35]

Where the financial institution is non-resident of Singapore for income tax purposes, the customer will have to comply with the withholding tax obligations under the Income Tax Act, as in the case of interest payments made to non-residents.

Goods and Services Tax

The sale of property (other than residential real estate) in a Murabaha financing has GST implications on both the customer and the financial institution. The customer would have to pay GST based on the marked-up price. To rectify the situation, GST is exempted on the mark-up price.[36] The financial institution is also allowed to claim GST on the full purchase price of the property.

The tax invoice issued by the financial institution should give sufficient information to track the selling price and the mark-up.[37]

---

[34] Section 34B of the Income Tax Act.
[35] Section 13(1)(zd) of Income Tax Act.
[36] MAS Circular dated 27 July 2006 (Circular FDD Cir 11/2006).
[37] Paragraph 3.11 of MAS Circular dated 27 July 2006.

Stamp Duty

Where the underlying asset in a Murabaha arrangement comprises real estate situated in Singapore, additional stamp duty is payable on the sale of the property by the financial institution to the customer. The amount of stamp duty payable has been reduced from 3% of the sale price to S$500. Stamp duty on the initial purchase of the property by the financial institution will continue to be paid, in line with conventional financing. The transaction will have to be endorsed by the Shariah Board.

Mudaraba

In the Islamic financing arrangement based on Mudaraba, the financial institution manages money deposited by the customer and makes payment on a pre-agreed basis out of the profits arising from the use of the money. The payment received represents the customer's effective return on the deposit. The customer bears any loss of capital. The financial institution receives a fee for its management services. The arrangement is equivalent to a conventional deposit on which interest is paid to the customer.

The effective return paid by the financial institution to the customer for the use of the money is accorded the same treatment as interest for income tax purposes. The payment to the customer must be proportionate to the amount deposited by the customer.

In Singapore, interest income received by individuals (both residents and non-residents) from approved Singapore banks are exempted from income tax.[38] The effective return received by the customer from the financial institution will similarly be tax exempt.

---

[38] Such exemption also extends to interest income earned in Singapore by an eligible family-owned investment holding company (FIHC) incorporated in Singapore before 1 April 2013, where the shareholders are individuals related to one another — see Section 13(10) of Income Tax (Amendment) Act 2008.

Double Tax Treaty Implications

As at 31 December 2008, Singapore has entered into Double Tax Treaties with 69 countries, including the United Kingdom, Australia and Japan. The standard Interest Article of the tax treaty based on the OECD model defines 'interest' as 'income from debt–claims of every kind'.

The 'effective return' under the Murabaha, Mudaraba and Ijara contracts referred to in Section "Creation of Islamic Finance Products" falls within the definition of 'interest' under the Interest Article of the tax treaty. Where the effective return earned by the investor from a financial institution in Singapore is subject to Singapore income tax, such tax will be capped at the treaty concessionary rate (usually 10%). The investor must be a tax resident in a country with which Singapore has a Double Tax Treaty and he or she must not carry on any business through a permanent establishment in Singapore.

Tax Concessions for Islamic Financial Arrangements

At a glance:

Islamic finance transaction endorsed by Shariah Board	Stamp duty on Singapore real estate	Income tax on effective return	GST on effective return
Sukuk	Capped at S$500 for each instrument	QDS — 100% tax exemption Non–QDS 100% tax exemption	

(Continued)

(Continued)

Islamic finance transaction endorsed by Shariah Board	Stamp duty on Singapore real estate	Income tax on effective return	GST on effective return
		for individuals concession available for others	
Ijara Wa Iqtina	Capped at S$500 for each instrument, except for initial purchase	Effective return of financial institution treated as interest income	Effective return not subject to GST
Murabaha	Capped at S$500 for each instrument, except for initial purchase	Effective return treated as interest income	Mark-up of price exempted from GST capital provider can claim GST on full purchase price
Mudaraba	No real estate involved	Effective return of capital provider treated as interest income Effective return received by individuals are tax exempt	

**Incentivising Financial Institutions to Carry on
Shariah-Compliant Financial Services**

Singapore has in place since 2003, a Financial Sector Incentive (FSI)
Award Scheme to promote its growth as an international financial
centre. The qualifying activities are of two categories:

(1) the standard tier — which enjoys a 10% concessionary tax rate
    on income derived from designated qualifying activities;[39] and
(2) the enhanced tier — which enjoys 5% concessionary tax rate on
    income derived from high growth and value-added designated
    activities.

A new enhanced tier award — the Financial Services Incentive —
Islamic Finance (FSI-IF) — scheme was introduced with effect from
1 April 2008 to incentivise financial institutions to carry on Shariah-
compliant financial activities from Singapore.[40] Under this award, a
5% concessionary tax rate will apply for 5 years to income from qualifying activities, which has been endorsed by the approved Shariah
Board of the financial institution.

There are two types of FSI-IF awards:

(1) lending and related activities; and
(2) fund management and investment advisory services.

The award is open to all existing FSI award holders and new appli-
cants. In the assessment for the grant of the award, the number of
experienced professionals who are significantly involved in the qualifying activities as well as the business development plans in
Singapore will be taken into consideration.

---

[39] The updated designated qualifying activities are set out in MAS Circular No. FDD
Cir 03/2008 dated 30 May 2008.
[40] MAS Circular No. FDD Cir 03/2008 dated 30 May 2008.

Lending and Related Activities

Only licensed banks and approved merchant banks in Singapore may apply for the FSI-IF award under this category. The qualifying activities include:[41]

- granting of foreign currency loans (other than by way of bonds and debentures);
- secondary trading in foreign currency loans;
- foreign currency trade transactions;
- trade financing activities in foreign currency; and
- providing services to non-resident credit card holders in foreign currency.

The qualifying activities must be structured using one of the following Shariah concepts:

- Murabaha;
- Mudaraba;
- Ijara Wa Iqtina;
- Musharaka;
- Istisna; and
- Salam.

Funds Management and Investment Advisory Services

The applicant for this FSI-IF award must be a Singapore incorporated company holding a capital market services licence under the SFA or is exempted under that Act from having to hold the licence.

---

[41] For full list of qualified activities, see MAS Circular FDD Cir 02/2008 dated 30 May 2008.

The qualifying activities for this category include:[42]

- managing a qualifying fund[43] for designated investments,[44] which is Shariah-compliant;
- providing investment advisory services to such qualifying fund; and

---

[42] *Ibid.*

[43] A qualifying fund refers to:

(a) A company not resident in Singapore, and where the value of issued securities of the company is not 100% beneficially owned, directly or indirectly, by investors in Singapore (including investors who are resident individuals, resident non-individuals and permanent establishments in Singapore), and where the company:

  (i) does not have a permanent establishment in Singapore (other than a fund manager); and
  (ii) does not carry on a business in Singapore.

(b) A trust administered by a trustee not resident in Singapore, and where the value of the fund is not 100% beneficially held, directly or indirectly, by investors in Singapore (including investors who are resident individuals, resident non-individuals and permanent establishments in Singapore), and where the trustee of the trust:

  (i) does not have a permanent establishment in Singapore (other than a fund manager); and
  (ii) does not carry on a business in Singapore.

(c) An account of an individual, who is neither a citizen nor a resident of Singapore with any fund manager in Singapore for the management of monies in that account.

MAS Circular No. FDD 04/2007 dated 31 August 2007.

[44] 'Designated investments' are as defined in the Income Tax (Income from Funds Managed for Foreign Investors) Regulations 2003 and include:

(a) Shares denominated in any foreign currency of companies, which are neither incorporated in Singapore nor resident in Singapore (other than listed shares of Malaysian incorporated companies);
(b) Securities (other than stocks and shares) denominated in any foreign currency (including bonds, notes, certificates of deposit and treasury bills) issued by foreign governments, foreign banks outside Singapore and companies, which are neither incorporated in Singapore nor resident in Singapore;
(c) Futures contracts held in any futures exchange; and
(d) Any immovable property situated outside Singapore.

- arranging the lending of designated securities on behalf of a qualifying fund with another FSI award holder.

Takaful (Islamic Insurance) and Re-takaful (Islamic Reinsurance)

Under a separate Offshore Insurance Business Scheme, a 5% concessionary tax rate will be granted to relevant income from Shariah-compliant activities. This scheme is open to companies incorporated in Singapore licensed to carry on insurance business under the Insurance Act and a foreign insurer permitted under that Act to do insurance business in Singapore.

The relevant income includes:[45]

- income from general insurance business derived from accepting offshore risks;
- income from life insurance business derived from life insurance surplus;
- dividends and qualifying return in lieu of interest derived from outside Singapore;
- gains or profits derived from the sale of offshore investments; and
- qualifying return in lieu of interest on ACU deposits derived from the insurance and shareholders' funds in relation to offshore insurance business.

Other Changes that Benefit the Islamic Finance Industry

Apart from changes that have been made specifically to promote Islamic finance, Singapore has made other significant changes for its development as an international financial centre, which would enhance the growth of the Islamic finance industry.

---

[45] Paragraph 4 of MAS Circular FDD 02/2008 dated 30 May 2008.

Asset Management

Asset management was given a boost through recent changes that were made.

Increase in the Array of Funds' Vehicles

Through new legislation passed since 2006, Singapore now has:

- the Business Trust Act (Cap. 31A), which allows the creation of trust vehicles that combine trustee and management capabilities;
- the Limited Liability Partnership Act (Cap. 163A), which allows for the creation of partnerships with all partners having limited liability; and
- the Limited Partnership Act 2008, which allows for the creation of partnerships with general and limited liability partners.

Modernising the Trust Legislation

The Trustees Act (Cap. 337), which has its roots in the UK Act of 1872, was updated in 2004 by:

- scrapping the rule against perpetuities and allowing trusts to be created for up to 100 years;[46]
- abolishing the rule against accumulations; and
- widening the investment powers of trustees.

An interesting new provision that has been included in the Trustees Act in 2004 reads as follows:

Section 90

(1) Subject to subsection (3), where a person creates a trust or transfers movable property to be held on an existing trust

---

[46] Section 89 of the Trustees Act.

during his lifetime, he shall be deemed to have the capacity to so create the trust or transfer the property if he has capacity to do so under any of the following laws:

(a) the law applicable in Singapore;
(b) the law of his domicile or nationality; or
(c) the proper law of the transfer.

(2) No rule relating to inheritance or succession shall affect the validity of a trust or the transfer of any property to be held on trust if the person creating the trust or transferring the property had the capacity to do so under subsection (1).

(3) Subsection (1):

(a) does not apply if, at the time of the creation of the trust or the transfer of the property to be held on trust, the person creating the trust or transferring the property is a citizen of Singapore or is domiciled in Singapore; and
(b) applies in relation to a trust only if the trust is expressed to be governed by Singapore law and the trustees are resident in Singapore.

This would allow non-citizens of Singapore who are domiciled in overseas jurisdictions, which do not recognise trust arrangements (such as the Middle East) to set up valid trusts governed by Singapore law.

Regulating the Trust Industry

The Trust Companies Act (Cap. 336) was completely revamped to provide for licensing of companies providing trust services, to enhance the 'know your clients' rules and to introduce reporting requirements to MAS.

Abolishment of Estate Duty

With effect from February 2008, no duty is payable on the estate of deceased persons, whether they are domiciled in Singapore or elsewhere. Previously assets situated in Singapore were subject to estate duty.

Shariah-Compliant Stock Indices

With the development of the Shariah-based asset management industry, Shariah-compliant stock indices have been listed:

- in 2006, Singapore Stock Exchange together with FTSE and Yasser Research launched the FTSE SGX Asia Shariah 100 Index; and
- in May 2007, the Daiwa FTSE Shariah Japan 100 was listed as a Shariah-compliant exchange-traded fund on the Singapore Stock Exchange. The fund is based on Japanese equities.

These indices serve as benchmarks for the creation of Islamic financial products and the performance of index-linked funds, exchange tradable funds and over-the-counter products.

Islamic Real Estate Investment Trusts (REITS)

Singapore has a thriving REITs market. As at the end of 2007, there were 20 listed REITs with market capitalisation of S\$27 billion. As part of Singapore's vision to position itself as an international funds management centre, several attractive tax stamp duty exemptions are available. These include:

- stamp duty waiver on the transfer of Singapore real estate into listed REITs (or those about to be listed); and
- distributions made to individuals will not be subject to tax and those made to contain other qualifying unit holders are taxed at a 10% concessionary rate up to 2010.

In 2008, one of Singapore's listed REITs announced its intention to become Shariah-compliant. The Islamic finance industry would do well to leverage on the favourable infrastructure to launch Islamic REITs or real estate funds in Singapore.

Financial and Economic Integration

Singapore has taken significant steps to strengthen financial and economic ties with the Middle East. Free Trade Agreements and Double Tax Treaties have been concluded with:

Free trade agreements

- GCC in 2008; and
- Jordan in 2004.

Double tax treaties

- Qatar in 2006,
- Bahrain in 2004,
- Oman in 2003,
- Kuwait in 2002,
- Egypt in 1996; and
- The United Arab Emirates in 1995.

With closer integration, Singapore aims to promote trade and becomes the gateway for the funding of projects in the Middle East and Asia through Islamic financing.

Singapore also plays an active role to support the global integration of the Islamic finance industry. As a full member of the Islamic Financial Services Board (IFSB), Singapore participates in establishing the uniformity in corporate governance, disclosures and accounting standards as well as consistency in legal documentation and the treatment of unresolved issues.

Conclusion

The carefully planned strategies and policies, reflected in the changes to the legal and regulatory infrastructure, are designed to ensure the presence of the 3 components essential for the development of the Islamic finance industry. They are the investors, the products and the market makers.

For the investors, the laws were changed to make Singapore a competitive tax jurisdiction. Sufficient flexibility was built into the legal framework to allow for innovative creation of Shariah-compliant products. More financial institutions were drawn to the Islamic finance industry through the offer of attractive tax incentives. With them in place, Singapore is well positioned to become an internationally recognised centre for Islamic banking and finance.

BRUNEI: A NICHE MONEY MARKET FOR OFFSHORE ISLAMIC FINANCE

Khairul A. Khairuddin and Sukor Ashak

Introduction

Brunei's economy is fully dominated by the oil and gas sector. Therefore, like so many other hydrocarbon economies, Brunei faces the challenge of diversifying its economy. Because of its huge hydrocarbon exports, Brunei has been able to achieve a high standard of living. With oil and gas production accounting for about 50% of GDP and 90% of exports and government revenue, the economy is fully dominated by oil and gas production.

Future growth will depend on the extent to which Brunei succeeds to diversify its economy, and new oil and gas wells will be found and the unsteady oil price. In its effort to diversify its economy, Brunei aims to become an international offshore financial centre with a niche in the Islamic financial and capital market sector.

With a total Shariah-compliant assets of US$31.5 billion, that places Brunei as the 6th largest Islamic banking and finance centre.[1]

The Brunei International Financial Centre (the BIFC)

The Brunei International Financial Centre (the BIFC) was established in July 2000 to diversify, expand and grow the value-added financial service sector of the Brunei economy and position Brunei as an equal partner in the globalisation of financial and commercial activities. The establishment of BIFC is aimed to focus its development on the niche Islamic market in the rapidly growing world of Islamic money market.

The BIFC is well equipped with a wide range of international legislation to facilitate international banking activities, international insurance and Takaful activities, Mutual funds and securities, and international trusts and company management activities. The BIFC is a regulatory body within the Ministry of Finance responsible in supervising the conduct of licensees and business activities within the ambit of the financial centre.

There were 10 legislations introduced since its commencement as an IFC which includes the International Business Companies Order 2000, International Limited Partnerships Order 2000, Registered Agents and Trustees Licensing Order 2000, International Banking Order 2000, International Trusts Order 2000, Mutual Funds Order 2001, Securities Order 2001, the International Insurance and Takaful Order 2002 and anti-crime Orders, namely, Money Laundering Order 2000, Criminal Conduct (Recovery of Proceeds) Order 2000 and Anti-Terrorism (Financial and other Measures). With the consent of His Majesty the Sultan and Yang Di-Pertuan of Negara Brunei Darussalam, the Brunei Government introduced 2 additional legislations, namely, the Islamic Banking Order 2008

---

[1] Country Report, Rabobank Economic Research Department, September 2008.

and Islamic Takaful Order 2008 in September 2008 to boost the nation's position as the growing Islamic banking and finance centre in the region.

Brunei Darussalam's objectives for establishing an International Financial Centre includes:

- To diversify economy away from oil and gas to service industry including financial industry;
- To catalyse the growth of other industries;
- To create employment opportunities to young qualified Bruneians in the financial services sector; and
- To establish Brunei Darussalam as a Regional Financial Hub.

The BIFC's main functions as regulatory body of the International Financial Centre are:

- Registration and supervision of International Business Companies (IBCs), registered agents and licensed trust companies;
- Licensing and supervision of securities and Mutual funds;
- Assemble guidelines and codes of conduct for all classes of licences and products;
- Facilitate the development of new products including Shariah-compliant products; and
- Work directly with law firms, accounting firms, trust companies and other ministries and governmental agencies in marketing and promotion activities and other related areas.

Shariah Financial Supervisory Board

The Government of Brunei Darussalam has taken an important step to centralise and streamline the decision-making process in respect of Shariah compliance of financial products and service through the establishment of the Shariah Financial Supervisory

Board (SFSB) in 2006 under the Shariah Financial Supervisory Board Order 2006.

The SFSB has been in charge with the task of ensuring that all Islamic banking and financial products offered in this country are Shariah-compliant. Chaired by the Permanent Secretary of the Ministry of Finance, the SFSB comprises of 9 members of the country's top scholars and Shariah experts.

The SFSB is empowered to approve Islamic financial products and to approve membership of the Shariah advisory body and Shariah consultant and advisor of a financial institution. Since its establishment, the SFSB is responsible in approving Islamic capital and money market products available in the country.

Islamic Banking and Finance Activities

Brunei Darussalam practises a dual banking system, which consists of Islamic banking and conventional banking. Over the past 15 years, Brunei has been actively promoting Islamic banking as an alternative to conventional banking. The initial step in developing its Islamic financial system in the country is by the establishment of the Perbadanan Tabung Amanah Islam Brunei (TAIB) or Brunei Islamic Trust Fund in September 1991. This is later followed by the conversion of the 2 conventional banks, the International Bank of Brunei to the Islamic Bank of Brunei (IBB) in January 1993 and the conversion of the state-owned Development Bank of Brunei to the Islamic Development Bank of Brunei (IDBB) in July 2000. Subsequently in 2006, the IBB and the IDBB were merged to form the Bank Islam Brunei Darussalam (BIBD).

Domestic Islamic and conventional banking activities in Brunei Darussalam are governed by the Islamic Banking Act 1999 and the Banking Order 2006 under the supervision of the Ministry of Finance, Financial Institution Division. With the recent introduction of the Islamic Banking Order 2008, aimed at expanding the Islamic banking sector in Brunei at the same time increasing the competitiveness among players by creating a level playing field as well as strengthening the supervision and regulation of Islamic banking activities.

In the keynote address delivered by the Minister of Finance 2, Pehin Orang Kaya Laila Setia Dato Seri Setia Awang Haji Abd Rahman Haji Ibrahim during the 6th Brunei Roundtable Meeting held in the country in November 2008, the new legislation aims to attract foreign participants to strengthen the Islamic banking industry as a whole and to nurture local knowledge and expertise.

With the introduction of the new Islamic Banking Order, all Islamic banks in the country are required to have a Shariah Advisory Body comprising at least 3 Muslim religious scholars. One of the interesting points about this regulation is that 2 of the religious scholars must be Bruneians.

Also mentioned that under the Islamic Banking Order 2008, the minimum paid-up capital for Islamic banks are B$100 million for local Islamic bank, or an amount equivalent to B$500 million for a foreign head office and B$30 million for a net head office fund. In addition, every Islamic bank will have to pay annual licence fees for its head office (B$50,000), branch ($10,000) and ATM (B$3,000).

International Banking Legislation

International Banking activities services to non-residents in Brunei are governed by the International Banking Order 2000 (IBO). While encompassing the traditional definition of banking by reference to taking of deposits, the IBO recognises that this is not the daily concern of a sophisticated International Bank. The IBO expands its horizons in line with the banking industry's modern development and trends. Four classes of licence are provided for:

- A full international licence for the purpose of carrying on international banking business generally;
- An international investment banking licence for the purpose of carrying on international investment banking business;
- An international Islamic banking licence or the purpose of carrying on international Islamic banking business, granted in respect of full investment or restricted activities; and
- A restricted international banking licence for the purpose of carrying on international banking business subject to the restriction that the licensee shall offer only the services agreed between the Bank and the Authority, and/or may offer, conduct or provide such business only to persons or a class of persons named or described in an undertaking embodied in the application for the licence.

'International Islamic banking business' is banking business, whose aims and operations do not involve any element which is not approved by the Islamic Religion. Provision for Shariah Law to over-ride a conflicting provision in the IBO is made, subject to good banking practice, and there is a requirement for the appointment of a Shariah Council. The restriction to local ownership which applies under the domestic Islamic Banking Act does not apply to the international regime.

Islamic Insurance and Takaful Activities

The 3 major Takaful companies operating in the country are Taib subsidiary Insurans Islam TAIB, Takaful IBB Berhad and Takaful IDBB. While negotiations over the merger of Takaful IBB Berhad and Takaful IDBB are still an ongoing process, Insurans Islam TAIB, which has been in the market for 15 years, holds 53% of the total Takaful market in Brunei Darussalam.[2]

Brunei's growing Takaful activities have given the country's conventional insurance companies plenty of competition especially ever since the first Shariah-compliant companies were established in the 1990s. To date, Islamic insurance or Takaful activities have captured 50% of the total market of non-life insurance sector[3] as motor coverage makes most of their business. The Insurance Order which was introduced in 2006 only regulates the conventional segment of the country's insurance sector. Although Takaful providers are not bound to the insurance order, they however tried to follow the same regulations as the conventional companies and have taken to following the guidelines provided by the General Insurance Association of Brunei Darussalam.

In September 2008, the Ministry of Finance launched the new Islamic Takaful Order 2008. The new order is an order to provide for the regulation of Takaful business in Brunei Darussalam and for the purpose relating thereto or connected with Takaful. The order is a new comprehensive legislation to govern the activities of the domestic Takaful industry and provide the legal platform for a level playing field between conventional insurers and Takaful operators. Under the auspices of the BIFC, the focus will be on 3 categories of insurance, namely, captive insurance, re-insurance centre, and Takaful and re-Takaful.

International Insurance and Takaful Activities

The BIFC also acts as the regulatory authority for institutions licensed under the International Insurance and Takaful Order 2002, which governs the conduct and business of international insurance

---

[2] The Report Brunei Darussalam 2007, Oxford Business Group.
[3] The Report Brunei Darussalam 2008, Oxford Business Group.

and Takaful activities. The purpose for the introduction of the IITO in 2002 is clearly defined in the long title, which is "An order which is to provide for licensing and regulations of person carrying on international insurance business and international insurance-related activities, to provide for the security and protection of long-term international insurance business and to provide for matters incidental thereto or connected to therewith".

It deals with all classes of general and long-term international insurance and Takaful, including specifically, financial loss, all classes of captive, linked long-term, pension and annuity and re-insurance as well as international Re-Takaful business. It introduces statutory protection (in the absence of fraud) of all long-term products and funds transferred to such contracts, and redefines concepts of insurable interest and enforceability.

International insurance business (i.e., non-domestic business, conducted with non-residents, with the exception of re-insurance) must be carried on by an IBC or a foreign international company incorporated under the International Business Companies Order 2000 (IBCO), a company incorporated under the (domestic) Companies Act (Chapter 39) or a company registered under Part IX of the Companies Act (Chapter 39), which holds a valid licence under IITO. Further, no person (including a corporation) may carry on any business as an international insurance manager, international underwriting manager or international insurance broker unless he holds a licence relating to such business. Services offered by a licensee are limited to those specified in the licence granted and may be provided only to other licensees under the Order. Services cannot be offered relating to domestic insurance business, but a licensed international insurance broker may, notwithstanding any other written law, handle the re-insurance of domestic insurance business (*Source: BIFC summary on IITO*).

Islamic Capital Market — Mutual Fund
and Investment Activities

Islamic capital markets are now gaining momentum to grow into a vibrant market place and Brunei has a niche in this sector especially in Islamic financial and capital market sector. Since the early 2006, Brunei has taken significant steps that are crucial in its effort to develop itself as one of the region's emerging Islamic capital markets. The success of Brunei to become one of the region's Islamic capital markets does not solely rely on the fact that it is an Islamic state, but also taking into consideration of its sovereignty, political and economic stability and importantly the sizable liquidity available. For the past couple of years, the country has developed the required infrastructure, policies, regulations and incentives that are conducive to the development of an Islamic capital market.

Brunei's seriousness and effort to develop its Islamic Capital Market can be seen when it became the first nation in the world to bypass conventional capital money markets by developing its first short-term investment Islamic commercial paper, the Sukuk Al-Ijara worth US$98.1 million in 2006. Most recently Brunei's Ministry of Finance announced that its 18th issuance of the short-term Sukuk Ijara has been successfully priced. The B$45 million (US$31.5 million) issue carries a 91-day maturity and has a rental rate of 1%, and as of 6th November 2008 the total value of Sukuks issued by the Ministry of Finance has totalled about B$1.299 billion. For an oil-rich nation that virtually has no debt and in fact has liquidity of great scale, this effort alone is a clear gesture of the country's sincerity in becoming a regional Islamic Capital Market.

There are currently over 200 funds being offered by the various financial institutions in Brunei with less than 10% of the funds Shariah-compliant. There are about 20 Mutual funds registered under the MFO of which only 7 are Shariah-compliant. There was a notable increase in the number of Shariah-compliant funds registered and licensed under the MFO, where the SFSB has approved a total of 6 Shariah-compliant funds in 2008 compared to only 1 the year before. It is expected that in year 2009, a number of Mutual Funds including both Shariah-compliant and conventional to be established and registered in Brunei are expected to increase.

Financial institutions such as the Brunei Investment Commercial Bank Capital through its subsidiary BICB Capital and Malaysia's CIMB are currently promoting and helping the development and establishment of Shariah-compliant funds in the country. The number of funds and financial institutions offering Shariah-compliant funds is expected to increase, as there is growing demand for such funds from both the public and private sectors.

Mutual Funds activities are regulated by the Mutual Funds Order 2001 (MFO) under the supervision of BIFC. The objective of the MFO is ascertained from its long title which reads, 'An Order to provide for the regulation of Mutual Funds in Brunei Darussalam, the supervision and licensing of such funds and/or persons promoting and providing services in connection therewith and for other matters related to Mutual funds'. With the introduction of the MFO, efforts are being made to ensure that these funds are registered and regulated by the BIFC.

The MFO provides the legal framework for the regulation of Mutual Funds both conventional and Shariah-compliant, the supervision and licensing of such funds and of persons promoting and providing services in connection with funds-related activities in Brunei Darussalam. It allows fund operators such as fund managers and fund administrators to be licensed and to operate from and within Brunei. The MFO allows the registration funds, where funds being offered in Brunei are required to be approved and regulated under the Order.

Unlike most regulations available, the MFO does not only regulate conventional funds. There are important provisions in the

MFO, which are important in the promotion and development of Shariah-compliant funds in Brunei Darussalam. For example, it is clearly mentioned in Section 8(1), where the Authority will only issue or give a Mutual Fund licence or permissions for an Islamic fund only if provision is made for the appointment of an appropriate Shariah Council. The BIFC is working to improve the legislations and at the moment in the process of updating the MFO to make it in line with current international standards and to attract more Shariah-compliant funds to be registered and established in the country.

The Securities Order 2001 (SO)

While the MFO provides the legal framework for fund-related activities, the Securities Order 2001 provides the regulation and administering activities relating to financial exchanges and investment-related activities in the country. It regulates intermediaries, who provide advice in respect of, or manage or deal in securities including those offered and traded on such an exchange.

The SO commenced on March 2001 with its objectives as derived from the long title "An Order to make provision with respect to financial exchanges, dealers and other person providing advice in respect of, managing or dealing in securities, for certain offences relating to securities, and for other purposes connected therewith".

Securities are defined inclusively rather than exhaustively in the definition provided in this Order is not limited. It is defined to include stocks and shares, in a public or corporations, debt instruments such as debentures and bonds, depository receipts, loan stock, bills, notes, financial instruments or other debt instruments of any government or of any body, whether corporate or unincorporated.

The most important aspect of the SO is that it allows intermediaries, who are interested to provide investment-related services in Brunei particularly to provide services as Investment Advisers or

Investment Representatives to operate in and from Brunei and provide their services to both domestic as well as international businesses.

Benefit and Incentives for Setting Up Fund and Investment-Related Activities in Brunei

Funds and investment-related activities enjoy various benefits and incentives. For example, Shariah-compliant funds carefully structured under the IBCO can be offered to both local and international investors without restrictions on capital contribution. Alternatively, funds can also be established under the ITO for global investors. Investment and funds-related activities set up under the IBCO and ITO are 100% tax exempted. While those established under the domestic Companies Act may be subject to corporate tax, they may however benefit from pioneer status, which allows them to be exempted from corporate tax over a certain period.

Market development requires strong sponsorship and leadership of the host country government, especially in legal and regulatory issues, and Brunei's policy actions to promote and develop its Islamic capital market are already in place for the market to grow. By combining the various infrastructures, policies, benefits and incentives offered by the Government of Brunei and local player especially financial institutions, the potential of developing Brunei as a regional Islamic Capital Market is beneficial to the country as well as local and foreign players seeking to grab the opportunities in Brunei's emerging and exciting Islamic capital market.

Training and Education — University Brunei Darussalam, Centre for Islamic Banking, Finance and Management

The Centre for Islamic Banking, Finance and Management (CIBFM) is established under the supervision of the Universiti

Brunei Darussalam (UBD) with a close association with the BIFC. Established in March 2006, the Centre's mission is to have a sustainable and an unflinching commitment to the development of human resources in the area of Islamic banking and finance. To achieve this mission, the Centre works closely with many international core partners such as Islamic Research and Training Institute, Jeddah. It is intended to create a learning community of industry practitioners and academicians interacting in a stimulating environment.

The Centre dedicates itself to promoting Islamic banking and finance through the provision of training, research, consultancy and academic programmes at various levels. The training programme is a testament to one of the premier efforts of CIBFM to develop human capitals, who are experts in the banking and finance industry. It is structured to meet the needs of a wide spectrum of learners, from the beginners to the more seasoned learners.

Challenges

There are obstacles, however minor, which need to be overcome before Brunei can eventually implement an effective Islamic Money Market in this region. These are the few difficulties that are brought up and to be enlightened and ways for solutions to be found.

Brunei with its relatively small population of just over 385,000 has a small local market; hence, the Islamic money market in Brunei may tend to be relatively small. At present, there are 2 financial institutions that provide Islamic banking facilities and there are 3 Takaful firms providing Islamic insurance services. Additional players in the market will somehow reduce the market share of the current players and therefore may not be feasible.

Pace of product innovation is slow. Islamic banks in Brunei currently provide various savings and financing facilities based on known Islamic principles such as Al-Wadiah savings accounts and

Mudaraba investments. In the capital market sector, Brunei so far has only developed short-term Sukuk Al-Ijara. There is plenty of room that the Brunei money market can develop. One example is in the Takaful industry, where medical and family Takaful products are currently absent in the Brunei Takaful industry.

There is a lack of uniformity in Shariah principles between Islamic countries due to the absence of a universally accepted central authority on Islamic banking and finance. Therefore, Islamic banks form their own religious boards for guidance. Islamic banks need to consult their respective religious boards or Shariah advisors to seek approval for each new product with no exception to the Islamic money market instruments. Differences in interpretation of Islamic principles by different schools of thought may result in identical financial instruments rejected by one board but accepted by another; consequently, the same instruments may not be accepted in other countries.

Other issues concerning the development of Islamic money market in Brunei include the lack of a mechanism to ensure accessibility of information by the public on Islamic financial services and products, and the shortage of trained Islamic banking and finance expertise that can analyse and manage portfolios, and develop innovative products according to Islamic financial principles.

The hallmark of a well-developed financial infrastructure including the implementation of Islamic money market in Brunei is an effective legal regulatory and supervisory framework. It is in fact an indispensable and vital component of the financial structure. For the Islamic financial system to work this framework needs to be consistent with the requirements of the Shariah principles with the establishment of a Shariah Council to provide assurance that the strategic direction policies and conduct of financial transactions are in compliance with the Shariah principles. This would need to be supported by an efficient court system that can effectively deal with all Islamic banking and finance cases.

However, in Brunei all Islamic banking and financial cases are heard in the Civil Court and not in the Shariah Court, as Section 15 of the Shariah Courts Act 2000 only has jurisdiction to hear matters concerning Islamic family law.

THE RISK PROFILE OF MUDARABA AND ITS ACCOUNTING TREATMENT

Hajah Salma Latiff

Introduction

In both conventional and Islamic banking and finance, the broad range of products and services has helped support the growth of the industry. In the last decade or so, the innovative and creativity of industry players and academicians has successfully developed financial products that give support to the viability of the industry. Some of these products are complex and require risk analyst and accountants to respond adequately by studying the risks involved and how best to record and report the transactions in the financial statements.

In Islam, individuals are accountable for their actions. Actions by individuals inadvertently affect the community and the society. This implies that conscious effort is needed to ensure that the individual's actions, including individual business dealings, must be legitimate, fair and just. As quoted from Hadith Qudsi, Allah Subhanah Wa Ta'ala has declared that He will become a partner in a business between two Mushariks (*business partners*) until they indulge in cheating or breach of trust.[1] And on a broader level, an individual's actions must benefit and have a positive effect on improving the well-being of the society. Individuals therefore hold an implicit but real stewardship role in the society they live in.

This chapter reviews the application of these Islamic values to Islamic banking and finance. This review is done by considering the risk profile of a particular Islamic banking financial product, which is Mudaraba financing, and providing an assessment of the fairness and adequacy of the accounting treatment as practised by banks in 3 specific areas: information asymmetry, impairment of losses and displaced commercial risk viz-á-viz profit equalisation reserve account. The Accounting and Auditing Organisation of Islamic Financial Institution (AAOIFI) first introduced their accounting standards in 1993 as guidelines for Islamic financial institutions. The standards, developed over the years, have been successful in formalising and standardising the financial reports and statements for Islamic financial institutions. This review will therefore also attach references to the relevant standards introduced by the AAOIFI and make suggestions for improving information asymmetry, where needed.

Nature of Risks in Islamic Banks versus Conventional Banks

Islamic banks face significantly different risks as compared to an interest-based conventional bank because they operate primarily on profit-sharing basis. A businessman must be consciously aware that to gain a share in an investment, he must bear the risk of

---

[1] Usmani (2002, p. 87).

loss. The concept of risk is supported by the saying of the Beloved Prophet (peace be upon Him): 'Profit comes with liability'. This implies that profit can only be considered lawful gain if one also bears the risk of loss. It must be noted that this concept differs from a game of chance, where the outcome is not based on any calculated risk. An example would be the case of gambling where the extent of 'calculated risk' would be the probability of getting the right cards in hand or the right throw of the dice. Most importantly, the result of win/lose position of gambling is known almost immediately and the activity produces no real output.

The profitability of an Islamic bank is directly affected by the failure or success of their customers' businesses because the bank is in partnership with them. This is compared to a conventional bank, where the performance of the customers' businesses is of a secondary concern. Conventional lending is based on interest earnings; therefore, the bank's risk is directly linked to the non-receipt of interest due from their borrower on pre-agreed future dates. The performance of their customers' investments is therefore not related to the performance or profitability of the bank. Instead, conventional banks force their customers into deeper financial dilemma when they levy penalty charges for late interest payment in the event of a customer default.

The Structure of the Financial Statements of Islamic Banks

In their latest 2008 publication of "Accounting, Auditing and Governance Standards", AAOIFI presented 3 Statements of Financial Accounting (SFA) and 23 Financial Accounting Standards (FAS).

The Statement of Financial Accounting Statement No. 2 (Amended) and the Financial Accounting Standard No. 1 (FAS 1)[2] provide guidance for banks in structuring their financial statements.

---

[2] AAOIFI (2008).

FAS 1 presented the main 7 financial statements that make up the complete set of financial reporting. They are:

- Balance Sheet;
- Income Statement;
- Cash Flow Statement;
- Statement of Changes in Owners' Equity;
- Statement of Changes in Restricted Investments;
- Statements of Source and Application of Zakat; and
- Statement of Sources and Uses of Qard Funds.

The basic framework of a stylised Islamic bank's balance sheet is as follows:

Assets	Liabilities
Deposits mobilisations	Deposits collection — current and savings account
• Mudaraba	
• Musharaka	• Al-Wadiah
Funds mobilisation investments/sales receivables	Investment accounts — unrestricted or general IAH
	Restricted or special IAH
• Ijara	Private equity
• Istisna	Venture capital
• Murabaha	• Musharaka
	• Mudaraba
Trade-related financing	
• Murabaha	Profit equalisation reserve
• Bai Salam	Investment risk reserve
• Bai Muajjal	
Asset securitisation	Zakat and taxes payable
Fixed assets (net)	Capital owners' equity
Other assets	Other payables
	• Salam payables
	• Istisna payables
	• Proposed dividends
	• Other liabilities

The complete set of financial statement should be accompanied with the notes to the accounts and any statements, reports and other data which assist in providing information required by users of financial statements. When compared to the reports of a conventional bank, the additional financial information that is disclosed to the users of an Islamic bank's accounting report are the statement of changes in restricted investments, Zakat and Qard funds.

A New Risk — Accounting Risk

Risk can be classified as financial and non-financial.[3] Financial risks are those that directly affect the financial position of the company and will generally include credit, market, liquidity and operational risks. There are many other risks that may also directly affect the company such as management and reputation.

However, in recent years, we have seen many high net worth corporate accounting scandals such as Enron and WorldCom, which have resulted in bankruptcy due to manipulation of accounting information that comes only to public awareness after the management can no longer cover the wrongful acts of deceit and fraud. This new risk can be termed as 'accounting risk', which can be defined as 'the lack of disclosure in financial statements and improper assignment and allocation of accounting entries. This subsequently results in information asymmetry, thus misleading users of accounting information'.

Accounting risk can occur in a simple case where a company, wishing to evade taxes, may not disclose all the income earned for the year. It can also be a series of serious manipulation of accounting entries, where the company does not wish to disclose the actual severe losses due to the accumulation of many wrongful recording

---

[3] This classification is taken from Gleason (2000) and extracted from Tariqullah Khan (2001).

entries over the years. In most recent cases, the audit team is generally part of the scheme.

In the case of Enron, the company delayed the recording of their liabilities and the reporting of their revenues. According to accounting standards, revenue can only be recognised when the transaction is completed and where the ownership has been transferred to the buyer. The company however did not close their accounting books at the end of the accounting period with the objective of accumulating sales that were transacted after the accounting period. This affected sales turnover favourably, thereupon showing the management's achievements in meeting their 'annual' sales targets. They also recognised revenue prior to services being rendered and delayed recording payments.[4] These 'creative accounting' techniques boosted revenue and profit, to the satisfaction of the shareholders.

In the case of WorldCom, the company disguised $3.8 billion in expenses over 15 months with the objective of reducing costs substantially and reporting improved profit levels for the reported accounting period.[5]

Arguably, one can categorise the above risk as management risk, fiduciary risk or fraud risk. This, however, inadvertently undermines and trivialises the severity of accounting risk which, in some cases, emanates from the flaws and loopholes of established accounting standards. The accounting problems arising due to the lack of proper accounting disclosure or improper treatment of accounting entries are not uncommon. There arises a need, therefore, for accounting risk to be treated as a separate risk consideration, similar to legal risk issues. The severity of accounting risk calls for stringent accounting standards which are 'fraud-tight' and eliminates the possibility of corporate accounting frauds.

---

[4] http://www.ehcat.com/essay.php?t=26970, 9 March 2009.
[5] Ibid.

The Risk Profile of Mudaraba and Its Accounting Treatment

Mudaraba financing is a partnership arrangement whereby the financier or Rabb Al-Maal provides the funds to an entrepreneur or *Mudarib*, who utilises the funds in a business venture. Any profit arising from the business will be shared between the financier and the entrepreneur in a pre-agreed profit ratio. However, in the event of a loss, the financier absorbs all the losses and the entrepreneur loses the time and efforts expended in the business. The rule prevails but with the exception that if the entrepreneur proves to be negligent or has mismanaged the company, he will be legally responsible for the losses.

This simple business transaction is applied in banking operations in the form of deposit placements. The surplus monies of the customers are deposited in the bank on a profit-sharing basis. Here the customer acts as a Rabb Al-Maal and the bank as a *Mudarib*. Banks apply the Mudaraba mode of financing to attract investments from customers; these funds therefore fall under the liability side of the balance sheet.

The bank establishes itself as an intermediary between the suppliers of the capital and the users of the fund who need the money as a source of capital. In its intermediary capacity, the bank invests the funds in perceived lucrative and profitable businesses. At this

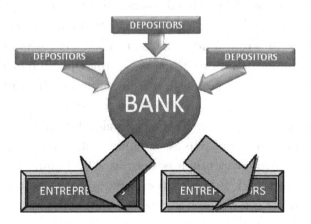

point, the simplified Mudaraba mode of financing becomes slightly complex with the introduction of a two-tier Mudaraba model to facilitate the intermediary role of the bank as a Rabb Al-Maal. The second tier will therefore fall under the asset side of the balance sheet.

As seen in the diagram, the bank, as an expert in assessing the viability of businesses, selects profitable businesses with the lowest risks and places them at the disposition of the entrepreneurs. Where the bank pools the depositors' fund into a single commingled investment, the total pool is then invested in the different sectors of the economy. The investment portfolio will comprise of various forms of investments, but the profit or loss is calculated in one lump sum, by adding all profits and deducting any investments that result in losses. Profit and loss to the bank will only be realised on closing of the accounts at the financial year-end or at the completion of the project. Profit is thereupon shared on the pre-agreed basis.

The Mudaraba investment accounts can either be unrestricted investment accounts or restricted investment accounts. In the case of unrestricted investment account, the holders allow the bank to invest their funds at the bank's discretion. Normally these funds are invested together with the deposits of current account holders and also the bank's own capital accounts. In restricted investment account, the account holders provide detailed instructions to the bank as to how and where the funds are to be invested. Banks are restricted from commingling their own funds with the restricted investment funds.

In the Mudaraba mode of financing, the Islamic banks are not dealing with lending of money to the entrepreneur. In conventional banking, banks afford banking facilities in the form of lending to the borrower and expect interest to be paid at regular intervals. In Islamic banking, the bank acts as a partner in a business venture and earns money through profit–loss sharing. The Islamic bank therefore earns a greater share of the profit of the company when compared to the interest received by the conventional bank. This is because the Islamic bank takes on the risk factor and earns greater rewards from the overall banking transaction.

The bank brings together the financier in the first tier and the entrepreneur in the second tier. The risk exposures for the financier in both tiers are the same. In the first tier, the depositor places his fund and submits to the expertise of the bank. Similarly, in the second tier, the bank hands the funds to the entrepreneur and submits to his expertise and business acumen after exercising necessary due care and diligence. The risk is high because the financier plays no further part in the usage and management of the fund. The execution of the fund is solely in the province of the entrepreneur. The question of trust is therefore of utmost importance. The financier must be confident that the Mudarib will invest the funds in *halal* and useful economic activities and thereafter will report a true and accurate profit. The Islamic values of trust, honesty and integrity are relied upon to have this transaction to result in a profitable transaction. Mudaraba is therefore a trust-based financial instrument.

Given the risk exposure, it is pertinent for accounting bodies to enforce accounting standards that can mitigate and reduce the transactional risk. AAOIFI's FAS No. 3 provides basic guidelines to the accepted method of recording the accounting entries for a Mudaraba transaction in its various forms and situations. It does not delve into the issues of risk and how to mitigate them through proper accounting methods. The AAOIFI's Shariah Standard No. 13 sheds some light in terms of accounting disclosures by requiring the parties of the Mudaraba contract to reach an agreement through a Memorandum of Understanding (MU). The MU should indicate the intention of the parties to use either unrestricted or restricted Mudaraba either through revolving transactions or separate transactions, the pre-agreed profit–loss ratio, and the type of guarantees that shall be presented by the Mudarib to cover cases of misconduct, negligence or breach of contract or other relevant issues in this regard.[6]

---

[6] AAOIFI Shariah Standards 2008, No. 13, p. 235.

In the year-end financial reports and statements of certain Islamic banks, the accompanying 'Notes to the Accounts' discloses the Mudaraba investments in terms of amount invested but little in the way of quality information. In some instances, the amount of investments in the 3Ms financial instruments — Musharaka, Mudaraba and Murabaha — are lumped together and represented by a single amount. The level of transparency is limited and grossly inadequate for the needs of the users and stakeholders. This is critical in cases where the bank has invested heavily in certain companies or where a large percentage of the portfolio comprised of companies concentrated in a specific industrial sector. Although AAOIFI's FAS No. 1 has indicated that disclosure should be made in the financial statements of the magnitude of assets invested or deposited in concentrated economic sectors or concentrated in a certain customer or in certain foreign countries, this requirement has not been practised fervently. The low level of transparency gives little access for interested individuals to gauge the risk profile without formally requesting for more specific information directly from the bank.

Regardless of whether it is a restricted or unrestricted investment, users should be privy to information that affects the riskiness of a bank's investment portfolio. For the benefit of both first- and second-tier financiers, information has to be more detailed and regular to facilitate the monitoring of the entrepreneur's activities and to prevent the likelihood of the funds being misused. An example is the recent March 2009 case where the Dubai Islamic Bank foreclosed on a real estate project where several businessmen allegedly misused the bank's fund amounting to about US$501 million.[7]

The bank plays an important intermediary role. The fact that depositors are willing to invest their funds in the bank stresses that the bank, as their Mudarib, should not fail them. Any slight negative outcomes will disrepute the bank's position as a *Mudarib*. The investor does not know whose projects/companies they are financing

------

[7] Borneo Bulletin's report dated 11 March 2009.

and the entrepreneurs/companies are clueless on where the funds are derived from originally.

To enable the monitoring of investments, banks established agreements and covenants to ensure that customers' funds are secured. If the funds are invested in a project venture, the bank will ensure that one of the covenants in the terms and conditions will require the entrepreneur to submit timely reports on the progress of the project. The Accounts Relationship Manager will make regular visits to the project site and analyse reports issued by the entrepreneur. In cases where the funds are used for purchase of specific equity investments such as Sukuk or in the shareholdings of companies, then research studies and monitoring of the performance company will be conducted by the Funds Managers to ensure that due dividends or returns will be received quarterly, half-yearly or on any agreed time intervals. Although these internal measures are carried out diligently and effectively by the banks' personnel and internal auditor, the issue remains that the information gathered by the bank is not cascaded to the interested parties and stakeholders. Why? This is because there is no statutory or legal requirement for such disclosure and there is no standardised format as recommended by accounting bodies to make such disclosure.

In the financial report of some banks, the disclosure for deposits from customers (which is in most cases comprised of more than 60% of the bank's total liabilities) is limited to a footnote that is reference to the notes of the financial statements. An example of the information provided in the notes to the financial statements is as follows:

> Deposits from customers represents short and medium term deposits accepted from the customers. The main categories of the deposits are deposits under Al-Muajjal, Al-Wadiah and Al-Mudaraba.... Liability Side of the Balance Sheet.

> Financing to customers represent short and medium term financing facilities granted to personal and corporate customers of which the main categories are Al-Ijarah.... Asset side of the Balance Sheet.

In an IMF working paper, Sundararajan and Errico (2002)[8] lucidly mentioned that in a conventional investment company, the share-holders of the company own a proportion of the company's equity capital and are given the right to vote, to receive a constant flow of information on the developments of the company's business and allowed to influence issues such as changing the investment policy of the company. In the case of Mudaraba depositors or investors, although owners of the fund, their involvement or knowledge in the application of their funds are limited and therefore they are unable to make any informed investment decisions.

The Statement of Changes in Restricted Investment, AAOIFI's FAS No. 1 has imposed certain disclosure items for a period of accounting, as summarised:

- Segregate the restricted investments by source of financing;
- Disclose the balance at beginning, during and end of period and to separate balances resulting from revaluation of restricted investments to their cash equivalent values;
- The number of investment units in each of the investment port-folios and the value per unit at the start and end of period;
- Deposits received or investment units issued by bank;
- Withdrawals or repurchase of investment profits as a *Mudarib* or its fixed fee as an investment agent;
- Overhead expenses from bank to restricted investment accounts or portfolios; and
- Profit or losses during the period with separate disclosure for revaluation of restricted investments.

A cursory review of the disclosure requirement indicates that the information so required or recommended to be disclosed is quanti-tative and restrictive in nature. Taking the view that accounting risk can be detrimental to depositors and stakeholders in general, it is

---

[8] Sundararajan V. and Errico L. (2002).

timely to insist that more detailed and regular information must be forthcoming for both restricted and unrestricted Mudaraba investments. It may be suggested that for high value restricted investments, only relevant depositors must be privy to the qualitative information. With regard to generic depositors, however, quantitative information should be accompanied with qualitative information gathered by the fund managers and accounting relationship managers. These reports should be produced regularly and made accessible to all interested depositors. The accounting bodies should table out standard formats for qualitative information reporting which all banks and financial institutions must adhere to as a legal requirement. The requirement of legal disclosure of such information will also act as a deterrent for banks and cause them to be more cautious in their investment decisions.

Accounting Treatment for Impairment Losses

In Mudaraba financing, the funds of the depositors are invested in assets, and their current values are therefore liable to changes. In the event the value of the assets increases, gain arising from the increment will only be realised at the point of liquidation of the assets. AAOIFI's Shariah Standards No. 13, Section 8.8 provides an accounting basis by stating that:

> ...It is permissible to distribute the realised profit among the parties on account, in which case, the distribution will be revised when actual or constructive valuation takes place. The final distribution of profit should be made based on the selling price of the Mudaraba assets, which is known as actual valuation. It is also permissible that the profit be distributed on the basis of constructive valuation, which is valuation of the assets on the basis of fair value.

On the other hand, in the event of a diminution of asset value, how will the asset be valued during the life of the investment?

The impairment of losses arising from the decreasing value of the asset has to be reflected in the accounts, in order for depositors to be aware that their deposits are currently exposed to valuation risk. AAOIFI has stated that losses due to liquidation are recognised at the point of liquidation by reducing the Mudaraba capital. Any provision made in the decline in the value of Mudaraba assets should be disclosed in the notes to the accounts and balance sheet as follows:

Mudaraba Financing	XXXXXX
Less: Provision for Decline in	
Value of Assets	XXXX
Net Mudaraba Financing	XXXXXX

Although the provision for the decline in value is noted as part of the financial statement, the information is vague and completely inadequate. It does not make mention of the provision as derived, what basis for measuring the diminution of assets, or which assets in the portfolio were affected by the lessening in value. It must be remembered that the Mudaraba portfolio comprises of many small investments.

The International Accounting Standards (IAS) recognises this diminution in value of debts. Under IAS 39, certain accounting guidelines have been issued to assist accountants in the valuation and reporting of the true asset value in the final accounts. The standard recognises that even when loans are apparently performing, some of the debts will be impaired even if these specific debts that have become impaired cannot be identified yet.[9]

Under IAS 39,[10] 2 different types of portfolio of loans are assessed for impairment. One type is where a portfolio of a large

---

[9] http://www.hmrc.gov.uk/manuals/bamanual/bam36070.htm.
[10] Ibid.

number of small loans has not been assessed individually, and these may or may not be performing. The second type is the portfolio of loans which have been assessed individually for impairment and have been identified as performing, but where there are indications of impairment in a group of similar assets.

The IAS 39 Standard provides ways of treating the impairment losses in the accounts. The bank may choose groupings or cohorts based on the material drivers for impairment; whether by region, by product or by value to loan ratio. The banks may also choose to apply more than one method to come to a more accurate figure. The calculation of impairment of loss is normally used for mortgage loans, which normally have a high loan to value ratio.

Although it is clear that Mudaraba investment is not a loan and no debt is involved in the investment, the concept of providing for decreasing value in Mudaraba investment can be applied in a similar manner to IAS 39. Mudaraba financing consists of investment assets such as investments in the stock market, real estate and project developments or in trade of goods. The values of these assets are liable to price fluctuations. Information asymmetry will therefore occur if banks fail to report impairment losses, which may result in inaccurate reporting in the final statements.

The different methods of quantifying impairment losses can be applied in the same way as IAS 39. For example, if certain commodity stocks are declining in value or that the property market is suffering from economic downturn, then the bank may choose this grouping of commodity stocks or property respectively and make a provision for the decline in line with the observable downward trend. The bank will definitely need to invest in the engagement of personnel to read the market and obtain the observable data. The continuous monitoring of these markets will provide a realistic measurement of the downward turn and expected future prices.

Displaced Commercial Risk and Profit Equalisation
Reserve Account

As previously mentioned, the funds from the depositor and investment account holders form more than 60% of the total source of
funds for the bank. To ensure that the account holders remain with
the bank, depositors and investors must be assured of a competitive
rate of return for their fund placements. Due to the pressure on the
banks to retain the account holders and continue attracting new
depositors, the banks may choose to waive their rights to receive part
of the entire share of their profit as Mudarib (first tier). This therefore displaces the risk from the account holders at the expense of
the bank shareholders. This can therefore be viewed as a payment
by the bank to maintain customers' loyalty.

In the long run, however, such an approach would be to the disadvantage of the shareholders. To overcome this practice, therefore,
the Profit Equalisation Reserve[11] or PER was introduced to the liability side of the bank's balance sheet. The purpose of PER account
is to shift the displaced commercial risk back to the account holders
by transferring a proportion out of the Mudaraba income, before
allocating the Mudarib share. The reasoning behind this accounting
manipulation is to maintain a certain level of return on investment
for the investment account holders as well as to increase owners'
equity.[12] By doing so, the bank is able to smoothen the returns of the
account holders and continue paying competitive returns especially
in times when their investment portfolio has underperformed. This
accounting treatment is in line with AAOIFI's FAS No. 11 under the
Provision and Reserves Standards.

---

[11] The PER issue from the perspective of corporate governance is well discussed by
Simon Archer and Rifaat Ahmed Abdul Karim (2007), pp. 310–341 ((IFSB),
Guiding Principles of Risk Management for Institutions (other than Insurance
Institutions) offering only Islamic Financial Services, December 2005).
[12] AAOIFI Financial Accounting Standards No. 11, Provision and Reserves.

This method of managing account holders funds by the creation of PER may have ethical implications. To fulfill its fiduciary duty, the bank should give the account holders the actual profit amount due to them as per the pre-agreed profit ratio. Since the transfer of the amount may differ from one year to another depending on the accumulated balance in the PER account, the account holders may either benefit or disbenefit from this accounting treatment. While it is important to ensure that account holders should get exactly what is due to them, it is also pertinent to ensure that viability of the bank remains intact as an ongoing concern for the benefit of the account holders.

To overcome this paradox, the Islamic Financial Services Board (IFSB) recommended that the basis for appropriating an amount to be transferred to PER should be pre-defined in accordance with contractual conditions. These conditions should be accepted by the account holders after a formal review by the directors of the Islamic financial institution. In addition, a written agreement should be obtained from the account holders prior to depositing the fund with the Islamic financial institution. Yet another solution would be for the bank to absorb the transferred amount in their appropriation account and accept a reduced amount as profit to be distributed to shareholders. Since the shareholders are the members who would normally continue to be with the financial institutions, it is fair that their profit fluctuates with the performance of the bank. In the long run, their profit will be 'smoothened out' by the performance of the investments and the effectiveness of their management.

In the event that PER practice is to be adopted by all Islamic financial institutions, it is also recommended for AAOIFI to place a ceiling on the percentage that can be transferred out of the Mudaraba income in any one accounting year. This is to ensure that the bank does not abuse this practice in view of the interest of the account holders.

Conclusion

Mudaraba financing is one of the modes of finance approved by Islam. This mode of financing, although well used in the liability side of the balance sheet, has proved unattractive to banks in the asset side of the balance sheet. This is due to the fact that Mudaraba is a trust-based contract and therefore vulnerable to moral risks and others. This chapter views the issue of risk from the point of view of the customer and the bank as Rabb Al-Maal based on first- and second-tiers of the Mudaraba financing mode. It highlights the issues of Mudaraba risks and how accounting, as an information tool, can be utilised to reduce information asymmetry. Although the bank operates in a risky and uncertain environment, it is important to be transparent and improve the quality and regularity of information to assist accounts holders in making informed decisions.

Finally, it must be stated here that AAOIFI has provided valuable contributions in the area of corporate governance by drafting the accounting standards for Islamic financial institutions to comply. Unfortunately, AAOIFI cannot enforce the implementation of the Standards since it is not a statutory body. Due to its lack of legal muscle, many banks have not strictly adhered to its accounting requirements. It is timely that these standards be made a legal requirement and be accepted in the same status as IAS. This will undoubtedly improve and bring uniformity in the financial reporting standards amongst the Islamic financial institutions.

Bibliography

(IFSB), I. F. (December 2006). *Guiding Principles of Corporate Governance for Institutions Offering only Islamic Financial Services (Excluding Islamic Insurance (Takaful) Institutions and Islamic Mutual Funds)*. Kuala Lumpur.

(IFSB), I. F. (December 2005). *Guiding Principles of Risk Management for Institutions (Other than Insurance Institutions) Offering only Islamic Financial Services.* Kuala Lumpur.

AAOIFI. (2008). *Accounting, Auditing and Governance Standards for Islamic Financial Institutions.* Manama, Bahrain: AAOIFI.

AAOIFI. (2008). *Sharia Standards for Islamic Financial Institutions.* Manama, Bahrain: AAOIFI.

Khan, T. (2001(1422H)). *Risk Management. An Analysis of Issues in Islamic Financial Industry.* Jeddah-Saudi Arabia: Islamic Research and Training Institute.

L., S. V. (2002). *Islamic Financial Institutions and Products in the Global Financial System: Key Issues in Risk Management and Challenges Ahead.* Paper presented in a conference in Tehran, Republic of Iran.

Simon, A. and Rifaat, A. A. K. (2007). *Islamic Finance — The Regulatory Challenge.* Singapore: John Wiley & Sons (Asia) Pte. Ltd.

Usmani, D. M. (2002). *Meezanbank's Guide to Islamic Banking.* Karachi: Darul-Ishaat Publishers.

LEGAL AND REGULATORY ISSUES CONCERNING ISLAMIC FINANCE'S DEVELOPMENT IN MALAYSIA

*Dato Dr Nik Norzrul Thani Nik Hassan Thani
and Madzlan Hussain**

Introduction

A sound legal and regulatory framework is fundamental in the development of any financial system. This has been acknowledged by the Malaysian government, which shows its commitment by formulating industry-friendly policies, amending existing laws as well as enacting new laws to promote Islamic finance. The coming years would see Islamic finance in Malaysia continue to break new ground. This chapter will discuss and illustrate the development of the legal and regulatory framework for Islamic finance in Malaysia. It will *inter alia* analyse the development of an effective legal framework within the context of growing internationalisation of Islamic finance.

---

* The authors would like to thank Mohd Hariz Daud, Senior Associate at Zaid Ibrahim & Co. Kuala Lumpur, for his invaluable assistance.

Malaysia has been in the forefront between Muslim countries in terms of economic development. It has shown admirable political will in putting into place the necessary infrastructure for a more conducive development of Islamic banking and finance (IBF). To further pursue a comprehensive Islamic financial system and complement the IBF industry, the government has also implemented initiatives towards an Islamic financial market comprising an Islamic capital market (ICM) and an Islamic money market (IMM).

Acknowledging that a sound legal and regulatory framework is fundamental in the development of any financial system, the government has shown its commitment by formulating industry-friendly policies, amending existing laws as well as enacting new laws to promote Islamic finance, generally.

Primary Legal Infrastructure

The framework that caters specifically for the development of Islamic finance was initially conceptualised with the enactment of the Islamic Banking Act 1983 (IBA). The IBA applies to full-fledged Islamic banks and imposes requirements for Islamic banks to conform to practices of prudent banking.

The central bank, Bank Negara Malaysia (BNM), is vested with similar powers of supervising and regulating Islamic banks as in the case with other banks. IBA requires an Islamic bank to have its own Shariah Advisory Council comprising qualified Shariah experts to ensure that its operations conform to the Shariah.

This was followed by amendments to the Banking and Financial Institutions Act 1989 (BAFIA) that governs conventional banks. By virtue of Section 124 of BAFIA, conventional banks may operate Islamic banking business and Islamic financial business subject to compliance with rules and guidelines of BNM. Having opened the door for IBF products to be offered by a larger number of players,

BNM has set up its own Shariah Advisory Council to assist it in monitoring the industry practices and standards.

Islamic insurance industry was launched by the enactment of the Takaful Act 1984 (TA). The TA allows the operations of Islamic insurance (Takaful). The basic concept of Takaful highlighted by the TA is the provision of insurance as a form of business in conformity with Shariah and is based on the Islamic principles of Al-Takaful (assurance) and Al-Mudaraba (commercial profit-sharing contract). The introduction of Takaful business complements the needs for Shariah-compliant insurance within the financial system.

On the capital market front, the securities and futures industry including in relation to Islamic securities are now governed by the new Capital Market Services Act 2007 (CMSA), which has consolidated the Securities Industry Act 1983 (SIA), the Futures Industry Act 1993 (FIA) and Part IV of the Securities Commission Act 1993 (SCA). The Securities Commission (SC) established under the SCA regulates the industry including issuing licences and introducing the relevant guidelines. The CMSA which came into force on 28 September 2007 is seen as the move towards the enhancement of investor protection by the introduction of a single licensing regime and the enhancement of the Securities Commission (SC) enforcement powers.

There is also an initiative made by the CMSA in facilitating the country to become a global Islamic financial hub. Section 316 of the CMSA empowers the Minister of Finance to make such modification in the prescription on the usage of expressions in the securities laws as may be necessary to give full effect to the principles of Shariah in respect of such Islamic securities. This provides the groundwork for the Minister to prescribe modifications to the securities laws to give effect to Shariah principles.

In addition, Section 316 also empowers the SC to specify guidelines to such Islamic securities in giving the full effect to the principles of Shariah to such Islamic securities. Thus, from time to time the SC issues guidelines that regulate various types of Islamic capital market products including Islamic debt securities and Shariah-compliant stocks. Therefore anyone who, for example, wishes to issue Islamic asset-backed securities, becomes an Islamic fund manager or qualified Shariah adviser, or even includes his company's shares in the list of halal (permissible) counters would have to comply with the relevant SC guidelines. For example, the SC Guidelines on the Issuance of Private Debt Securities provide that a qualified Shariah adviser must approve an Islamic private debt securities before it can be issued.

The operation of offshore financial institution (OFI) in Labuan is subjected to a different set of legislations independent of the laws governing financial activities in the domestic market although Labuan is part of Malaysia. OFIs establishing or conducting business in the Labuan International Business and Financial Centre (Labuan IBFC) are subjected to the various offshore legislations among others such as the Offshore Companies Act 1990, Offshore Banking Act 1990, Offshore Insurance Act 1990, Labuan Offshore Securities Industry Act 1998, Labuan Trust Companies Act 1990 and Labuan Offshore Trusts Act 1996. Although there has yet to be specific statutes regarding IBF or ICM industry in Labuan, the Labuan Offshore Financial Services Authority Act 1996 (LOFSA 1996) empowers the Labuan Offshore Financial Services Authority (LOFSA) to issue directives to ensure that OFIs conduct offshore financial transactions in accordance with the laws and norms of good and honourable conduct to preserve the good repute of Labuan as a centre for offshore financial services. In 2003, the LOFSA pursuant to its power under Section 4(5) of the LOFSA 1996 issued a directive in relation to the requirements that OFIs have to observe in offering Islamic financial products and services in the Labuan IBFC.

IBF and ICM Products

The specific legal framework creates new opportunities in IBF and ICM and encourages Malaysian financial institutions to launch a wide range of new IBF and ICM products and services. The laws applied in the Labuan IBFC have also been reviewed to ensure comprehensive and continuous improvement to the legal framework.

At the early stage, home financing facilities based on the principle of Bai Bithaman Ajil (deferred sale) as well as saving and investment accounts based on the principles of Al-Wadiah (safekeeping) and Mudaraba (profit-sharing) were introduced. Later, various trade financing products based on Murabaha (cost plus profit sale), Ijarah (leasing), Bai Al-Takjiri (leasing ending with ownership), Kafalah (guarantee) and Qardhul Hassan (benevolent loan) were offered. Personal financing based on Bai Al-Inah, another deferred sale instrument, also became available.

The last decade has seen the rapid growth of ICM products whereby Islamic debt securities (IDS) known as Sukuk have gained popularity to the extent of dominating the debt securities issuance in Malaysia. As of November 2006, the IBF industry's total assets in Malaysia stand at approximately RM122 billion with annual expansion average rate of 19.3% since 2003. The performance of the Malaysian Islamic financial market, in particular the ICM, has been encouraging. A total of 22 new IDS/Sukuk issues totalling to RM17.7 billion were announced in the first half of 2007, representing 31% of the Malaysian domestic market's rated corporate bond issues for that period. By the end of the year 2007, 76% of private debt securities approved in Malaysia are Sukuk. Profits of Malaysia's Islamic banks have surpassed RM1 billion (US$272 million, EUR227 million) since the year 2005.

The first IDS were issued in 1990 by Shell MDS Sdn Bhd based on the principle of Bai Bithaman Ajil. Since then IDS based on Ijarah or Murabaha were also issued. The IDS are traded in the secondary market under the principle of Bai Al-Dayn (sale of debt). Mudaraba and Musharaka (joint venture) arrangements have also gained some momentum for equity-based financing products such as unit trust and venture capital. Musharaka Mutanaqisah (diminishing partnership) has also been widely used.

The issuance of global Sukuk by Kumpulan Guthrie Bhd and the Malaysian government respectively proves that Malaysia can come up with IBF and ICM products that are recognised and accepted internationally. Since the inception of Malaysia Global Sukuk in 2002, significant progress has been achieved. In 2007, Malaysia accounted for about 60% of the global Sukuk outstanding, amounting to about US$64 billion. The total volume of Sukuk issued 2007 amounted to US$82 billion with a strong average growth rate of 40% since the year 2006. Malaysia not only represents the largest Sukuk market in terms of outstanding size, but also in terms of number of issuance. The year 2006 saw the issuance in Malaysia of more globally accepted Sukuk employing the concepts of Mudaraba, Musharaka and Ijara. Government-linked companies (GLCs) also demonstrated their commitment and support in this regard with several Sukuk being issued benchmarked to globally acceptable structures. These include the Khazanah Nasional Berhad exchangeable Sukuk, the world's first Islamic exchangeable Sukuk. The world's largest Sukuk issued in 2007 amounting to approximately US$5 billion was also issued in Malaysia, a testament of the country's success of becoming the international hub of Sukuk origination.

Incentives for Islamic Finance

The government has shown no hesitation in amending its tax regime to facilitate the development of Islamic finance. Since Islamic banking products such as Murabaha and Bai Bithaman Ajil mainly involve trading instead of merely lending, unlike conventional banks, the financing documents would comprise of sale and purchases. The documentation to the transaction would be repetitious.

Therefore, the Stamp Act 1949 (SA) was amended to provide that for the repayment of moneys provided under a scheme of financing made according to the Shariah, the stamp duty chargeable shall be calculated on the principal amount provided by the financier or financing body. This avoids the double stamp duty which otherwise would be payable since there are two sale and purchase agreements entered into in Bai Bithaman Ajil and Murabaha transactions.

Another example of stamp duty incentive is in the form of the Stamp Duty (Exemption) Order 1996. This Order gives stamp duty exemption for any documents in relation to the refinancing of conventional loans with Islamic financing facilities. Meanwhile, the Stamp Duty (Remission) (No. 4) Order 1996 provides for remission of excess duty for instrument of loan agreement. It states that 'Instrument of loan agreement for the purchase of goods made under the principle of Al-Bai Bithaman Ajil of the Shariah Law is subjected to stamp duty of RM3.00 or RM10.00 only if executed under seal and the excess duty is remitted'.

Recently another stamp duty incentive was provided in relation to approved Islamic financing instruments by virtue of Stamp Duty (Remission) (No. 2) Order 2007. Based on this Order, 20% stamp duty exemption will be provided in relation to the stamp duty payable on the principal or primary instrument of financing made according to the principles of Shariah and chargeable pursuant to subparagraph 22(1)(a) or subparagraph 27(a) of the First Schedule of the SA subject to the condition that the instrument is approved by the Shariah Advisory Council of BNM or the SC. In addition, effective from the year 2007 until the year 2016, instruments relating to Islamic banking and Takaful activities conducted in currencies other than Ringgit as well as non-Ringgit Islamic securities approved by the SC and executed under the Malaysian International Islamic Financial Centre are exempted from stamp duty.

The Real Property Gains Tax Act 1976 (RPGTA) imposes tax on gains from disposal of real property situated in Malaysia. Hence, in normal circumstances, a sale and purchase of property for the purpose of Islamic financing should attract gains tax on the party disposing the property. However, the RPGTA has been amended to the effect that in the case of the disposal of an asset by a person to the bank under an Islamic financing facility, the disposal price shall be deemed to be equal to the acquisition price thus not attracting any gains tax. Currently, pursuant to the Real Property Gains Tax (Exemption)(No. 2) Order 2007, any disposal of chargeable assets after 31 March 2007 is exempted from any gains tax.

Income Tax Act 1967 (ITA) is the main legislation governing the tax regime in Malaysia. From time to time the government in its annual budget provides tax incentives to encourage the private sector to finance their business using Islamic principles. There were 5 tax exemptions in relation to IBF and ICM being granted by the government in the year 2007.

An example of this is the Income Tax (Deduction for Expenditure on Issuance of Islamic Securities) Rules 2007, which provides that for the purpose of ascertaining the adjusted income of a company from its business for the basis period for a year of assessment, there shall be allowed a deduction of an amount equal to the expenditure incurred on the issuance of Islamic securities approved by the SC established under the SCA pursuant to the principle of Mudaraba, Musharaka, Ijara, Istisna, or any other principle in accordance with the Shariah principle approved by the Minister from the year of assessment 2007 until the year of assessment 2010.

Another notable exemption is the Income Tax (Exemption) (No. 14) Order 2007. The Order provides that a special purpose vehicle company established solely for the purpose of issuing Islamic securities approved by the SC is exempted from the payment of income tax in respect of income derived from the issuance of Islamic securities. Further, the Income Tax (Exemption) (No. 15) Order 2007 exempts companies managing Shariah-compliant funds of foreign investors approved by the SC from tax derived on the management fees received for 10 years beginning from the year of assessment 2007 until the year of assessment 2016. In the subsequent year, the Income Tax (Exemption) (No. 6) Order 2008 was issued to extend such exemption to companies providing

Shariah-compliant fund management services approved by the SC to local investors effective from the year of assessment 2008 until the year of assessment 2016.

Regulatory Bodies

The success of the ICM and IBF in Malaysia lies primarily in the helm provided by the two regulatory bodies, namely BNM and the SC.

BNM was established on 26 January 1959, under the Central Bank of Malaya Ordinance, 1958. In particular, BNM ensures that the availability and cost of money and credit in the economy are consonant with national macroeconomic objectives. In this respect, BNM acts as the banker for currency issue, keeper of international reserves and safeguarding the value of the ringgit, banker and financial adviser to the government, agency responsible for monetary policy and management of the financial system and banker to the banks.

The sound economic fundamentals of Malaysia — even during the slowdown of the economy in 1997 and 1998 — as well as the growth achieved by Islamic banks in Malaysia are the best evidences on the capability of BNM to steer the IBF industry in Malaysia. BNM has managed to create a ground breaking model of dual-banking system whereby Islamic banking and conventional banking complement each other without affecting the stability of the Malaysian financial system.

The SC is the regulatory body overseeing the development of capital market in Malaysia. It was officially set up on 1 March 1993, marking a significant milestone in the government's commitment to have a central authority in the regulation and development of the securities and futures industries in Malaysia. The SC's ultimate responsibility is of course protecting the investor. Apart from discharging its regulatory functions, the SC is also obliged by statute to encourage and promote the development of the securities and futures markets in Malaysia.

Its commitment and dedication towards the promotion of ICM highlight the uniqueness of the SC from other similar regulatory bodies throughout the world. Apart from coming up with a policy document as comprehensive as the Capital Market Masterplan and setting up a specialised Islamic Capital Market Unit (ICMU) within its Market Policy and Development Division to carry out research and development activities including formulating and facilitating a long-term plan to further strengthen the ICM in Malaysia, it is also the first capital market regulatory body to have its own Shariah Advisory Council (SAC).

As a result, international recognition has been achieved as the SC was mandated by the Executive Committee of the International Organisation of Securities Commissions (IOSCO) to lead a task force on ICMs at the 2002 IOSCO Annual Conference and meetings in Istanbul, Turkey which were held from May 18–24, 2002.

In the offshore financial industry, the main regulatory body is the LOFSA. The island of Labuan was declared as an International Offshore Financial Centre on 1 October 1990. Subsequently, LOFSA was established on 15 February 1996 pursuant to LOFSA 1996. Primarily, the Labuan IBFC (formerly known as the Labuan International Offshore Financial Centre) was developed towards catering for activities relating to offshore banking business. However, having a significant benefit from its strategic location at the heart of the fastest growing region in the world, the activities in Labuan IBFC have now become more diversified and comprehensive including trust, insurance business, investment banking, and capital market activities as well as the IBF and ICM industry.

LOFSA's dedication towards developing Labuan IBFC as the premier regional Islamic financial centre in the Asian Pacific region was shown by the development of a robust, effective and efficient legal and regulatory framework enabling conducive environment to support the development of the Islamic financial services industry in the Labuan IBFC. In 2006, LOFSA has taken a parallel effort with BNM and the SC by establishing its own SAC to advise LOFSA on issues relating to the development of Shariah-compliant products and instruments in Labuan IBFC. In addition, LOFSA has also established the Task Force on Islamic Finance (TFIF). The TFIF is part of the consultative approach of LOFSA to engage with OFI for more effective development of business in Labuan IBFC. TFIF's main role is to provide counsel on the development of Islamic finance business by assisting LOFSA in reviewing existing rules and regulations to ensure optimum environment for the growth of Islamic finance as well as recommends new products to be endorsed by the SAC.

Framework for the Future

The inauguration of the Capital Market Masterplan (CMM) by the SC on 22 February 2001 and the Financial Sector Masterplan (FSM) by BNM on 1 March 2001 mark the first comprehensive strategic policy document issued by regulatory bodies duly empowered by a government for the benefit and advantage of ICM and IBF.

The FSM envisions that the Islamic banking and Takaful industry landscape in 2010 would evolve in parallel with conventional banking and insurance to achieve the following:

- Constitute 20% of the banking and insurance market share with an effective contribution to the financial sector of the Malaysian economy;
- Represented by a number of strong and highly capitalised Islamic banking institutions and Takaful operators offering a comprehensive and complete range of Islamic financial products and services;
- Underpinned by a comprehensive and conducive Shariah and regulatory framework;
- Supported by a dedicated institution (Shariah commercial court) in the judiciary system that addresses legal issues related to Islamic banking and Takaful;

- Supported by a sufficient number of well-trained, high calibre individuals and management teams with the required expertise; and
- Epitomise Malaysia as a regional Islamic financial centre.

To realise the set-out objectives, the FSM seeks to build the necessary foundations in terms of capacity building, the provision of infra-structure and regulatory framework development. The efforts by BNM need to be complemented by that of the Islamic banking insti-tutions and Takaful operators to bring about the crystallisation of an efficient, progressive and comprehensive Islamic banking and Takaful industry.

Meanwhile, the CMM under its Chapter 3 sets out as one of its objectives and strategic initiatives the aim 'to establish Malaysia as an international Islamic capital market centre'. This is basically in recognition of ICM as one of the niche areas in which Malaysia has a comparative and competitive advantage following the significant development and expansion in its Islamic equity and bond markets over recent years.

Henceforth, the following strategic initiatives have been ear-marked to achieve the aforesaid objectives:

- Facilitating the development of a wide range of innovative and competitive products and services related to the ICM;
- Creating a viable market for the effective mobilisation of Islamic funds;
- Ensuring that there is an appropriate and comprehensive accounting, tax and regulatory framework for the ICM; and
- Enhancing the value recognition of the Malaysian ICM internationally.

On 1 November 2006, the BNM Governor Tan Sri Dr Zeti Akhtar Aziz held a dialogue with members of the financial services frater-nity within the IBF industry in Kuala Lumpur on the Malaysian

International Islamic Financial Centre (MIFC). First announced on 14 August 2006, MIFC is the government's initiative to capture the current globalising momentum of Islamic finance and institution-alise the country as the major international Islamic finance hub serving ASEAN, East Asia, South Asia and the Middle East. The BNM Governor took the opportunity to announce a series of strategies formulated to achieve this aim. They include some significant legal changes and concessions, and the reason behind them is the rapid growth of IBF industry in Malaysia and worldwide. Among the key measures and strategies that have been outlined to promote MIFC are as follows:

- Liberalising the Islamic banking, Takaful and retakaful markets with the issuance of new licence to allow for increased foreign participation;
- Attracting international entities by allowing foreign equity up to 49% in existing Islamic banks and Takaful companies;
- Issuing International Islamic Bank (IIB) and International Takaful Operator licences to qualified Malaysian and foreign companies to conduct the full range of businesses in inter-national currencies and enjoy a 10-year tax exemption under the Income Tax Act 1967 beginning from the year of assess-ment 2007 to year of assessment 2016. This is effective from 15 September 2006;
- Allowing the existing Malaysian institutions to set up International Currency Business Units (ICBUs) to offer Islamic financial services with a similar 10-year tax exemption to enable them to compete with IIBs, also effective from 15 September 2006; and
- Giving greater flexibility to Labuan offshore entities offering Islamic financial services to open operation offices anywhere in Malaysia, without the requirement of having to maintain a Labuan management office. According to LOFSA's MIFC announce-ment dated 12 October 2006, there is also no limitation on the

staffing and number of operation offices to be opened outside of Labuan. This would allow the 6 existing offshore Islamic banks and Islamic investment banks and 2 retakaful companies operating there to participate in the MIFC.

Bank Negara Malaysia and the SC have continued the extensive efforts in ensuring that the country remains as a global key player in the IBF and ICM industry. To allow international issuers to issue multi-currency Sukuks and having the flexibility to swap domestic currency funding into other currency, BNM has issued two circulars that have liberalised the Foreign Exchange Administration Rules (FEAR). In 2007, the threshold of 50% of the net asset value (NAV) on the investment of Islamic funds in foreign currency assets is abolished. Hence, Malaysian unit trust and fund management companies with Shariah-compliant funds would be free to invest 100% of such fund in foreign currency denominated assets, whether within or outside Malaysia. Further liberalisation of the FEAR was seen when BNM on May 2008 announced that companies are allowed to borrow any amount in foreign currency from licensed Islamic banks and licensed international Islamic banks. On 11 August 2008, the Governor of BNM during the Malaysian Islamic Finance 2008 Issuers and Investors Forum had mentioned that Malaysia has implemented the Prudential Standards developed by the Islamic Financial Services Board (IFSB) in support of moving towards consistent development of Islamic finance across different jurisdictions to ensure its soundness and stability.

Meanwhile, the SC in ensuring the sustainability of ICM in Malaysia has to date, through its SAC published 4 guidelines and 5 practice notes in relation to the ICM industry and between them is the world's first guidelines for Islamic REIT in 2005. In 2007, the IBF industry's total assets constitute to 15.4% of the total banking industry's assets in the country. In December 2007, the SC issued its first guideline in relation to the ICM industry pursuant to its power under Section 377 of the CMSA, which is the Guidelines on Islamic

Fund Management. The guidelines provide for the requirements to be complied by the Islamic fund managers carrying on Islamic fund management.

The Director General of LOFSA, in the Global Islamic Finance Forum 2007, has announced on several key efforts taken up by LOFSA to ensure the progress of Labuan IBFC as the centre for Islamic finance and innovative Islamic financial solution. The role of the SAC under LOFSA has been expended to cover the endorsement of Islamic financial products and instruments submitted by OFI. In addition, LOFSA has also published the framework for conducting Shariah-compliant trust as well as Takaful and retakaful businesses in the Labuan IBFC. LOFSA has also seen the need to establish the Labuan International Financial Exchange (LFX) as a focal point for dual listing and trading of both Islamic and conventional financial instruments. The huge potential of the LFX was seen by the listing of 37 instruments in the LFX since 2001 with a market capitalisation of US$14.2 billion. Out of this number, 7 are Shariah-compliant investments with market capitalisation of more than US$2.0 billion. In achieving the said objective for LFX, strategic alliance with other international bourses has been made to cross-list Shariah-compliant products across markets. As a result, some Malaysian and Bahraini Sukuk are cross-listed in Labuan and Bahrain. LOFSA, being a member of the International Islamic Financial Market (IIFM) since 2001 is also actively involved in the promotion of cross-border secondary trading of Islamic financial instruments.

The MIFC Initiative Key Achievements

Since its announcement on August 2006, BNM has made it known that MIFC is more than just a series of initiatives. It is to be a one-stop centre that will not only handle all queries from interested quarters, such as clarifications on foreign equity, tax exemptions, immigration policies, and so forth, but will also facilitate the requisite processes. The MIFC initiative is set to position Malaysia as an internationally recognised platform of Islamic financial hub in key sectors of Sukuk origination, Islamic wealth and fund management, Islamic international banking, international Takaful and human capital development. The platforms prepared by the MIFC initiative to achieve the nation's aspiration of becoming a global Islamic financial hub are as follows:

- A comprehensive and competitive Islamic financial market;
- Becoming the hub for Sukuk origination;
- Progressive Islamic legal, regulatory and Shariah infrastructure;
- Quality human capital development infrastructure; and
- Conducive business environment.

The steps and proposals outlined in relation to the MIFC are being followed through by the authorities and have been complemented by assertive marketing efforts. Malaysia looks poised to overcome its competition and emerges as the hub for Islamic banking and finance for the region. The MIFC has so far achieved, among others:

- Average annual growth of 18–20% of Islamic banking assets since the year 2006 and currently accounting for 15.4% of total banking assets in Malaysia;
- A strong growth in assets and net contributions of the Takaful and retakaful industry with average annual growth rate of 19% in 2007;
- Over 85% of securities listed on Bursa Malaysia are Shariah-compliant, which represents about 60% of the total market capitalisation;
- Shariah-compliant unit trust funds have chalked up sales totalling to RM2.96 billion in 2007, a growth of 84% from the year 2006; and

- Becoming the first ever country in the world to provide professional certification in Islamic finance via the Certified Islamic Finance Professional (CIFP) programme, which saw its first batch graduating by the end of the year 2008.

In June 2008, the MIFC was selected as the Best International Islamic Finance Centre 2008 at the Second Annual London Sukuk Summit Awards of Excellence. The summit was endorsed by the UK Treasury, UK Trade & Investment (UKTI), City of London Corporation and the London Stock Exchange. Moving forward, the MIFC now aims of strengthening the international interlinkages in the global Islamic financial system by launching the Global Communication Campaign (GCC) at the Third Malaysian Islamic Finance Issuers and Investors Forum 2008 on 11 August 2008. The GCC will highlight opportunities and offerings available in Malaysia for investors, issuers, industries in the economic sectors and for professionals and practitioners with interest in the Islamic financial services industry.

Conclusions

Currently, in Malaysia, there are 13 full-fledged Islamic banks, which includes 4 Islamic banks with presence in the global Islamic banking industry, namely, Al Rajhi Banking & Investment Corporation Berhad, Kuwait Finance House (Malaysia) Berhad, Asian Finance Bank Berhad, and HSBC Amanah Malaysia Berhad. The coming years would see Islamic finance in Malaysia continue to break new ground, among others, the government's plan to spur the overall development of the Islamic financial system in the country by promoting Malaysia as a regional and international Islamic financial hub for IBF via MIFC, the expansion of Labuan as an international Islamic financial centre and the liberalisation of the markets as planned under the FSM.

In terms of legal infrastructure, a dedicated High Court has been established to handle cases on Islamic banking and finance, and a law review committee has been formed as an extension of this initiative. In addition, the Shariah framework would also be further strengthened to complement the development of the IBF industry in the country. A working group on Shariah has been formed to conduct a comprehensive review of Islamic banking issues, as well as to formulate a guide for the innovation of IBF products.

In meeting the growing global demands for competent and qualified human capital of the industry, BNM has initiated the establishment of a dedicated university called the International Centre for Education in Islamic Finance (INCEIF) which came into operation in March 2006 with an aim to be an international nucleus for tertiary education in Islamic finance, training and research.

BNM also established the International Shariah Research Academy for Islamic Finance (ISRA), as a specialised research outfit funded and backed by an endowment from BNM to conduct research concerning issues in the fast-growing field of Islamic finance and support existing local and international standard-setting bodies.

The changing worldviews in the aftermath of the 9/11 incident have required Muslims to strengthen their economic position and review their investment options, more than ever before. Malaysia provides an alternative not only in terms of investment opportunities which are halal and with good potential returns, but also assures stability and security in terms of adequate legal and regulatory framework. Under the 10-year Masterplan for Islamic finance, the legal and regulatory framework will continue to be revised and improved while market players are encouraged to lend their experience and expertise to develop the industry.

RECENT LEGAL AND REGULATORY DEVELOPMENTS FOR ISLAMIC BANKING AND FINANCE IN INDONESIA

*Hanim Hamzah**

Introduction

Being only available from the mid-1990s, it is often claimed that Islamic banking and finance has been slow to take up in Indonesia — the world's most populous Muslim country, with nearly 90% or approximately 220 million Muslims.[1] The relative delay is perhaps ironic, but it is not a unique state of affairs for there are various Muslim countries dealing with respective colonial heritages of dual

* The author would like to thank senior associate Harly Siregar, Roosdiono and Partners, for his research assistance.
[1] At the legal-doctrinal level, Indonesian Muslims are generally followers of the Shafi'i school of Islamic law, although other schools (*Madhhab*) such as Maliki, Hanafi and Hanbali are also recognised.

or 'competing' legal systems, so that introducing and developing Shariah law has rarely, if ever, been a simple matter.[2] In Indonesia, several leading scholars and the general public have not generally perceived conventional banking to be *haram*, or recognised *riba* (interest/usury) to be identical with the interest charged or offered by modern banks.[3]

This 'low awareness' arguably dates back to concerns, of the country's founders and subsequent Presidents, about overt support for Shariah law. Indonesia gained its independence in 1945. In its constitution (specifically the initial draft of the preamble) was the statement: 'Belief in one Supreme God with the obligation for followers of Islam to perform Shariah (Islamic) law'. However, the last words — 'with the obligation for followers of Islam to perform Shariah law' (*dengan kewajiban menjalankan Shariah Islam bagi pemeluknya*) — were removed after protests by some who felt that the statement amounted to discrimination against other religions.[4] So the line stayed as 'Belief in one Supreme God', without mention of Shariah. Especially at that time, the founders' support was largely for the Pancasila (five principles) ideology to include the country's many ethnic groups.[5]

---

[2] See 'The effectiveness of the legal and regulatory framework for Islamic financial services' by Nik Norzrul Thani Nik Hassan Thani and Aida Othman in *Islamic Finance: Global Issues and Challenges* (Islamic Financial Services Board, 2008), pp. 1–37.

[3] 'Islamic Banking and its potential impact' by Thomas A. Timberg in *Risk Management: Islamic Financial Policies*, pp. 1–12, presented at 'Paving the way forward: An international conference on best practices'. See also *Islamic Banking — Fiqh and Financial Analysis* by Ir Adiwarnan A. Karim (PT Rajagrafindo Persada, 2005).

[4] 'Introduction' in *Shari'a and Constitutional Reform in Indonesia* by Nadirsyah Hosen (Institute of Southeast Asian Studies, Hongkong, 2007), pp. 1–27.

[5] The five principles are (i) Belief in one supreme God (*Ketuhanan Yang Maha Esa*); (ii) a just and civilised humanity (*Kemanusiaan Yang Adil dan Beradab*); (iii) the unity of Indonesia (*Persatuan Indonesia*); (iv) democracy guided by decision-making through consensus (*Kerakyatan Yang Dipimpin oleh Hikmat Kebijaksanaan, Dalam Permusyawaratan Perwakilan*), and (v) social justice for all the peoples of Indonesia (*Keadilan Sosial bagi seluruh Rakyat Indonesia*).

These 'plural' concerns still exist today, albeit in slightly different terms. As stated by the Finance Minister, Sri Muliyani Indrawati, Indonesia's option for Shariah-compliant banking and finance is simply one of many, neither the only nor necessarily the best, but more can be done to support the sector.[6]

While there has been little impetus from the public for Islamic finance, it is the government, as in other Muslim countries, that has taken the initiative to expand Shariah services. But the influential stakeholders of banks, finance companies, pension funds, mutual funds and assurance companies have also played their part by pushing for change, and taking advantage of laws and regulations passed to develop Islamic finance.

Global influences have also left their mark. After 9/11, and following the boom in oil prices, US$1 trillion of 'Gulf money' began to flow towards 'home countries' including Indonesia. By 2007, countries from the Middle East had invested some US$2.25 billion in the country.[7] Efforts to attract these funds have helped spur more regulations to be reviewed and reforms to be put in place for Shariah-compliance.

What with an arguably increased awareness of the Muslim Ummah on a global scale, both the international and domestic contexts have changed. So that in the wake of the downfall of the repressive Soeharto regime in 1998, there has been more impetus by Islamic parties to try and succeed where secular ones have failed. In the House of Representatives (*Dewan Perwakilan Rakyat*, DPR), legislators have been busy. Regarding Islamic finance, it can be said that more laws have been changed or added in the last ten years, or so, than in the last 50.

This chapter will provide an overview of some of the key legal and regulatory developments that are stirring real change in the financial landscape of this vast archipelago of 17,000 islands.

---

[6] Opening speech presented at the 'Financing of Infrastructure Projects Developments Using Islamic Financing Instruments: Sharing of lessons learnt from Malaysia' workshop dated 29 August 2006, Jakarta; and guest panelist speech presented at the 5th World Islamic Economic Forum, 2–5 March 2009, Jakarta.
[7] *The Jakarta Post*, 5 January 2008.

Definitions

First: a word about definitions. In Indonesia, 'Shariah banking and finance' is the common term for Islamic banking and finance and therefore will be used throughout this chapter.

To minimise confusion, in 2005, Bank Indonesia (BI), the central bank, provided key terms for Shariah transactions in Indonesia that were to be taken as standard.[8] They are as follows:

Akad — a written contract setting forth an offer (*ijab*) and acceptance (*qabul*) between the bank and another party that sets forth rights and obligations for each party in accordance with Shariah principles.

Wadiah — an agreement for placement of funds or goods made between a holder of funds or owner of goods and a custodian of the funds or goods with the obligation for the party accepting the placement to return the entrusted funds or goods at any time.

Mudaraba — funds placement from a holder of funds (*shahibul maal*) with a manager (*Mudarib*) to conduct a specified business, applying the method of profit and loss sharing or revenue sharing between the two parties at a ratio agreed in advance.

Musharaka — the placement of funds by holders of funds or capital for combining their funds or capital in a specified business with profit share at a ratio agreed in advance, while any losses are also borne by all holders of funds or capital, according to their respective portion of funds or capital.

Murabaha — a sale and purchase of goods at cost price plus an agreed profit margin.

Salam — the sale and purchase of goods by means of order placed with certain requirements and full cash payments in advance.

---

[8] BI Regulation No. 7/46/PBI/2005 regarding Fund Mobilization and Financing Agreements for Banks Conducting Business Based on Shariah Principles.

Istisna — the sale and purchase of goods comprising an order for production of goods according to certain agreed criteria and requirements, with payment on agreed terms.

Ijara — a transaction for leasing of goods and/or hire of labour over a specified period through lease payments or remuneration for services rendered without option; with the option of transfer of ownership of goods being leased from banks to other parties (*ijara wa iqtina*).

Qardh — the lending and borrowing of funds, without remuneration, in which the borrowing party is required to repay the loan principal in a lump sum or installments over a specified period.

Sukuk — this separate definition refers to *bonds*; securitised assets belonging to the category of asset-backed securities. Sukuk require an underlying tangible assets transaction either in ownership or in a master lease agreement. Characteristics of Indonesian Sukuk include ownership of tangible asset or beneficial title; revenue in the form of coupon, margin and a profit sharing referring agreement with no elements of *riba* (interest/usury), *gharar* (short selling) and *maysir* (gambling or games of chance); the Sukuk must be issued by a special purpose vehicle; must have underlying assets and must be Shariah-compliant.

All these provisions have been formulated under the guidance of fatwas issued by the National Shariah Council of Indonesia (*Dewan Shariah Nasional* or DSN).

Current Developments — Focused Efforts on Legal Certainty

As definitions have been made clearer by key organisations such as the National Shariah Council and Bank Indonesia, other larger, legal reforms have also been ongoing.

Among the earlier, most influential laws was the Banking Law (No. 7 of 1992), which provided for a dual banking system of conventional and Shariah, as well as Shariah units. This enabled the establishment of Bank Muamalat as the pioneer Shariah bank in the same year. The 1992 Banking Law, as amended by the 10/1998 Law, led to the opening of other Shariah banks.

In 2008, both the Sovereign Sukuk Law (Law No. 19 of 2008) and the Shariah Banking Law (Law No. 21 of 2008) were passed, leading to significant stimulus for both the Shariah capital market and Shariah banking. These latest Acts serve to 'iron out' irregularities or loopholes that arose out of earlier legal reforms, and further strengthen the legal certainty for the Shariah banking and finance sector.

The latest Shariah Banking Law (No. 21 of 2008) seeks to facilitate still wider opportunities for the development of Shariah banking. The main highlights of this Law include a clearer process for conventional banks to convert their conventional licences into Shariah licences. The Law also places a new deadline for existing Shariah banking units to obtain licences as full Shariah banks — either within 15 years or when the Shariah unit's assets surpass 50% of its parent's asset value, whichever is sooner.

Increased Role by the Central Bank

The Bank of Indonesia Law No. 23 of 1999, as amended by Law No. 3 of 2004, provided the central bank with the authority to develop policies, instruments and regulations that comply with Shariah principles for all Shariah banks in Indonesia.[9] By 2006, Bank Indonesia had 17 regulations relating to Shariah banking with more than 14 circular letters and 2 guidance books distributed in the

---

[9] BI Regulation No. 8/3/PBI/2006 regarding 'Conversion of Business of Conventional Commercial Banks to Commercial Banks Conducting Business Based on Shariah Principles and Establishment of Bank Offices Conducting Business based on Shariah Principles by Conventional Banks' (amended by BI Regulation No. 9/7/PBI/2007).

effort to standardise and enhance the awareness and practice of Shariah banking and finance in the country. As may be expected, the central bank has been integral in attempts to establish a consistency and integrity of Shariah principles in practice. With the passing of a new Shariah Banking Regulation in early 2009, the central bank now regulates the minimum capital and shareholding requirements of the new Shariah commercial banks (*Bank Umum Shariah*, BUS). The central bank has also put in place additional regulations and distributed circular letters, all within the same year.[10]

Master Plan for 2015

In 2006, the central bank also launched the Shariah Banking Development Acceleration Programme to fast-track the role of Shariah banking in the national banking industry.

The Programme's six 'pillars' or objectives involve the strengthening of: (i) Shariah bank institutions; (ii) Shariah bank product development; (iii) Public education and Alliance of Strategic Partners; (iv) The governmental role and Shariah bank legal framework; (v) Shariah bank human resources; and (vi) Shariah bank supervision.

---

[10] Bank of Indonesia Regulations No. 10/17/PBI/2008 regarding Products of Shariah Bank or Bank Shariah and Shariah Business Unit or Unit Usaha Shariah ('PBI No. 10/17/PBI/2008'); No. 11/3/PBI/2009 regarding Commercial Bank or Bank Umum ('PBI No. 11/1/PBI/2009'); No. 11/3/PBI/2009 regarding Shariah Commercial Banks or Bank Umum Shariah ('PBI No. 11/3/PBI/2009'); No. 11/10/PBI/2009 regarding Shariah Business Unit or Unit Usaha Shariah ('PBI No. 11/10/PBI/2009'); No. 11/15/PBI/2009 regarding Conversion of Business Activities of Conventional Banks to Shariah Banks ('PBI No. 11/15/PBI/2009'); Circular Letter No. 6/15/DPNP dated 31 March 2004 regarding Fit and Proper Tests ('BI Letter No. 6/15/DPNP'); and Circular Letter No. 11/9/DPBS dated 7 April 2009 regarding Shariah Commercial Banks or Bank Umum Shariah ('BI Letter No. 11/9/DPBS').

The Acceleration programme targeted the assets of Shariah banking to increase up to 5.25% of national banking assets by December 2015.

As an earlier target, the official projection of Shariah assets was to reach 2% of total banking assets by the end of 2008 from 1.5% (or IDR 22.7 trillion) in 2006.[11] As it turned out, this target was not met. Still, it should be noted that the annual growth rate of Islamic banking was 65% in 2006, compared with the much lower average growth of conventional banking at approximately 7%.[12] Although there was a lull in 2007, momentum has again picked up.

Uptake by Commercial Banks, Increase in Authoritative Bodies

Following the mid-1990s Law and regulations that permitted Shariah units, banks were not sluggish to set them up. PT Bank Nasional Indonesia (Persero) Tbk opened its Shariah unit called BNI Shariah and over 20 other banks followed suit, including Bank BRI, Bank BII, Bank Danamon, Bank CIMB-Niaga and other provincial banks.

As of May 2008, there were 3 full-fledged Islamic Banks (Bank Muamalat, Bank Shariah Mega and Bank Shariah Mandiri), 25 Shariah units within the national and regional banks, and 120 rural banks operating under Shariah principles.[13]

While the central bank has played a significant role, other institutions have grown in number as part of the attempt, if not the race, to establish their authority in the changing landscape of Shariah banking and finance.

A Directorate of Shariah Financial Policy has been established under the Ministry of Finance, Indonesia. Private sector initiatives

---

[11] *Gatra*, 11–24 October 2007, pp. 10–11.
[12] A Brief History of the Islamic Banking Industry in Indonesia: Legal Perspectives (Bank Muamalat, 2007).
[13] 'Islamic finance in Indonesia: Cleared to take off?' by Mahmoud Abushamma in *Islamic Finance News*, 8 August 2008, pp. 19–20.

include the independent association, the Indonesia Shariah Banking Association (ASBISINDO), established in 1992 with members of pioneer banks, namely, Bank Muamalat Indonesia, Bank Shariah Mandiri and Bank Shariah Mega Indonesia.

As pointed out by many, developing a legal and regulatory framework should not mean excessive attention paid to drafting issues without due consideration of enforcement. Indonesia already has a mechanism in place, although it has yet to be fully tested. The Religious Court Law No. 7 of 1979, as amended by Law No. 3 of 2006 enlarged the court's jurisdiction in handling Shariah economic cases.

To date, however, parties still generally prefer the option to settle out of court. The National Shariah Arbitration Board (*Badan Arbitrase Shariah Nasionah* or BASYARNAS), initially known as the Indonesian Muamalat Arbitration Board, was established by the Indonesian Islamic Scholars Council (*Majelis Ulama Indonesia* or MUI) on 21 October 1993.

BASYARNAS is the only arbitration council that serves by Shariah principles to settle any disputes arising. Up to 2003, it had settled 16 cases and released rules and procedures pertaining to disputes within Shariah banking. It should be noted that conventional banking is also allowed to settle the disputes at BASYARNAS.

BASYARNAS' procedures are based on *ukhuwah Islamiyah*, namely, being closed to the public; disputes are to be settled in a period no longer than 6 months (180 days); the award is to be made by experts of particular knowledge; to be final and binding; and with full executorial and enforcement legitimacy.[14]

Meanwhile, to facilitate matters if and when more cases come before the courts, the Supreme Court, in 2008, issued the much-anticipated *Compilation of Shariah Economic Law* (*Kompilasi Hukum*

---

[14] See 'The role of BAMUI in developing national law' by Mariam Darus Badrulzaman in *Islamic Arbitration in Indonesia*, ed. Abdul Rahman Saleh *et al.* (BAMUI/Bank Muamalat Indonesia, Jakarta, 1994), pp. 58–60.

Ekonomi Shariah), a set of guidelines for judges on the interpretation and application of Shariah principles related to economic matters.

Clearer Scope of Work in Banking, Finance and the Capital Market

It was a critical early step to define a clear relationship between Bank Indonesia and Shariah scholars so that the National Shariah Council was confirmed with the duty to issue basic guidelines (fatwa) for the central bank to proceed to develop and issue proposed Islamic laws and regulations. This step allowed each body to get on with its own expertise. Under the Fatwa of DSN No. 3 Year 2000, for example, the National Shariah Council is required to appoint any member of the Shariah Supervisory Council (*Dewan Pengawas Shariah* or DPS) for each Shariah financial institution (including Shariah banking). Every Shariah Supervisory Council should have four members and is responsible for overseeing the implementation of Shariah principles and fatwa in Shariah financial institutions.[15]

Besides the main players of Bank Indonesia and the National Shariah Council, there is also the Capital Market Supervisory Board (*Badan Pengawas Pasar Modal — Lembaga Keuangan* or BAPEPAM-LK), established in 2003.

The Jakarta Islamic Index (JII) is another development of the last decade. This Shariah investor benchmark for equity investment was launched in 2000 and officially established on 14 March 2003, following the signing of a Memorandum of Understanding between BAPEPAM-LK and the National Shariah Council. The JII seeks to help investors wanting to invest in Shariah-compliant products in the capital market.

---

[15] www.mui.co.id.

The first Shariah-based Mutual Fund was launched on 3 July 1997 by PT Danareksa Investment Management. PT Indosat Tbk, the telecommunications company, offered a Shariah-compliant Islamic bond in September 2002. Shariah Ijara (Shariah-based bonds with a rent agreement system) were introduced on the Jakarta Islamic Index in 2004. A year later, in 2005, the first Shariah syndicated facility in Indonesia was developed — a US$312 million Islamic Murabaha financing facility agreement for Pertamina Indonesia (the national oil and gas corporation).

The Indonesian Capital Market and Sukuk — the Current 'Star'

It used to be that savings and deposit accounts were the mainstay of Shariah banking in the country. That was the case in the mid to late 1990s. However, capital market products have been developed, involving increasingly larger capital. Sukuk (bonds) are presently the most successful capital market instrument to help raise funds. As of April 2008, there were 22 Sukuk and 3 Shariah MTNs issued with a total value of IDR3.9 trillion.[16] They are expected in the near future to help underwrite urgent infrastructural development in the country. Globally, the US$10 billion market for listed Sukuk is also expected to grow to more than US$20 billion by 2010.[17]

In April 2008, the landmark Sovereign Sukuk Law was finally passed. (It could not be passed earlier as it had to be harmonised with prevailing laws, including the Treasury Law, the State-Owned Enterprise Law, the Limited Liability Law, and the Capital Market Law as well as the Package of Tax Law.) Its structure does not differ markedly from Sukuk structures currently accepted in the market, namely Ijara (sale and lease back scheme) and Istisna (the sale and

---

[16] 'Islamic finance in Indonesia: Cleared to take off?' by Mahmoud Abushamma in *Islamic Finance News*, 8 August 2008, pp. 19–20.
[17] 'Watch out' by Tom Young in *International Financial Law Review* (June 2007).

purchase of goods comprising an order for production of goods according to prior agreed criteria).

Following its passing, the government issued its first state Sukuk in August 2008, giving over the titles of state-owned assets (land and buildings owned by the Ministry of Finance in all regions) to a special purpose vehicle (SPV), known as Perusahaan Penerbit SBSN Indonesia. Unfortunately, the fund only raised IDR2.71 trillion, due to tight liquidity.

Six months later, in February 2009, a time when the market was more liquid, the government sold retail Sukuk certificates to individual investors, using the same Ijara structure. This time, the issuance was oversubscribed by 314%.[18] Despite the global economic crisis, domestic investors were drawn to the offer with its attractive coupon value of 12% per annum. Until maturity (25 February 2012), investors will receive coupon payments or fees in monthly installments. At maturity, the SPV will buy back the retail state Sukuk certificates from investors, and then sell the Sukuk assets back to the government. Bank Indonesia, the central bank, acts as the agent, paying the coupons and the total amount back to investors at maturity.

The government's focus on Sukuk has been multi-purpose — to help expand the sources of financing for the state budget; support expansion of the Shariah financial market; create a benchmark in the Shariah financial market; enable diversification of the investor base; develop an alternative for investment instruments; optimise on using state-owned assets; and use any funds from consumers not collected by conventional banking system to date.

It should be noted that the new Sukuk Law introduced two key new legal concepts: the first is usufruct rights (*hak manfaat* or beneficial rights). There is no concept of beneficiary ownership in Indonesian law, therefore no differentiation between legal and beneficial ownership. So the transfer of assets is usually understood as the transfer of the legal title of those assets, which requires re-registration

---

[18] *The Jakarta Post*, 6 February 2009.

and most prohibitively, being subject to land transfer tax. The new law confirms that the sale of usufruct rights will not, in fact, involve any transfer of title or physical transfer of assets. There are other advantages that result in the process of issuing Sukuk being much smoother for the government.

The second new legal concept introduced is that of the SPV. However, grey areas exist because there is little information about the setting up procedure, capital requirements and who can be shareholders. Possible conflict of interest may arise because for the government to issue state Sukuk, it could later get caught between being a trustee to protect holders' interest, and being responsible to the Finance Minister. Still, the Sukuk law created new opportunities to raise capital.

New Players

The sovereign Sukuk issued so far, and all the discussion prior to their actual issuance, have helped raise awareness and prompted more assurance, mutual funds, pension and Takaful organizations to get involved by offering new products. At the time of writing, Prudential, for example, is widely advertising a 'PruShariah' product on national television.

But while there is significant momentum in setting up the legal and regulatory framework, common problems remain.

Common Problems — Lack of Qualified Shariah Scholars and 'Double Taxation' (recently amended)

Although the National Shariah Council has been very active, the fact remains that there is a shortage of skilled advisors in Shariah-compliance and modern banking, finance and economics. This hampers all stages of the legal and regulatory framework including drafting, implementation and enforcement. (Nevertheless, this is not a unique problem for Indonesia.[19]) Various initiatives by colleges and universities have been taken to offer new courses. Air Langga University, one of the earliest universities with a Shariah Economics faculty, now offers a new Master's course in Shariah Economics in association with the Global University in Islamic Finance (INCEIF) Malaysia.

Another critical problem, but again relatively common with several other Muslim countries which have a dual or multiple legal framework, has been the matter of 'double taxation'. In 2003, the central bank issued new regulations as well as the Guidelines of Shariah Banking Accountancy (*Pedoman Akuntansi Perbankan Shariah* or PAPSI) to regulate transactions of Mudaraba as transactions of sale and purchase between the bank and customer, whereby the bank is the seller and the customer is the buyer. Unfortunately, these guidelines included the imposition of Value Added Tax (VAT) on transactions of Mudaraba.

In 2005, Bank Indonesia stated that the terminology of *Mudaraba* was correct in accordance with the prevailing Banking Law and the central bank did not and could not revoke the regulation that entailed VAT to be imposed on Shariah banking transactions. In 2006 and 2007, however, the central bank did revoke the 2003 regulations but PAPSI remained unchanged, thereby allowing conflict to arise as to whether VAT must be imposed or not.

While the government expects to raise revenue by the VAT, detractors correctly argued the VAT was a 'double tax', a crucial barrier making for prohibitive costs that prevented Shariah banking from growing, compared with conventional banking. There was then pressure on the government to amend the PAPSI rather than set up a new regulation on tax for Shariah banking.[20] Finally, on 15 October 2009,

[19] 'Wanted: More scholars to help sell Islamic bonds' in *New Straits Times*, 4 May 2007, p. 44.
[20] *Gatra*, 11–24 October 2007, pp. 10–11.

the government passed the amendment to the VAT Act which effectively removes the 'double taxation' bind. Please note however that this amedment only comes into force on 1 April 2010.

Conclusion — from Political Maneuver to 2015 Master Plan and Beyond

The founding statement of 'Belief in one Supreme God' notwithstanding, Shariah banking and finance have been developing at a much faster rate in the world's most populous Muslim country. It is generally acknowledged that the late President Soeharto only began to support Shariah banking in the late 1980s as a way to woo the increasingly vocal Muslim vote. But it was not supported in a significant way for two reasons: firstly, that it conflicted with Pancasila ideology, and secondly that Shariah banking and finance were generally understood to mean exclusively for Muslims, hence deemed controversial in a country that officially recognised five religions including Buddhism and Christianity.

However, by 2002 with Bank Indonesia's 'blue print' launch for the Shariah Banking Industry until 2015, it can be seen that national aims and estimates to create a viable and developed Shariah banking sector have gone beyond simple political expedience. Given the financial collapse of many reputable banks in the most recent crisis, there has been occasion for Shariah bankers to claim a far superior product to conventional banking, at least compared to particularly more 'high-risk' instruments such as derivatives. The Shariah Banking Director of Bank Indonesia, Ramzi Zuhdi, said the structure of Indonesia's Shariah banking system, relying heavily on actual assets and conservative financial instruments, had made it less exposed to recessional impact. Ramzi also noted that to date, no Shariah bank had filed an appeal for emergency funding from the central bank.[21] Of course, Shariah banks are arguably shielded because they currently control only 3% of the market in terms of assets.[22] As at the end of 2007, there were 26 Islamic mutual funds with a net asset value (NAV) of IDR946 billion, or a mere 1% of total mutual funds NAV. Even the Takaful industry, which at the end of 2007 comprised three companies and no less than 35 Takaful units, accounted for only 1.1% of the national insurance market share. But these figures can only expand. Efforts are underway in the firm belief that a stronger foundation must be established for an expected groundswell of Shariah financial opportunity and the opportunity of profit for all Indonesians, whether Muslim or non-Muslim.

Bank Indonesia's blue print for the development of the Shariah banking and finance sector by 2015 is expected to be achieved via political will and efficient implementation. Of course, such an achievement is dependent on a trustworthy and efficient legal environment, as well as constant and favourable macroeconomic factors outside the country.

While significant progress has been made in the last decade, it is evident that if Indonesia is to keep pace with neighbouring and global competitors (all interested to be another 'gateway' or 'hub' of some kind for Shariah finance), then reform and development of Shariah banking and finance in Indonesia must continue at an all the more urgent pace. To be sure, global Islamic finance has slowed down, in tandem with the global credit crunch, though not to the same extent. The present risk aversion amongst investors is likely to be temporary. A giant has stretched its legs but running with it will take some time yet.

---

[21] *Tempo Interaktif*, 28 April 2009.
[22] 'Shariah finance provides bridge between Middle East and Indonesia' in *Jakarta Globe*, 14 March 2009.

MAKING SENSE OF THE FAST-GROWING ISLAMIC FINANCE MARKET

Tadashi Maeda

Introduction

As global crude oil prices soar, oil-producing countries in the Middle East hold ever-increasing financial assets. It is against this backdrop that Islamic finance has expanded sharply and begun to receive more attention. It is a well-known historical fact that the second oil shock of 1979 brought large current account surpluses to oil-producing countries in the Middle East, and that these funds, known as 'petrodollars', were recycled in the form of investment in international financial assets. The concept of Islamic finance also came into being during this period. Indeed, it was in 1979 that the Bahrain Islamic Bank was established as the first Islamic bank in Bahrain, and played a pioneering role as an international financial market in the Gulf states. Further development came in 1983 when the Islamic Banking Act was passed and Bank Islam Malaysia

Berhad (BIMB) was established in Malaysia. Today, Malaysia has exceeded Bahrain in scale as a market for Islamic financial services.

Here, a brief overview of petrodollars is presented, as they are closely related to the evolution of Islamic finance. Petrodollars are defined as 'surplus foreign currency assets generated from net oil revenues in oil-producing countries'. Since there are no adequate statistical data covering this definition, the scale of petrodollar assets is merely an estimate. Its peak in terms of flow lasted from 1980 immediately after the second oil shock through the 1990s, reaching about US$100 billion. The data supporting this figure is the sum of the current account surpluses of the four OPEC countries: Saudi Arabia, Kuwait, the United Arab Emirates, and Qatar. Their combined current account surpluses peaked in 1980 and 1981, reaching US$60 billion in 1980 and 1981. This was followed by a long period of declining crude oil prices dissipated the flow of current account surpluses, and petrodollars seemed to have become a thing of the past. However, in 2000, oil-producing countries in the Middle East recorded surpluses as large as in 1981, and since then sharply climbing crude oil prices have enabled these 4 OPEC countries in the Middle East to postcurrent account surpluses in excess of the peak figures in 1981, exceeding US$90 billion by 2004. Their surpluses underwent an additional sharp increase to exceed US$160 billion in 2005. In 2006, while the rate of increase slowed down, the total figure is estimated to have reached a level beyond US$180 billion.

There is no doubt that rapidly expanding Islamic finance after 2000 is closely linked to the swelling of petrodollars against the backdrop of soaring crude oil prices since 2000. Today, financial institutions offering Islamic financial services are not only limited to the Islamic world, but also extended to more than 300 financial institutions in 75-plus countries across the world, including European countries. Their total financial assets are expanding at an astounding rate of more than 15% annually, and it is estimated that they will reach the range of US$750 billion to US$1 trillion.

Malaysia Leading the Islamic Financial Market

One of the factors behind the sharp expansion of Islamic finance is attributable to the positive contributions of Malaysia, one of Asia's Islamic countries. Malaysia has been actively promoting the spread of Islamic finance, and has become the centre of Islamic finance in the world by establishing the inter-bank market of Islamic financial institutions, developing Islamic money market instruments, issuing Sukuk bonds or Islamic securities, as well as developing their secondary market and creating institutional infrastructure for Islamic finance. Bank Negara Malaysia (the central bank of Malaysia) issued the first global sovereign Sukuk (Islamic bonds) in 2002, which were listed in the international stock exchanges, following the first-ever issuance of sovereign Sukuk by the Bahraini government. Since then, the Malaysian government and government agencies have continued to issue Sukuk regularly.

The Government of Malaysia has also been working on the systematic compilation of guidelines for issuing Sukuk along with ordinary securities. Since the government drew up the Capital Market Master Plan, which includes Islamic finance, in 2001, it issued guidelines on the Offering of Private Debt Securities and of Islamic Securities in July 2004, which systematically compiled the previous laws and regulations on security issues. Furthermore, Bank Negara Malaysia and the Securities Commission released a decree on the issuance of ringgit securities to promote the issuance of nonresidents such as multilateral development banks (MDBs) and financial institutions (MFIs). Following these measures, the Securities Commission issued Practice Note 2 on the guidelines for MDBs and MFIs in November 2004 and Practice Note 2A on the guidelines for foreign governments and government agencies in March 2006. These efforts to develop institutional infrastructure for Islamic securities markets by the Malaysian government helped increase Islamic financial assets in Malaysia to US$30 billion, accounting for 70% of the total Sukuk issuance market. Malaysia has thus firmly established its position as the centre of Islamic finance.

Overview of Islamic Finance

Discussion has thus far dwelled on factors behind the rapid expansion of Islamic finance. This section gives the definition of Islamic finance, and describes the various instruments of Islamic finance. Islamic finance refers to finance mechanisms in compliance with Shariah, which is based on two major sources: the Qur'an and the Sunnah, a compendium of practices from the days of the Prophet Mohammad. It is also called Shariah-compliant finance.

One outstanding characteristic of Shariah is prohibition of lending money for interest (riba). In other words, a conventional loan contract whereby money is lent to earn interest is prohibited. However, Shariah recognises the concept of capital as a factor of productive activity producing economic value. What it prohibits is a contract where part of earnings produced by capital is acquired in advance by the supplier of capital.

Therefore, the basic structure of Islamic finance is 'the sharing of profit and loss' between lenders who provide capital funds and borrowers who engage in economic activities by using them. Taking this point, the view is often expressed that since the fundamental tenet of Islamic finance is sharing profits and losses, it has high-risk preferences, seeking high risks and high returns. This is a total misunderstanding. Shariah does not encourage speculative activities and gambling. On the contrary, Shariah does not admit speculation (Maisir) without a rational basis.

As a result, Islamic finance takes the form of asset trading. This so-called underlying asset cannot include business areas prohibited by Islamic law such as those involving alcohol, pork, gambling, and pornography. In the project loan in which the author has been involved, more specifically in the Islamic finance technique called

Ijara which corresponds to a lease agreement, it came to light that part of the asset covered by Ijara included a cafeteria of a hotel and that alcoholic drinks are provided for the customers in this cafeteria. For this reason, it was excluded from the lease asset based on the advice of a Shariah scholar.

The first finance technique developed for financial transactions for the purchase of real assets was the Murabaha, which corresponds to an installment sales contract. Typically, this is a contract for selling automobiles and articles of high value by deferred payment or in the form of installments. The purchaser of an automobile enters into a Murabaha contract with an Islamic financial institution. This contract charges a certain fee on the purchase price. The Islamic financial institution then purchases the good from the seller and the purchaser pays the total cost by installments.

Furthermore, as in the case of purchasing a new house, when a real asset does not exist at the time of the contract because it is to be built afterwards, a variation of the Murabaha called the Istisna, originally meaning 'let one build' in Arabic, is used. In this way, the practice of Islamic finance to meet the needs of individual consumers purchasing relatively small-scale assets gained ground during the 1990s, mainly in the Islamic world.

However, the appearance of Sukuk, or Islamic bonds, and the development of their secondary markets, led to a rapid expansion of the Islamic finance that had been provided on only a small scale until the 1990s. Sukuk have made it possible to mobilise huge amounts of funds. In Arabic, Sukuk is the plural form of the word Sakk, meaning a check. Medium-term sovereign Sukuk were first issued by the Government of Bahrain in 2001. Since then, governments and government agencies in the Islamic world, including Bank Negara Malaysia, and Governments of Qatar and the Emirate of Dubai, have issued increasingly huge amounts of Sukuk, with some exceeding US$1 billion.

A typical structure often used as Sukuk is Sukuk Al-Musharaka, which is akin to a joint venture for projects that cover assets specified beforehand, and Sukuk Al-Ijara, in which a special purpose company (SPC), which is set up by a Sukuk issuer to obtain funding, acquires assets enters into a lease contract with the Sukuk issuer. Another form of Sukuk is a variation of Sukuk Al-Musharaka called Sukuk Al-Mudaraba, a form of investment trust in which a Sukuk issuer does not participate in the management of a joint business venture. At the time of writing, however, there is no issuance of Sukuk Al-Mudaraba. In 2004, the World Bank and the International Finance Corporation of its group issued Sukuk in Malaysia. Their Sukuk was called Bai Bithaman Ajil, which means that the investment instrument of Mudaraba constitutes a money market instrument (MMI), as transaction assets.[1] Since securities rather than real assets were taken to be transaction assets, there are different interpretations regarding this Sukuk in Shariah and it was accepted in Malaysia but not in the Middle Eastern Islamic countries. As this has indicated, Islamic finance still seems to be halfway to becoming a global international finance modality, given its origin in the enclave of local markets and differences among the Islamic countries regarding how strictly Shariah has to be interpreted.

A Move Toward International Standardisation of Islamic Financial Services

As the presence of Islamic finance has increased in the world of international finance, there has been growing recognition of the need to set unified standards governing Islamic financial services, whose origin is traced back to limited local markets, and harmonise them with the supervisory rules of traditional international finance. An organisation expected to play a central role in international

---

[1] Mudaraba investment instrument (MII) is a short-term security approved by Malaysia as a security traded in its inter-bank market. MII securities are traded in Islamic financial markets.

supervision of Islamic finance is the Islamic Financial Services Board (IFSB). The IFSB was established in 2002 as an international supervisory body of Islamic finance based on an agreement among central banks and bank supervisory agencies in Islamic countries. Bank Negara Malaysia played a leading role in its establishment. Its Articles of Agreement stated: 'To promote the development of a prudent and transparent Islamic financial services industry through introducing new, or adapting existing, international standards consistent with Shariah principles'. Its full members include 16 central banks and bank regulatory and supervisory agencies primarily in Islamic countries, and 9 organisations, mainly multilateral institutions, such as the International Monetary Fund (IMF), the World Bank, and the Bank for International Settlement (BIS), constitute its associate members. Furthermore, 69 financial institutions offering Islamic financial services have participated as observers. Between non-Islamic countries, the Monetary Authority of Singapore has participated as a full member, and the People's Bank of China and the Bangko Sentral ng Pilipinas (the central bank of the Philippines) have participated as associate members. Japan Bank for International Cooperation (JBIC), with which the author is affiliated, has also participated in IFSB as an observer since November 2007.

With technical assistance from the IMF, the IFSB set up working groups of experts and these groups have been mainly working on setting standards of Islamic financial services to be consistent with international standards in financial services in the banking, securities, and insurance services. In the arena of international finance, Islamic finance is no longer a peculiar finance modality used in the enclave of the Islamic world. In terms of volume and prevalence across the world, it has become an important constituting segment of global international finance, a force to be reckoned with. The working groups of the IFSB are preparing standards and guidelines consistent with Shariah principles, while drawing on, as reference, international financial regulatory and supervisory standards, including those of the Basel Committee on Banking Supervision. The IFSB has already prepared Guiding Principles on Risk Management and Capital Adequacy in December 2005 and recommended their adoption to Islamic financial institutions. It is also drafting guidelines on corporate governance and guiding principles on investment funds.

UK Keeping Its Eye on Becoming a Gateway to Islamic Finance

With the fast growth of Islamic finance, the United Kingdom, which has the City as its major international financial centre, took note of its importance early on. The Financial Services Authority (FSA), the financial regulatory body, granted a banking license to the Islamic Bank of Britain, the first bank specialising in Islamic financial services, in August 2004. In fact, the Eurodollar market was formed primarily in the City of London in the 1980s when petrodollars in the Middle East, which dominated international financial markets, were channeled back to destinations all over the world through the City. Having the historical recognition that this has consolidated the position of the City as *the* international financial market, Her Majesty's Treasury (HMT) and FSA moved quickly.

About 1.8 million Muslims are living in the United Kingdom, roughly 3% of the total population. The City of London, priding itself on its tradition of working as an international financial market, has served as a secondary market of such Islamic financial products as Sukuk and commodity Mudaraba. In March 2007, a banking license was granted to the European Islamic Investment Bank as the second financial institution specialising in Islamic financial services. Then Chancellor of the Exchequer Gordon Brown stated in June 2006 "the ambition to make Britain a gateway to Islamic finance". Indeed, since then, 3 more Islamic finance institutions have applied for banking licenses, one of which obtained a license. These Islamic banks are able to open branches in other countries within the European Union without hindrance.

Reflecting the positive stance of UK authorities toward Islamic finance, financial flow sharply increased from the UK to the US capital market, the world's largest market. Such unprecedented financial flows from the United Kingdom should be seen as an inflow of petrodollars in the Middle East into the US market through UK investment funds.

Such positive attitude toward Islamic finance attested to the foresight of the UK government. However, when the author had an interview with a manager responsible for Islamic finance in the FSA, he said, "We do not think that making London a gateway to Islamic finance means distinguishing Islamic finance from conventional finance and governing it under special regulations. FSA encourages Islamic finance but does not promote it. We are ensuring a level playing field, and that there is only a single regulatory framework". This single regulation is the Financial Services and Market Act 2000. As mentioned above, Islamic finance takes the form of asset trading. Therefore, for example, Ijara is close to a finance lease contract, and Murabaha is close to an installment sales contract. These are more or less equivalent to the leasing and lending business activities in Japan. In these cases, the supervisory authority is not the Financial Services Agency but the Ministry of Economy, Trade and Industry. In this way, whereas in the United Kingdom, the FSA supervises Islamic finance under a single law, by contrast there is no single supervisory authority in Japan, where multiple laws govern these businesses. Article 12 of the private banking law of Japan prohibits banks from doing asset trading, which is likely to prove one of the hindrances for Japanese banks opening terms of opening the door to Islamic finance in Japan.

Thus, if Japan wishes to make serious efforts to encompass Islamic finance, it has to clear many hurdles. It is of urgency that the Japanese administrative authorities follow the example of the United Kingdom and seriously study Islamic finance.

THE GROWTH OF ISLAMIC FINANCE IN SOUTHEAST ASIA: REGULATORY CHALLENGES AND OPPORTUNITIES FOR THE UNITED STATES

Mercy A. Kuo

Introduction

The objective of this chapter is to provide a broad outline of how practitioners and regulators in Southeast Asia and the United States are managing the growth of Islamic finance amid turbulent shifts in the international financial landscape. The contractions in the global economic system beginning in the fall of 2007 with the Subprime mortgage crisis in the United States grew increasingly acute in the latter half of 2008 with the capital hemorraghing of American behemoth blue chip companies, such as American International Group, Bear Stearns, Citigroup, and Merrill Lynch, with a few — Lehman Brothers and Washington Mutual — fully collapsing along the way. With the long-term impact of the current economic downturn still unfolding, Washington DC, Wall Street, and the American public are grappling with the pitfalls and perturbations of national economic stabilisation and recovery efforts. Their counterparts in Asia, Europe, and the Middle East are also pursuing measures to curtail further domestic economic gyrations. More than anything, the cascade effect of these contractions has magnified the vulnerabilities and inefficiencies of the global financial regulatory system in mitigating systemic risk. Amid this undulating backdrop, it is particularly timely and policy-relevant to examine developments of the Islamic finance industry in Southeast Asia and the United States and to assess the regulatory challenges and opportunities for the United States in managing the industry's rapid developments.

From the Southeast Asian perspective, the United States represents nearly half of the world's equity markets by capitalisation with the Dow Jones Islamic Market Indexes covering more than US$10 trillion market capitalisation in over 40 countries.[1] More importantly, decisions and actions from Washington DC and Wall Street invariably affect capital markets and the global financial system at large — this recognition is a prime motivating factor for key Southeast Asian countries to engage the United States. In the United States, understanding of Islamic finance varies depending on vantage point. Awareness and curiosity in the private sector is slowly growing. Among US regulators, interest and receptivity toward learning more about Islamic finance is increasing. In examining Southeast Asian and US perspectives, this chapter will explore how leaders in the field can leverage their respective countries' strengths and capabilities in forging areas of cooperation.

This chapter is divided into four sections. The first section examines the evolution and characteristics of Islamic finance in Southeast Asia, focusing specifically on Malaysia's strategy to fashion itself as a regional and global Islamic finance industry leader and

---

[1] Governor Zeti Akhtar Aziz, Bank Negara Malaysia. Speech on 'Enhancing Interlinkages and Opportunities — The Role of Islamic Finance' in 'Islamic Finance in Southeast Asia: Local Practice, Global Impact' Conference Report by The National Bureau of Asian Research (NBR), 18 October 2007, Washington, DC.

Singapore's efforts to establish itself as a regional Islamic finance hub by carving out a niche-market position in Islamic finance wealth and asset management and other financial services. The second section surveys Islamic finance developments in the United States and identifies key industry players and leaders. The third section highlights fundamental challenges facing US regulators. The final section identifies common areas of cooperation between the United States and Southeast Asia in advancing efforts to raise awareness and facilitate exchange of expertise on Islamic finance.

The Evolution and Characteristics of Islamic Finance in Southeast Asia

The evolution of the Islamic finance industry in Southeast Asia reflects the heterogeneous histories, cultures, societies, ethnicities, and religions of this region. Southeast Asia's Muslim population — 250 million — accounts for approximately 15% of the world's total Muslim population of 1.5 billion. According to historical records, Islam began to take root in Southeast Asia between the 12th and 13th centuries through Muslim traders from India and West Asia. Sufis contributed significantly to the further spread and propagation of Islam across Southeast Asia. Sufism's mystic quality and tolerance for coexistence with earlier animist, Hindu, and Buddhist beliefs and rituals allowed Southeast Asians to localise Islam, which further facilitated the establishment of Muslim centres of learning and interaction across the Archipelago.[2] Of the four schools of Islamic jurisprudence (Fiqh) within Sunni Islam, Shafii Islam is predominant throughout Southeast Asia and is the official school of law (Madhab) of the governments of Malaysia and Brunei Darussalam. The Indonesian government adheres to Shafii Madhab for Indonesia's Compilation of Shariah (Islamic law). Imam Shafii

---

[2] 'The Spread of Islam to Southeast Asia', http://history-world.org/islam7.htm.

developed a systematic methodology in interpreting Islamic law, yet
sought to balance tradition with pragmatism.

In modern-day Southeast Asia, the diverse interpretations and
applications of Islam in individual countries are indicative of a deeply
diverse blend of Shafii Islam with indigeneous cultural norms, values,
beliefs, and practices, which in many ways has fostered a tolerant, plu-
ralistic pursuit of Islam in much of Southeast Asia. This pragmatic
and even entrepreneurial practice of Islam is intricately interwoven
into the political culture of Southeast Asia's ruling elites. In the case
of Malaysia, though a secular country, Islam has served as an integral
ideological underpinning of the government's modus operandi.
During his tenure as Malaysia's Prime Minister from 1983 to 2003,
Mohammad Mahathir exhorted Islamic scholars (ulama) and Islamic
jurists (fuqaha) to be practical and innovative in interpreting Islamic
law with a view of advancing Malaysia's national economic development. 'The Malaysian brand of Islam does not fit typical Western
perceptions and stereotypes … It is fused with other influences
(nationalism, capitalism, 'Asian value') producing a unique ideology
of development. Rather than being an obstacle to change, religion
was to be an engine of growth and modernisation and a tool to
promote financial innovation'.[3]

This top-down, centralised nature of leadership that imbues
Islam into all aspects of public life in Southeast Asia also charac-
terises the main piston of the rapid growth of the Islamic finance
industry in Southeast Asia. The upper echelons of governments in
Malaysia and Singapore are developing and pursuing coherent,
multisectoral, and local–global strategies in framing the regulations
and standards that facilitate a marketplace conducive to the industry's
long-term expansion.

Furthermore, the infusion of capital from petrodollar investors
into Asia has contributed to the accelerated growth of Southeast

---

[3] Ibrahim, W. (2006) *Islamic Finance in the Global Economy.* Edinburgh: Edinburgh
University Press, p. 195.

Asia's Islamic finance industry over the past two decades. As of 2006, the total Islamic finance market was worth US$500 billion, of which US$70 billion were Sukuk (Islamic bonds). Standard and Poor's estimates that by 2010 the Sukuk market will grow to US$170 billion and the overall Islamic financing market to US$4 trillion.[4] Malaysia has emerged as a major force in Islamic finance innovation and expertise, and Singapore is developing its capabilities as a top-choice Islamic finance services provider. Both countries' strategies for positioning themselves as critical players in attracting liquidity could provide indicators of how the industry is developing in the region and globally. Let us take a closer look at developments in Malaysia and Singapore.

Malaysia on the Move

With the founding of the Muslim Pilgrims Saving Corporation in 1963 to help Malays save for performing the *haj* and its evolution into the Pilgrims Management and Fund Board, or popularly known as Tabung Haji, Malaysia's leadership in setting the pace for developments in Islamic finance has contributed to major advances in product innovation. Malaysia's pioneering initiatives in the field — such as issuing the world's first global sovereign Sukuk in 2002 and the landmark issuance of the exchangeable Sukuk in 2006 by Khazanah Nasional, the Malaysian sovereign wealth management group and the inaugural ringgit-denominated Sukuk issue by the International Finance Corporation — have positioned Malaysia as an increasingly sought-after provider of industry expertise.

The Malaysian government is pursuing a course of further market liberalisation to create an environment attractive to foreign

---

[4] McKinsey Global Institute, 'New Power Brokers — Petrodollars: Fueling global capital markets' (October 2007), pp. 65–66.

investment in the Malaysian bank market and position Malaysia as a
centre for origination, distribution, and trading of Sukuk. Profits or
income received by non-residents for investments in ringgit and
non-ringgit Islamic securities issued in Malaysia are exempted from
withholding tax; in addition, the Malaysian government has granted
tax neutrality measures to accommodate the Sukuk issuance.[5] Malaysia
spurred further liberalisation in the Islamic banking sector by issuing new licences to select foreign Islamic financial institutions, such
as the Kuwait Finance House, the Saudi-backed Al Rajhi Bank, and
the Asian Finance Bank Berhad, supported by shareholders representing Qatar Islamic Bank, RUSD Investment Bank of Saudi Arabia
and the Global Investment House of Kuwait.

As a critical move to expand Malaysia's reach as a global Islamic
finance hub, Bank Negara Malaysia (BNM) has initiated plans to
establish the Malaysia International Islamic Financial Centre
(MIFC). BNM is gaining support from the Malaysian Bar Council to
allow 'foreign law firms to operate independently or through joint
ventures with local firms to facilitate and support the conduct for
international currency in the Islamic finance business in Malaysia...
and to attract and retain the best talents in international Islamic
finance'.[6] Malaysia's impact on virtually all segments of the Islamic
finance industry — product innovation, education and training,
regulatory and legal expertise — stems in large part from what
appears to be a top-down, coherent effort led by the Malaysian
government in branding Malaysia as a pivotal industry player and
placing it strategically at the nexus of capital flows between the
GCC and Asia.[7]

---

[5] Zeti Akhtar Aziz, Bank Negara Malaysia. Speech on 'Enhancing Interlinkages and
Opportunities — The Role of Islamic Finance' in 'Islamic Finance in Southeast
Asia: Local Practice, Global Impact' Conference Report by The National Bureau of
Asian Research (NBR), 18 October 2007, Washington, DC.
[6] Islamic Finance Legal Eagles Back Open Door Policy (17 December 2007),
Malaysian Reserve.
[7] Bank Negara Governor Dr. Zeti Akhtar Aziz to address the inaugural London
Sukuk Summit (14 May 2007) http://www.zawya.com/printstory.cfm.

Singapore as a Financial Services Centre

As an international financial centre, Singapore is a recent entrant in the Islamic finance industry. Recognising the long-term growth potential of the Islamic finance industry combined with increasing financial flows between the Middle East and Asia, the Monetary Authority of Singapore (MAS) is taking steps to create a regulatory environment conducive to extending the reach of Singapore's wealth, investment, and asset management expertise into the Islamic financial services sector. With the growing need for Islamic finance instruments in project financing, trade financing, capital raising, and investments in Shariah-compliant equity stocks and real estate products, MAS in 2005 adjusted regulations to allow banks in Singapore to offer financing according to the Murabaha concept.[8] In addition, MAS waived the imposition of double stamp duties in Islamic transactions involving real estate and accorded the same concessionary tax treatment on income from Islamic bonds that are afforded to conventional banks.[9]

The establishment of the Financial Times Stock Exchange (FTSE)-Singapore Stock Exchange (SGX) Asia Shariah 100 Index Series in February and the Islamic Bank of Asia in May of 2007 marked two critical steps in cementing Singapore's intention of becoming a major industry player. The FTSE-SGX Asia Shariah Index is the first index of the series and is designed to represent the performance of Shariah-compliant companies in Japan, Singapore, Taiwan, Korea, and Hong Kong.[10] The Islamic Bank of Asia, a subsidiary of the

---

[8] A sales contract made between the bank and the customer for the sale of goods at a price which includes a profit margin agreed to by both parties. As a financing technique it involves the purchase of goods by the bank as requested by the customer. Repayment is conducted by installments within a specified period.

[9] Opening Remarks, Mr. Ng Nam Sin, Executive Director, Monetary Authority of Singapore at the IQPC Islamic Finance Summit, Singapore 2006, http://www.mas. gov.sg/news_room/statements/2006/Opening_Remarks.

[10] FTSE SGX Shariah Index Series, http://ftse.com/Indices/FTSE_SGX_ Shariah_Index_Series/index.jsp.

Development Bank of Singapore Limited (DBS), has DBS as the major stakeholder along with 22 other investors from prominent families of the GCC countries. DBS Chief Executive Jackson Tai said in a statement, "Singapore is becoming a convenient stopover for GCC investors and capital flows bound for Asia. Against this backdrop, the Islamic Bank of Asia is strategically well positioned not only at the financial crossroads of Asia, but also in Singapore, an Asian capital market centre renowned for its effective regulatory and corporate governance framework".[11]

Though accurate aggregate data are not publicly available, Singapore's stable investment climate also appeals to high net worth individual Muslims and non-Muslims — including Chinese and Indians — who are seeking alternative investment avenues in Asia.[12] The demand for Islamic financial services is expected to rise exponentially with the Muslim population forecast to grow to 1.6 billion within the next 10 years and the increase in the wealth of high net worth individuals in the Middle East, which is expected to reach US$1.8 trillion by 2010.[13] Singapore is leveraging the capabilities of its multiethnic society, solid financial infrastructure, and geographic location as an entrepot for GCC capital flows into Asia.

Islamic Finance Developments in the United States

In contrast to Malaysia and Singapore's centralised, state-driven efforts in directing the course of Islamic finance developments in the region, the United States has seen a more localised development of Islamic finance as a small, but growing industry that has arisen primarily from local needs of Muslim Americans. More a grassroots outgrowth, than a top-down, systematic initiative, the

---

[11] http://www.iht.com/articles/ap/2007/05/07/asia/AS-FIN-Singapore-Islamic-Bank.php [7 May 2007].
[12] Interviews with officials of various Islamic banks in Singapore (December 2007).
[13] 1e finance Blog, http://gbe-i-finance.blogspot.com/2007_10_01_archive.html.

American brand of Islamic finance is being shaped by a small cluster of local and regional Islamic finance providers. This path of development is not unique to Islamic finance, rather it reflects the US regulatory practice in general to allow market forces to innovate, and then ensures that innovation accords with law and regulation. Islamic finance services have primarily revolved around Shariah-compliant financing for home and auto purchasing and small business start-up funding to Muslim-American communities throughout the United States. This section focuses on the demographic composition of consumers and key providers of Islamic finance products.

US Islamic Finance Consumer Market Composition

According to the Pew Research Centre's 2007 Study on Muslim Americans, the total Muslim-American population is estimated at 2.35 million, based on data from the Pew survey and available US Census Bureau data on immigrants' nativity and nationality, and of these, 1.5 million are adult Muslim Americans, 18 years of age and older, who compose 0.6% of the US adult population.[14] More than a third (37%) of all foreign-born Muslim Americans arrived from the Arab region, including Arabic-speaking countries in the Middle East and North Africa. An additional 27% emigrated from South Asia — Pakistan, India, Bangladesh, and Afghanistan. Another 8% come from European countries and 6% from other parts of Africa. More than 3/4 (77%) of Muslim Americans say that they have always been a Muslim, while 23% say that they converted to Islam. 9-in-10 converts (91%) to Islam were born in the United States, and almost 3/5 (59%) of converts to Islam are African Americans. A 55% majority converts identify with Sunni Islam,

---

[14] Pew Research Centre Report, 'Muslim Americans: Middle Class and Mostly Mainstream' (22 May 2007), www.pewresearch.org, p. 3.

another 1/4 (24%) identify with no specific tradition, and only 6% of Muslim converts identified themselves as Shia.[15]

In terms of financial composition, family income among Muslim Americans is comparable with that of the US population as a whole. Among adults nationwide, 44% report household incomes of US$50,000 or more annually, as do 41% of Muslim-American adults. At the highest end of the income scale, Muslim Americans are about as likely to report household incomes of US$100,000 or more as are members of the general public (16% for Muslims compared with 17% among the public).[16] In relation to the purchasing potential of Muslim Americans reflecting that of middle-class American at large, another factor generating demand for Islamic finance products is the degree of religious observance, which can be categorised on three levels:

(1) the most devout Muslims who do not use conventional forms of financing — this group represents the core market for Islamic financing products;
(2) observant Muslims who use conventional financing but would choose Islamic financing mechanisms, if the option existed; and
(3) the least observant Muslim who currently uses conventional financing products and who given the choice would not use Shariah-compliant products.[17]

Domestic markets for Islamic products have emerged from concentrations of Muslim-American communities spread across the nation. Current available data indicate that as of 2001, 1,368 mosques — usually the centrepoint for Muslim communities — exist

---

[15] Ibid. p. 22.
[16] Ibid. p. 18.
[17] Chiu, Shirley and Newberger, Robin. (2006) Islamic finance: Meeting financial needs with faith-based products. In *Profitwise News and Views: Research Review*, pp. 8–14.

in the United States. The states with the greatest number of mosques include California, New York, New Jersey, Michigan, Pennsylvania, Texas, Ohio, Illinois, and Florida. Between 1986 and 2001, California, New York, New Jersey, Michigan, and Pennsylvania experienced the greatest growth in the number of mosques, according to demographic surveys.[18]

Providers of Islamic Finance Products

Islamic finance service and product providers reflect the demographics in their respective communities. According to a 2005 report by the Federal Reserve Bank of Chicago on Islamic finance in the United States, there are 9 institutions that offer formal Islamic asset finance products (see Table 1).[19] Of the 9, LARIBA Finance House, founded in 1987, was the first organisation, primarily funded by Muslim-Americans and is licensed to sell Islamic finance products in 49 states. Guidance Financial Group began operations in 2003 in Reston, Virginia, and is licensed in 18 states. Devon Bank in Chicago, Illinois and University Bank in Ann Arbor, Michigan are privately owned community banks with 6 branches between them. University Bank formed the University Islamic Financial Corporation, the first Islamic banking subsidiary run entirely according to Shariah principles. State-chartered community banks, such as Devon and others, are supervised by their state regulator. HSBC is the only large bank that offers Shariah-compliant products — home financing, deposit accounts, and credit cards — in the United States. Home financing and real estate acquisition

---

[18] Kosmin, B. A., Egon, M. and Ariela, K. (2001) *CUNY American Religious Identification Survey and Hartford Seminary's Hartford Institute for Religious Research.* New York: The Graduate Centre, CUNY.

[19] Chiu, Shirley, Newberger, Robin and Paulson, Anna. (2005) Islamic finance in the United States: A small but growing industry. In *The Federal Reserve Bank of Chicago, Chicago Fed. Letter, Essays on Issues,* No. 214.

Table 1   Islamic finance providers in the United States.

Institution	Location	Type of institution	Products
LARIBA Finance House	Pasadena, CA	Finance house	Home, auto, business financing
Guidance Financial Group	Reston, VA	Finance house	Home financing
Devon Bank	Chicago, IL	Bank	Home financing, business financing
University Bank	Ann Arbor, MI	Bank	Interest-free deposits, home financing
HSBC	New York, NY	Bank	Home financing, interest-free checking, credit/debit
Neighbourhood Development Centre	Minneapolis/ St. Paul, MN	Non-profit	Small business financing and training
World Relief	Nashville, TN	Non-profit	Small business financing
SHAPE Financial Group	West Falls Church, VA	For profit wholesaler/ consultant	Home financing, savings accounts, and consulting
Reba Free	Minneapolis/ St. Paul, MN	For profit wholesaler/ consultant	Small business financing models and consulting

Source: Chicago Fed. Letter, Federal Reserve Bank of Chicago, May 2005, Number 214.

comprise the 2 core Islamic finance products for these organisations. The US Islamic finance institutions usually offer 3 types of Shariah-compliant financing structures: Musharaka (co-ownership), Ijara (lease to purchase), and Murabaha (installment credit sale) (Table 1).[20]

---

[20] (1) Musharaka (co-ownership) — the firm and the individual jointly purchase the home with the firm owning the larger stake because it provides most of the money. The individual then makes monthly payments that include a fee to cover use of the firm's share of the property. With each payment, the individual gains equity in the house until he owns it. (2) Ijara (lease to purchase) — the firm buys and then rents the home to the individual; the monthly payment covers rent and a fee; the balance accumulates toward the purchase; the parties agree that the firm will sell the home

In the area of small business financing, the Neighbourhood Development Centre and World Relief are non-profit, small-volume lenders that cater mainly to the needs of Somali refugees in Minneapolis and St. Paul in Minnesota and Nashville, Tennessee, respectively. Organisations such as SHAPE Financial and Reba Free are for-profit enterprises that work with financial institutions to provide predesigned Shariah-compliant financing products and consultation. Asset management groups such as Saturna Capital, Azzad Asset Management, and Allied Asset Advisors offer a suite of Islamic finance investment products including mutual funds, growth funds, and income funds that are considered halal (permissible) in that they do not support producers of alcohol and pork-related products, suppliers of conventional financing, and providers of entertainment services. Islamic finance investment products are also increasingly being offered for private equity, hedge funds, real estate investment trusts (REITs) and exchange traded funds. In the commercial real estate-financing sector, Zayan Finance began offering Shariah-compliant financing in 2007. "Over 25% of Muslim Americans earn $100,000 or more, compared to 15% of the overall US population. A majority of this segment are professionals and business owners, with over 65% completing college or graduate degrees. The markets credit worthiness is marked by the fact that over 1/2 of Muslim Americans have an excellent credit score (above 700 where maximum score is 850)", according to Naveed Siddiqui, CEO of Zayan Finance.[21] As the Islamic finance industry in the United States steadily grows, it would be worthwhile to examine a few fundamental challenges facing US regulators.

---

to the individual by a certain date. (3) Murabaha (installment credit sale) — the firm buys a house and then sells it to the individual for the purchase price plus an agreed-upon profit; the amount remains fixed for the buy-out period; the full price may be paid at the time of purchase, at a fixed point in the future, or through a series of deferred payments. http://www.washingtonpost.com/wp-dyn/content/article/2006/10/20/AR2006102000788_2.html.

[21] 'Islamic Finance Gaining Traction in the US', http://dinarstandard.com/finance/IF_NorthAmerica112107.htm [21 November 2007].

Challenges Facing US Regulators[22]

With the multiple regulatory agencies and the multilayers of bureau-
cracy between state and federal jurisdictions in the United States, US
regulators face various challenges in handling Islamic finance developments. How US regulators manage Islamic finance developments in
the United States and in relation to cross-border financing transactions
is integrally linked to how the US government revises standards and
regulations for financial institutions. In his March 2009 speech on
'Financial Reform to Address Systemic Risk', Federal Reserve
Chairman Bernard Bernanke underscored the need to craft "a strategy
that regulates the financial system as a whole, in a holistic way, not just
its individual components. In particular, strong and effective regulation and supervision of banking institutions, although necessary for
reducing systemic risk, are not sufficient by themselves to achieve this
aim".[23] Bernanke also highlighted 4 key elements of this strategy:

(1) address the problem of financial institutions deemed too big —
    or perhaps too interconnected — to fail;
(2) strengthen the financial infrastructure — the systems, rules, and
    conventions that govern trading, payment, clearing, and settle-
    ment in financial markets — to ensure that it will perform
    under stress;
(3) review regulatory policies and accounting rules to ensure that
    they do not induce excessive procyclicality; and
(4) consider whether the creation of an authority specifically
    charged with monitoring and addressing systemic risks would
    help protect the system from financial crises.[24]

---

[22] The author wishes to thank anonymous reviewers at the Federal Reserve of
New York for their feedback.
[23] Federal Reserve Chairman Bernard Bernanke, 'Financial Reform to Address
Systemic Risk', Speech to Council on Foreign Relations, (10 March 2009)
http://www.federalreserve.gov/newsevents/speech/bernanke20090310a.htm.
[24] Ibid.

As US regulatory reforms take shape, determining the impact on US domestic developments of Islamic finance should be understood in the context of 2 fundamental challenges — relating to religion and supervision — with a primary focus on depository institution regulation.

While the First Amendment to the US Constitution provides that "Congress shall make no law respecting an establishment of religion, or prohibiting the free exercise thereof", which in essence preserves the separation of church (or mosque) and state, a corollary of the principle of religious freedom enshrined in the Constitution is that the secular law should adapt, as much as possible, to accommodate different religious practices.[25] Although the US legal system is broad and sophisticated enough to allow the use of Shariah-compliant structures, US regulators must manage preserving the free exercise of religion while executing the secular mandate of common law, which includes enforcing disclosure requirements and maintaining supervision over transparent and sound financial practices, whether in a faith-based or conventional context. Introducing Islamic finance principles into the US financial and banking system poses the challenge of finding ways to accommodate certain aspects of Islamic law in US legal frameworks pertaining to cross-border transactions, contracts, tax codes, and so forth. A corollary challenge in this regard is identifying the experts who possess depth and breadth of knowledge in US common law, Islamic law and international finance and are qualified to advise on regulatory supervision and product integrity. Shariah supervisory boards assume this independent role for their respective banks, but not as an integrated entity within the US regulatory structure.

Maintaining oversight, transparency, supervision, and enforcement of regulatory and prudential standards is another major challenge for US regulators, who must manage a variety of risks and

---

[25] Baxter Jr. and Thomas, C. (2005) Executive Vice President and General Counsel, Federal Reserve of New York, 'Regulation of Islamic Financial Services in the United States' (2 March 2005), http://www.newyorkfed.org/newsevents/ ssspeeches/2005/bax050302.html.

vulnerabilities while concurrently accommodating the industry's efforts to establish credibility and sustainability. The official inception of the Islamic finance industry in the United States emerged from two key decisions by the Office of the Comptroller of the Currency (OCC) in the Department of Treasury. OCC charters, regulates, and supervises all national banks. It also supervises the federal branches and agencies of foreign banks. The OCC issued two interpretive letters in 1997 — a response to a proposal submitted by the United Bank of Kuwait for a resident net lease-to-own home finance product — and in 1999 — a proposal to offer certain Murabaha-based financing products. The OCC concluded that because the purchase and sale occurred simultaneously, the bank would be as a 'riskless principal' in such transactions. In allowing the transactions, the OCC determined that the structures were equivalent to conventional products.[26] Both cases demonstrate how the US regulatory framework can ensure compliance while allowing for flexibility.

On an operational level, bank supervisors have to become familiar with the internal mechanisms of Islamic finance institutions, specifically in the areas of risk management — credit, market, investment, operational, and legal — compliance and control, corporate governance, and capital policy. According to Ibrahim Warde, "Because of the religious injunction against *gharar* [risk], financial institutions and their Shariah boards tread carefully around all issues involving risk, including complicated financial instruments designed to control risk. Thus, although such products are supposed to control risk and reduce it, they do not always pass to muster with Shariah boards. Islamic banks have thus been lagging in their efforts to devise the risk management techniques required by regulators".[27] In the

---

[26] Rutledge, W. (19 April 2005) Regulation and supervision of Islamic banking in the United States. Remarks at the 2005 Arab Bankers Association of North America (ABANA) Conference on Islamic Finance: Players, Products and Innovations. New York.

[27] Warde, I. (2006) *Islamic Finance in the Global Economy.* Edinburgh: Edinburgh University Press, p. 195.

United States, as in many other countries, bank examiners follow a supervisory regime based on legal and regulatory requirements. More training and education on supervisory approaches are needed to accommodate the growing needs of Islamic finance and banking in the US domestic context and for developing international supervisory standards.[28]

Opportunities and Outlook for the United States and Southeast Asia

Islamic finance in the United States is still in its nascent stages. US expertise and experience in Islamic finance is concentrated among a limited pool of private and public sector experts scattered throughout the country. For those in the US banking, financial, legal, and regulatory sectors, basic education and awareness of Islamic finance and banking could be considered the first prerequisite in demystifying general misconceptions about Islamic finance and understanding the factors that make it an appealing alternative to conventional modes of banking and finance. If data projections on the Islamic finance industry's growth trajectory are borne out over the next decade, US expertise in standardising financial practices, structures, and contracts and commitment to enforcing legal frameworks are essential to facilitating efforts toward convergence of international regulatory standards for the industry.[29] The potential cost of inaction or remaining on the sidelines of industry developments could hinder US players from being key stakeholders in influencing the direction and volume of Islamic capital flows,

---

[28] Ibid.

[29] DeLorenzo, Y. T. and McMillen, M. T. J. (2007) Law and Islamic finance: An interactive analysis. In *Islamic Finance: The Regulatory Challenge*, Simon Archer and R. A. Abdel Karim (eds.), pp. 132–197. Singapore: John Wiley & Sons (Asia); Regulation-lite belongs to a different age (21 January 2008). *Financial Times*, p. 9.

particularly between the GCC and Asia, and in a broader context, the norms and practices of the industry.

With Asia's accelerating gravitational pull as a centre of economic dynamism and investment opportunities, the liquidity from petrodollars is finding the growth destinations in Southeast Asia. To facilitate greater US involvement in Islamic capital markets, cooperation between the United States and key Southeast Asian countries, such as Malaysia and Singapore, could take the form of working group expertise exchanges between US regulators and their counterparts at Malaysia's Central Bank and Securities Commission, the Monetary Authority of Singapore, the Accounting and Auditing Organisation for Islamic Finance Institutions (AAIOFI) in Bahrain, and the Islamic Finance Services Board (IFSB) based in Kuala Lumpur. In the area of education and training, Malaysia's International Centre for Education in Islamic Finance (INCEIF) — established in 2006 as a professional certification body and education institute for post-graduates in Islamic finance — offers a certification course in Islamic finance for international professionals. Subject-matter expert exchanges on professional and institutional levels — law firms, corporations, and research institutes — could also foster cross-fertilisation of knowledge and practices among industry practitioners and analysts.

Looking ahead, it is foreseeable that developments in the Islamic finance industry will sustain growth in major infrastructure projects, real estate acquisition, insurance, and mortgage lending, and likely expand into industries such as aerospace, estate planning, philanthropy, tourism, transportation, among others.[30] As the industry grows, regulatory challenges will become more complex — a theme particularly punctuated at the G-20 Finance Ministers and Central Bank Governors meeting in March 2009, where US Secretary Treasury Tim Geithner and other countries' government financial

[30] http://www.janes.com/news/transport/business/jtf/jtf080125_1_n.shtml [25 January 2008].

leaders pursued a fundamental rethinking of how to retool the global financial system for greater effectiveness in mitigating the systemic risks and laid the ground work to build a framework to increase transparency, accountability, and efficiency in the global regulatory system. Their measures underscore how the throes of current global economic climate are testing the viability and resilience of traditional financial structures and practices.[31] With uncertainty and fluidity as constants in capital markets, governments and practitioners will need to reassess their current approaches toward Islamic finance in the context of larger transformative trends unfolding in the global financial system.

---

[31] Prepared Statement by Treasury Secretary Tim Geithner at the G-20 Finance Ministers and Central Bank Governors' Meeting (14 March 2009) http:// www.treas.gov/press/releases/tg56.htm.

AN INTRODUCTION TO THE LAWS AND PRACTICES OF ISLAMIC TRUSTS AND THE DISTRIBUTION OF A TRUST UPON MATURITY

Angelo M. Venardos and Aimi Zulhazmi Abdul Rashid

Overview

Contracts are drawn to ensure the existence of clearly recognised guidelines for all parties involved. They state the standings of all those involved and the condition(s) of the transaction(s) that are to take place. This occurs in both conventional and Islamic banking. The general principle of the Islamic law of contract is contained in the Quranic verse: "O you who believe, fulfill all obligations".[1] The definition of contract (Al-Aqd) in Shariah law is similar to that in English common law, but is wider in that it includes dispositions which are gratuitous as well as endowments and trusts.

---

[1] Quran 5:1.

A contract in Islamic law consists of an agreement made between two or more parties and the basic elements are quite similar to those of English common law:

  (i) **Offer and acceptance** — a contract requires an offer (*Ijab*) and acceptance (*Qabul*). The contract can be oral or in writing, made by signs or gestures, by conduct or through an agent. If the offer is made in writing it remains in force until received by the other party, who must then reply promptly.

 (ii) **Consideration** — as in common law, consideration may consist of money, goods or services. It must be something which is capable of being given, or, in the case of a service, capable of being performed, and it must not involve materials or acts which are prohibited according to Islamic law.

(iii) **Capacity** — the parties entering into a contract must be legally competent. A minor, a person of unsound mind, an insolvent person, a person legally declared a prodigal, an intoxicated person or a person suffering from an illness which leads to his or her death (*Mard Al-Mawt*) cannot enter into a binding contract.

(iv) **Legality** — the purpose of the contract must be legal in terms of the Shariah. A contract to grow grapes for winemaking, for example, would be illegal, as would a contract to sell firearms to criminals or to make a loan with interest.

 (v) **Absence of duress** — the parties must enter into the contract of their own free will. A contract concluded under duress is null and void.

Types of Contract in Shariah

There are 7 types of contract recognised by Shariah law and they are as follows.

Al-Tamlikat (Acquiring of Ownership)

This kind of contract relates to the acquisition of ownership of properties, or the rights to the benefits of properties. The kinds of contract which fall into this category can be further divided into 2 sub-groups, namely:

(a) *Uqud Al-Muawadhat* (Contracts of exchange)
    In this instance, the acquisition of ownership involves some kind of exchange between 2 parties involving a sale, hire, money changing, compromise, partition, sale by order and the like.

(b) *Uqad Al-Tabarruat* (Contracts of charity)
    This kind of contract relates to situations where the ownership of a property is acquired without involving an exchange, for example as a gift, alms, endowment, benevolent loan (*Al-Qard Al-Hasan*) or the assignment of debt. Sometimes, a contract may be initiated as a contract of charity, but then later the receiving party is required to give an exchange. Examples of such a contract are guarantees requested by the debtor and gifts with the condition of an exchange. Contracts such as these are contracts of charity at the beginning, ending as a contract of exchange.

Al-Isqatat (Releases)

These contracts relate to the dropping of rights against others with or without exchange. If the release is without compensation from the other party, then the release is an absolute release and includes repudiation, remission of the penalty of talion, release from debt and withdrawal from the right to pre-emption. If the release is with compensation from the other party, then it is a release with exchange.

Al-Itlaqat (Permissions)

This kind of contract includes giving total responsibility to individuals, firms or agencies in the appointment of governors and judges; giving a person who is dispossessed of the power of administration, permission to administer his property, or giving permission to a minor to carry on trade; and the appointment of a nominee to take care of one's children after death.

Al-Taqyidat (Restrictions)

Contracts in this group prevent or terminate the performance of certain functions. They include the dismissal of governors, judges and supervisors; the termination of endowments; the termination of the appointment of nominees and agents; and dispossession of the administration of property because of insanity, mental disorder, prodigality or infancy.

Al-Tauthiqat (Securities)

This kind of contract is meant to secure debts for their owners and guarantee creditors of debts owing to them. They include guarantees and the assignment of debt and mortgage.

Al-Ishtirak (Partnerships)

These contracts relate to sharing in projects and profits. They include Al-Mudaraba, where a person gives an amount of money to another to trade or invest with the condition that they share in the profit while the loss is borne by the owner of the capital. They also include partnerships involving the cultivation of land and taking care of trees.[2]

Al-Hifz (Safe Custody)

Contracts in this group relate to keeping property safe for its owner and include some of the functions of agency.

Islamic Financing in a Contemporary Setting

Before the modern era, Mudaraba partnerships, in which some of the partners contribute only capital and the other partners only labour, worked perfectly well, especially in traditional settings which typically involved simple commercial, agricultural or manufacturing ventures, where the number of investors was usually limited and the size of capital invested relatively small. Today, however, contemporary economic circumstances require a much more flexible institutional framework, whereby a PLS company arrangement is able to accommodate itself to a huge number of investors, enormous financial resources and ever-expanding technological frontiers. The problem here has been one of adapting what are essentially medieval financial practices to the modern world of banking and investment. This is a challenge that has been met by modifying present-day financial institutions to the extent that they can embody the principle implicit in the former, while still remaining compatible with contemporary practices.

---

[2] Some financing principles of Islam stem from ancient practices in agriculture, which allowed parties to deal in crop-sharing for cultivable land and fruit orchards in accordance to Shariah law.

The Problem of Uncertainty (*Gharar*)

Risk-taking and uncertainty are a fact of life in the conventional world of business, even though most people will naturally seek to minimise the chances of something going wrong due to unforeseen circumstances. However, as we have seen, under Islamic law, risk-taking or uncertainty (*Gharar*) is expressly forbidden. In legal and business terms, *Gharar* means to enter into a commercial venture blindly, without sufficient knowledge, or else to undertake an excessively risky transaction, and it can apply in a number of different circumstances. They include:

- Transactions where the seller is not in a position to hand over the goods to the buyer;
- Transactions where the item or commodity for sale cannot be immediately acquired — for example the sale of fruit which has not yet ripened, or fish or birds not yet caught;
- Speculative investments such as trading in futures or on the stock market; and
- Transactions where the purchaser is not given the opportunity of inspecting goods before purchasing item.

However, minor uncertainties may be permitted in situations, provided certain necessary conditions are fulfilled, namely:

- The goods or services of the transaction be in existence;
- The characteristics of the goods or service are known;
- The parties to the contract should have such control over the subject as to be able to ensure that exchange will take place; and
- If the transaction or exchange is to take place in the future, then the date when it is to take place should be certain.

In Islamic law, the principle underlying most illegal contracts is to prevent benefitting from others for nothing and unfairly. A zero-sum exchange encapsulates precisely what is to be avoided: it is an exchange in which one party gains at the expense of another leading to a win–lose outcome. Naturally, no one of sound mind would enter into a game where losing was an absolute certainty. It is only when the outcome is uncertain that such a game is played. Uncertainty or risk is what tempts rational agents to engage in exchanges where they know in advance that only one party will gain, while the other must surely lose. It is this temptation which is best described by the term *gharar* and it follows that a *gharar* contract is characterised as a zero-sum game with uncertain payoffs.[3]

Commercial Law

It can thus be seen that there has always been a close historical connection between Islam and commerce. The attitude of Islam towards commercial activities is generally seen as a positive one. Hence, the rules regarding Islamic finance, in essence, can be simply summarised as follows:

(i) Any predetermined payment over and above the actual amount of principal is prohibited. Islam allows only one kind of loan and that is *Qard Al-Hasana* (literally a 'good loan') whereby the lender does not charge any interest or additional amount over the money lent. Traditional Muslim jurists have construed this principle so strictly that, according to one commentator, "this prohibition applies to any advantage or benefits that the lender might secure out of the *Qard* (loan) such as riding the borrower's mule, eating at his table, or even taking advantage of the shade of his wall". The principle derived from the quotation emphasises that associated or indirect benefits are also prohibited.

---

[3] Al-Suwailem, Sami, 'Towards an objective measure of ghararin exchange', Islamic Economic Studies, Vol. 7, Nos. 1 and 2, October 1999, April 2000.

(ii) Lenders must share in the profits or losses arising out of the enterprise for which the money was lent.

Islam encourages Muslims to invest their money and to become partners in order to share profits and risks in the business instead of becoming creditors. As defined in the Shariah, or Islamic law, Islamic finance is based on the belief that the provider of capital and the user of capital should equally share the risk of business ventures, whether those are industries, farms, service companies or simple trade deals. Translated into banking terms, the depositor, the bank and the borrower should all share the risks and the rewards of financing business ventures. This is unlike the interest-based commercial banking system, where all the pressure is on the borrower: he must pay back his loan, with the agreed interest, regardless of the success or failure of his venture.

The principle which emerges here is that Islam encourages investment in order that the community as a whole may benefit. It is not willing to allow a loophole for those who do not wish to invest and take risks, but rather are content with hoarding their money or else depositing it in a bank to receive an increase on their capital for no risk (other than the bank becoming insolvent). Within Islam, either people invest with risk, or else suffer loss through devaluation by inflation by keeping their money idle. Islam encourages the notion of higher risks and higher returns and promotes it by leaving no other avenue available to investors. The objective is that high-risk investments will act as a stimulus to the economy and encourage entrepreneurs to maximise their efforts.

(iii) Making money from money is not Islamically acceptable.

Money is only a medium of exchange, a way of defining the value of a thing; it has no value in itself and therefore should not be allowed to give rise to more money simply by being put in a bank or lent to someone else at a fixed interest rate. The human effort, initiative, and risk involved in a productive venture are more important than the money used to finance it. Muslim jurists consider money as potential capital rather than capital, meaning that money becomes capital only when it is invested in business. Accordingly, money advanced to a business as a loan is regarded as a debt of the business and not capital and, as such, it is not entitled to any return (i.e., interest). Muslims are encouraged to purchase and are discouraged from keeping money idle so that, for instance, hoarding money is regarded as being unacceptable. In Islam, money represents purchasing power which is considered to be the only proper use of money. This purchasing power (money) cannot be used to make more purchasing power (money) without undergoing the intermediate step of it being used for the purchase of goods and services.

(iv) *Gharar* (uncertainty, risk or speculation) is also prohibited.

Under this prohibition, any transaction entered into should be free from uncertainty, risk and speculation. Contracting parties should have perfect knowledge of the countervalues intended to be exchanged as a result of their transactions. At the same time, though, parties cannot predetermine a guaranteed profit. This is based on the principle of 'uncertain gains' which, on a strict interpretation, does not even allow an undertaking from the customer to repay the borrowed principal plus an amount to take into account inflation. The rationale behind the prohibition is the wish to protect the weak from exploitation. Therefore, options and futures are considered as un-Islamic and so are forward foreign exchange transactions because rates are determined by interest differentials.

A number of Islamic scholars disapprove the indexation of indebtedness to inflation and explain this prohibition within the framework of *Qard Al-Hasana*. According to those scholars, the creditor advances the loan to win the blessings of Allah and expects to obtain the reward from Allah alone. A number of transactions are treated as exceptions to the principle of *Gharar*; sales

with advanced payment (*Bai Bithaman Ajil*); contract to manufacture (Istisna); and hire contract (Ijara). However, there are
legal requirements for the conclusion of these contracts to be
organised in a way which minimises the risk.

(v)　Investments should only support practices or products that are
not forbidden — or even discouraged — by Islam. Trade in
alcohol, for example would not be financed by an Islamic bank;
a real-estate loan could not be made for the construction of a
casino; and the bank could not lend money to other banks at
interest.[4]

Thus, it can be seen that, ultimately the aim of the Islamic
financial system is to allow individuals to earn a living in a fair and
profitable manner, without exploitation of others, so that all
society benefits.

Trust Concept in Islam

The Majelle, one of the oldest Islamic literatures published over 200
years ago, is a popular source of reference on modern Islamic banking and finances. The literature initially written in Arabic was
translated in many languages, beginning with French and followed
by English, Malay and others. The Majelle in two Articles defined
trust from the perspective of Shariah, in Article 762,[5] in which
Al-Ameen is described as being in charge of something entrusted
with. Al-Ameen was also the nickname of Prophet Muhammad (saw)
given by his people before he was appointed Prophet. The name
describes someone fully trusted by the society, hence providing an
early example of *Trustee*. Furthermore, in Article 769,[6] the role of

---

[4] Nida'ul Islam magazine, 'Principles of Islamic Banking', www.islam.org.au,
November–December 1995.
[5] Article 762, The Mejelle.
[6] Article 769, The Mejelle.

Trustee is further defined in the area of responsibility — that if it is due to the negligence of the trustee the entrusted asset is damaged or destroyed, then the trustee shall be responsible.

The holy book of Muslims, the Al-Quran, also elaborates on the Trustee fundamentals. In the verse 23:8, God described good Muslims as those who faithfully observe their trusts and covenants.[7]

Furthermore, in verse 4:58, God directed Muslims that they must bestow their trust to the right people:

> Allah commands you to render back your trusts to those to whom they are due; and when you judge between man and man, that you judge with justices: verily how excellent is the teaching which He gives you! For Allah is He who hears and sees all things.[8]

Literary, *trust* is also described as Amanah, the action of a party to safe-keep the asset on behalf of another party. Another popular illustration is the Wadiah concept, used by Islamic bank to describe the act of holding the customers' deposits in saving accounts.

Islamic Trust Development

Islam certainly encourages Muslims to seek wealth, which is a very important point as there are certain quarters that believe Muslims should concentrate and focus on Ibadah (spiritual) alone for Akhirat or the hereafter. They are extremely rigid or interpret the divinely inspired injunctions literarily, in fact God instructed Muslims after completing their prayer that Muslims should work hard to obtain prosperity and become wealthy:

> And when the Prayer is finished, then you may disperse through the land, and seek of the Bounty of Allah: and celebrate the Praises of Allah often (and without stint): that you may prosper.[9]

---

[7] Al Mu'minun (23:8).
[8] Al Nisa' (4:58).
[9] Al Jumuah (62:10).

Wealthy people have more capacity in terms of monetary and time to help people, as illustrated by philanthropists establishing their foundations to help others. Such set up by a Muslim in Malaysia is Syed Mokhtar Al-Bukhary. As God certainly encourages sharing of wealth as described in verse 5:2 that Muslim should help others with full sincerity:

... You help one another in righteousness and piety ...[10]

The sharing of wealth in Islam during the days of Prophet Muhammad (saw) and his companions 1,400 years ago led to the establishment of an institution called Baitulmal, which is still being practised in the present day. Literally Bayt is a house and Mal is property — a public treasury where alms or Zakat are collected as a form of tax from the people. Zakat in their respective proportions were collected and then distributed to the needy. Later on, when Arab and Indian traders started to travel around the world especially in the Asian region, the role of Trustee became more prominent. The traders entrusted the assets and families to the trusted family members or heads of the clans/tribes until they return, and even laid out the distribution should the traders never return.

Since then, there had been rapid development of assets and issues that must be taken into consideration. Sophistication in the modern financial world gives rise to new asset forms, various moveable asset forms, such as bonds, debentures, company shares, gold certificates, safe-keeping receipt of craft, paintings and artefacts located at different countries and jurisdictions. Moreover, different laws govern the asset forms and locality from continental laws, common laws, civil laws, to offshore laws. The 11 September incidence

---

[10] Al Maidah (5:2).

had also changed the geo-political global landscape. Terrorism is now recognised as a major global treat. Anti-money laundering scope previously only covers drugs and arm trades, but now includes terrorism-related activities. The Western and Muslim worlds now are at more different polars of opinions than before. Muslims certainly have now greater awareness of their financial planning needs, wanting to oblige their faith on their financial requirements and thus opting for Islamic banking, insurance and financing. The introduction of Islamic banking and Takaful products, Sukuk, Islamic unit trust/Mutual Funds and REITs have expanded the varieties of Islamic financial services as well as pushing for more Shariah-compliant offerings. The sizable private wealth of Muslims especially in the Middle East (estimated at US$1.5 trillion in 2006) led to the demand for Islamic wealth management and Islamic private banking.

There are, however, some issues that need to be addressed in the setting up of trust and its compliance to the Shariah laws as the guiding principles, that is, from the Al-Quran and the teachings/ practices of the Prophet Muhammad (saw). Shariah describes 'Halal' as acceptable and the opposite is 'Haram', the forbidden ones; both attract good and bad deeds accordingly. Shariah provides guidelines on definitions and types of asset, debt and investment that are halal and haram. For example, income from business related to gambling, liquors or pig-rearing are haram; similarly, interest income received from savings in the conventional bank is also haram. When discussing Islamic trust, knowledge of Faraidh or forced heirship distribution must be attained at the beginner's level. Approval from the Shariah supervisory council must be obtained to provide credibility support on the Islamic products and services.

Before we move to the next area in the various Islamic Trust products, there is the need to emphasise the importance of witnesses in the execution. This is underlined by the Quranic verse that in making bequest, there should be two witnesses preferably fellow Muslims; however, non-Muslims can also act as witnesses should there be no Muslims around.

> ... when death approaches any of you, (take) witnesses among yourselves when making bequests, two just men of your own (brotherhood) or others from outside if you are journeying through the earth, and the chance of death befalls you... .[11]

The preferred order of witnesses are as follows:

(1) Two male witnesses;
(2) If not available then one male witness and two female witnesses; and
(3) If not available then four female witnesses.

Islamic Trust Products

Waqf

The first type of Islamic Trust is Waqf, also currently the most popular term to be used in illustrating Islamic Trust. The setting up of Waqf is normally intended for charitable persons. By definition, Waqf can be a dedication of assets in perpetuity for charitable and religious objectives; secondly Waqf can also be defined as the use of an asset for a specified cause. There are 2 categories of Waqf, that is, Waqf Am (general) normally for public causes and Waqf Azzuri (limited to family members). Four main areas need to be considered when structuring Waqf Trust:

(1) Waqif (the asset owner);
(2) Mauquf (asset to be Waqf);

---

[11] Al Maidah (5:106).

(3) Mauquf allaih (beneficiary); and

(4) Sighah (the contract).

One example of Waqf is Cash Waqf in Labuan, Malaysia, an offshore jurisdiction. The product had been launched in July 2004.

Islamic Will

Before we elaborate further on Islamic Trust products, we need to understand how a Will is prepared and executed according to Shariah rules. A Will is defined in Islam as an admission (Iqra) of honour made by a person during his or her lifetime; the purposes of preparing a Will can be of charitable nature or any other purposes permissible by Islam. Even the Al-Quran extensively elaborated the importance for Muslims to write a Will:

> It is prescribed, when death approaches any of you, if he leaves any goods, that he makes a bequest to parents and next of kin, according to reasonable usage; this is due from those who fear Allah. If anyone changes the bequest after hearing it, the guilt shall be on those who make the change, for Allah hears and knows (all things). But if anyone fears partiality or wrongdoing on the part of the testator, and make peace between (parties concerned), there is no wrong in him: for Allah is Oft-Forgiving, Most Merciful'.[12]

Writing of an Islamic Will would require 2 witnesses (as described earlier). The Will comprises of 2 main categories that are divided into portions of 1/3 and 2/3:

(1) One-third portion (1/3) is defined as up to one-third amount of the estate, meaning the portion must be met; however, not

---

[12] Al Baqarah (2:180–182).

necessarily to the maximum of 33.3%; it can be in lesser amount as long as the amount is allocated. The allocation is at the liberty of the testator (one who makes the Will) but must not be for those family members entitled under the forced heirship ruling (2/3). Examples of those entitled for the 1/3 portion are:

(a) Adopted children/foster parents/siblings;
(b) Non-muslim immediate family members (parents and siblings);
(c) Relatives not entitled under force heirship ruling, for example, in-laws and grandchildren; and
(d) Institutions and organisations, either charitable or non-charitable.

On the other hand, Islam recognises that more than 1/3 portion can be made to the above beneficiaries; however, such agreement would be required from those relatives entitled under the 2/3 portion after the death of the testator. If not being agreed than it would revert back to 1/3 portion.

(2) Two-third portion (2/3) or the balance after allocating the one-third portion is allocated to the relatives or family members. This distribution can be allocated according to the following:

(a) Directly follow Faraidh distribution or forced heirship, close family members of blood relations and spouses, who are also known as the main beneficiaries.
(b) The testator can also suggest or propose that instead of following Faraidh, the assets are to be distributed according to their wishes. However, the suggestion/proposition is subjected to the agreement of the main beneficiaries after the testator is demised.
(c) Conversely, the main beneficiaries may amicably agree to divide the asset according to their common agreement instead of following Faraidh distribution.

As commented by an Islamic scholar, one of the most important features of the Shariah is that of its flexibility, because the overriding objectives of Shariah is the preservation of human interest, its welfare and well-being.[13] In the above situation, Islam is not rigid by enforcing Faraidh but certainly encourages common agreement among the heirs. Only when the consensus fails Faraidh comes in as the provided solution by Shariah. However, certain objectives intended by the Will testator may not be realised due to the indifferences among the family members, under such a situation it is crucial to plan during the lifetime *vis-à-vis* setting up Islamic to achieve the intentions.

Hibah

Generally, an Islamic Trust product is called *Hibah*. By literal definition Hibah means gift. It is basically the transfer of ownership or conveyance of the asset from the Donor to the Beneficiary. The Donor, also known as Settlor of the Trust, creates the trust for the benefits of the Beneficiary. The creation is made voluntary by the Donor and without valuable consideration. The Trust must also be created during the lifetime of both the Donor and Beneficiary. Furthermore, the creation of trust in Islam is highly encouraged (given good deeds Sunat), as underpinned by both Quranic verse and the Prophet Muhammad (saw) hadith:

> … give away wealth out of love for Him, for your kin, for orphans, for the needy, for the wayfarer, for those who ask (beggars)….[14]
> Give a gift; you will be in love with each other'. Hadith of Prophet Muhammad.[15]

---

[13] Dr. Wan Azhar Wan Ahmad, "The moderate nature of Islam", *The Star*, Malaysia, p. 46, 8 April 2008.
[14] Al Baqarah (2:17).
[15] From Abu Hurrairah, narrated by Bukhari.

Hibah could be categorised into 3 applications:

(1) Sadaqah, as the name reflects, means giving something to the needy. It does not require intervivos, meaning that there should not be any requirement that the beneficiary must be in existence to receive from the Donor. As for its charitable nature, it is a voluntary act without any condition or any consideration. Donor can create Sadaqah Trust for his private charitable objective with an appointed trustee, then instruct the trustee to donate on his behalf to named beneficiaries.

(2) Gift is an absolute transfer without any consideration but intervivos is required whereby the Beneficiary must accept from the Donor as specified. It is a voluntary act, without condition and without valuable consideration. Donor creates the trust by appointing the Trustee and the named Beneficiary.

(3) Conveyance intervivos is the most sophisticated of the 3. It is a voluntary act without consideration. The execution is basically broken into 2 segments:

    (a) Offer and Acceptance (Sighah) action is required from both Donor and Beneficiary, then delivery is made by Donor to Beneficiary, and then Beneficiary must take possession of the assets. This action is documented in Sighah (contract).

    (b) Immediately, both Donor and Beneficiary must then agree to appoint the Trustee to act as the legal owner of the asset by signing another document called the Trust Deed. Any conditions can be included in the deed as it is now a contract among the 3 parties. Asset received by the Beneficiary is now transferred to the Trustee that is holding it in trust on behalf of the Beneficiary.

Distribution of Islamic Trust

In understanding the effect of distribution on the trust discussed earlier, we need to have preliminary knowledge of Faraidh or forced heirship ruling on asset distribution during estate administration. Faraidh ruling is highly prominent in the Al-Quran:

> Allah directs you as regard to your children (inheritance) to the male, a portion equal to that of two females: if only daughters, two or more, their share is two-third. The distribution in all cases is after the payment of legacies and debt. In what your wives leaves, your share is half, if they leave no child, but if they leave a child, you get a fourth; after payment of legacies and debt....[16]

The rationale of why the males get more than the females is because they are heavily entrusted and responsible for the females in the family. However in the current world we are living in, gender can be quite a topic in itself. Nevertheless, the Faraidh or Islam forced heirship formula should be looked at as the solution provided by God when there is disagreement among the heirs. Islam encourages mutual understanding or consensus among the heirs, which should be the first solution in the distribution process, and only when such consensus is not successful, the Faraidh will come in.

The Faraidh distribution formula is unique and predetermined in the Al-Quran. Beneficiaries include heirs from blood relations like brothers, sisters, father, and children and by marriage, that is, the spouse. Thus adopted children, in-laws and grandchildren are not entitled. An illustration of Faraidh:

A husband dies leaving a wife, a son, a daughter and parents; after deduction of legacies and debt, the distribution as follows:

(1) Wife 1/8;
(2) Father 1/6; and
(3) Mother 1/6.
(4) With the balance divided among the children:

    (a) Ratio of son to daughter 2:1, son 2/3 and daughter 1/3;

---

[16] Al-Nisa (4:11–12).

(5) When the children are daughters only, they are entitled only 2/3 of the balance with the remnant going to the father of the demised or siblings of the demised (in order of priority).

(6) When there is only a child who is a girl, she is entitled to a maximum of 1/2 of the balance, with the remnant going to the father of the demised or siblings of the demised (in order of priority).

On Islamic Trusts, the distribution of a Trust is not subjected to Faraidh if it is made irrevocable during the creation. This is due to the fact that:

- Transfer of ownership is made during the lifetime (including to Trustee as legal owner).
- Such examples are Waqf and Hibah, irrevocable instruments of Trusts.

On the other hand, revocable trust according to Shariah principles is certainly subjected to Faraidh ruling. These are people who created revocable trust for the purpose of overcoming lengthy estate administration process; although the assets are emplaced with the Trustee as legal titleholder, the Donor has the powers to revoke the trust and sell some of the assets as and when required.

Another important issue to be considered in Islamic Trust distribution is in a situation when the Beneficiary predeceases the Donor. For trusts like Waqf, Sadaqah, Gift, the asset becomes the estate of the Beneficiary. Take for an example when a father sets up a Gift Trust for the house he is living in to his only child. Should the daughter predecease him, the house he is living in becomes the estate of his daughter and needs to be distributed according to the Faraidh ruling. As a result he is entitled for 1/6 of the house. Maybe the house has to be sold to meet other heir's demands — for example, his ex-wife and the mother of his daughter requesting her

1/6 portion. This special situation is overcome by Hibah Conveyance Intervivos through the two conditions in the trust deed, Umra and Ruqba:

(1) *Umra* means age, that is, only when the Donor's age 'ends', the asset would be transferred by Trustee to Beneficiary.

(2) *Ruqba* means waiting — for example, should the child predecease the father, it is agreed by both parties that assets held by Trustee shall be Hibah to another Beneficiary, thus avoiding the assets to become the estate of Beneficiary.

Summary of Islamic Trust Products and Distribution

The Asset Filtering Model chart below illustrates the positions of the various Hibah Trusts and Islamic Will. In wealth management, it is very important to segregate a person's wealth as the assets would normally be in various classes and types. Based on the person's requirements, the assets are then segregated according to the suitable Trust instruments. The chart illustrates that various types of assets are initially filtered through the right Islamic Trust instruments. Hibah Conveyance Intervivos is on the top of the list because of the flexibility in earlier described Umra and Ruqba features, followed with Gift Trust, an absolute gift that is irrevocable in nature; and Sadaqah and Waqf Trusts for charitable purposes. For Trusts made during the lifetime of the Donor/Settlor, the assets distribution are not subjected to Faraidh ruling as the assets have been transferred to the Trustee or Beneficiary. For those assets not able to be emplaced within the Trust structure due to issues such as when the owner wants to obtain control of the assets or when the assets are still under financing, it is best to put the assets in the Will. The Will would not only cover those assets but also expenses like bereavement, pilgrimage and Umrah, Nazar or commitment and even testamentary trust that a person intends to be established upon his demise. The Will is only effective during the demise of the testator; hence, estate administration would take place. Normally the distribution follows Faraidh; otherwise, only by mutual consent from all heirs can other distribution methods be executed.

LESSONS FROM PAKISTAN'S MODEL

*Bilal Rasul**

Introduction: Pakistan's Capital Market
and the Islamisation Efforts

The Islamic Republic of Pakistan is home to a population of 160 million and a people of immense patriotic fervour. The country is 97% Muslim with a huge appetite for Islamic financial products. The country is 97% Muslim — potentially a large market for Islamic financial products which gives rationale to 'Islamising' the economy. The 1973 Constitution of Pakistan stipulates in Article 38, "*Promotion of social and economic well-being of the people* eliminate *Riba* as early as possible'.[1] The fathers of the Constitution were forthright for the creation of an interest-free financial system that would propagate the essence of Islam-social equality. The Presidential order to the local

---

* Director, Enforcement, at the Securities and Exchange Commission of Pakistan (SECP). The views and opinions expressed in this paper are his own and do not represent those of the SECP.
[1] Constitution of the Islamic Republic of Pakistan, 1973.

Council of Islamic Ideology on 29 September 1977 was followed, entrusting the Council with the task of preparing a report on such a system. Amendments were also made in the Banking Companies Ordinance, 1962 to include provisions of banking on a profit/loss sharing basis and Islamic leasing on markup. In 1999 the Supreme Court of Pakistan passed a judgement on *Riba* and ordered that an interest-free banking system be implemented from 2001.

At a time when Islamic finance was not delved upon beyond the government-to-government level, Pakistan was already afoot on establishing it on an industry-wide level within the country. In 1980, the Government introduced legislation for the establishment of Islamic financial institutions (IFIs), namely, the Mudaraba Companies and Mudarabas through promulgation of the Mudaraba Companies and Mudaraba (Floatation and Control) Ordinance, 1980. A tax-free financial institution based on the tenets of Islam, the Mudaraba was entrusted to cater to the needs of the entrepreneur as well as the small investor, equitably. It was the ideal model for conducting non-banking activities in an Islamic fashion. In the early 1990s, the Government of Pakistan launched a very successful privatisation, deregulation, and liberalisation campaign. The Islamisation efforts gained a lot of impetus through these policies of the Government and by 1994 52 Mudarabas had been floated with a paid-up capital of Rs. 8 billion (approximately, US$0.64 million — Rs. 80 = US$1). Pakistan was well on its way of assuming the lead role in Islamic finance.

Other efforts of Pakistan in the Islamisation process include: the Enforcement of Shariah Act, 1991, which was promulgated to Islamise the economy and implement Islamic fundamentals for trade and industry; the introduction of Islamic Mutual funds; the launch of Takaful companies or Islamic insurers; and the licensing of Islamic commercial banks. A basic fact sheet of each type of Islamic financial institution is in Table 1.

The efforts of the Government of Pakistan to Islamise the economy and financial industry cannot in any way be underrated. "Investors all over the world suddenly took notice of what could

Table 1 Information on Islamic Financial Institutions (IFIs) in Pakistan as on 30 June 2008.

	Islamic banks	Islamic mutual funds	Mudarabas	Takaful	Islamic pension funds	Total (Rs. in billion)	Total (US$ billion)*
No. of companies	6	9	41	5	4	61.00	0.89
No. of funds	—	14	27	—	4	41.00	0.60
Total equity	31.644	—	11.939	1.992	—	45.58	0.67
Total assets	235.343	24.242	29.703	2.461	0.465	291.75	4.28
Paid-up capital/ seed capital	29.137	—	7.88	2.141	—	39.16	0.57
Exchange rate as on 30.06.08 was US$68.20					Total	478.48	7.02

have been another 'tiger' market in the making".[2] Paradoxically and unfortunately, the growth of the Islamic financial sector in Pakistan does not reflect the effort made by the Government. The reasons are multifaceted, among which foremost was the absence of regulatory frameworks to ensure compliance to the enabling legislations that established these Islamic financial institutions. Political upheaval, policy inconsistencies, foreign exchange crises, and deep-rooted structural problems also added to the stunting of the overall financial sector. As a consequence, Islamic finance suffered. "A common observation made by the general public, conventional bankers, Muslims, and non-Muslims is that the modes of finance currently used by Islamic banks and some other financial intermediaries such as Mudarabas of Pakistan are primarily not very different from those of the conventional banks. The members of the Shariah Boards as well as the managers of the existing Islamic banks would, however, not accept this contention".[3] Such sentiment still persists and is typical of those unaware of the work being done in the field, but it is hardly a deterrent for further research and progress. While 100% Shariah compliance may not be realisable overnight, the *Ummah* must endeavour to achieve the maximum compliance to assimilate and strengthen the Islamic financial systems the world over.

Undoubtedly, Pakistan had been ahead of the times in attempting to put its financial system on Islamic modes but was constrained because it could not adopt Shariah financial guidelines and international best practices which were scantly existent at the time. To compound the dilemma, scholarly human resources and capacity were neither readily available at the regulator nor at the industry level.

In the absence of international Islamic regulatory and accounting bodies, the most well-intentioned Islamic models were destined

---

[2] C. Chou, *Reforming Pakistan's Capital Markets Director*, China Concept (HK) Limited.

[3] S. A. Siddiqui, Understanding and eliminating Riba: Can Islamic financial instruments be meaningfully implemented?, *Journal of Management and Social Sciences*, I(2) (Autumn 2005), 187–203.

to encounter bottlenecks. The Mudaraba sector too paid the price as a result of regulatory arbitrage. The sector attracted managements that were interested in exploiting the advantages of this type of financing vehicle for the secondary aspect — tax incentives and effortless resource mobilisation.

Today, when we consider Islamic finance at the national level, we look toward the Islamic Financial Services Board (IFSB) and its *Islamic Financial Services Industry Development: 10-Year Framework* for Islamisation and standardisation. For corporate Shariah compliance, we look toward the Accounting and Auditing Organisation for Islamic Financial Institutions (AAOIFI). The benchmark for Shariah compliance has become the adoption of AAOIFI's Islamic Financial Accounting Standards (FAS). A jurisdiction's financial compliance to Shariah is easily gauged by the number of FAS adopted by it. The International Islamic Financial Market provides the market for Shariah-compliant securities and the Liquidity Management Centre provides for the investment of surplus funds of the IFIs.

Islamic finance is universal; it is not restricted to the Muslim communities of the world. It is a system that preaches an equitable mode of financing and business in which the profits and the risks are shared. The collapse of the conventional financial industry all around the globe makes it an opportune time for the proponents of Islamic finance to emphasise the advantages of this benign financial system, which goes beyond the financial aspect and into the ethical realm of business.

The Mudaraba Companies and Mudarabas: The Envisaged Concept

The Mudaraba concept does not need to be redefined here since it is a commonplace mode. In Pakistan, as aforementioned, commercialisation of the concept was implemented in the shape of the Mudaraba Company and the Mudaraba forming a trust-like structure similar to that of an asset management company and a Mutual Fund. The Mudaraba Companies are vested with the function and duties of the *Mudarib*; the management. And the Mudaraba, or the *Rabb Al-Maal*, constitutes the funds pooled together by the general public/investors. To secure the interest of the *Mudarib* in the Mudaraba, a minimum statutory holding of 10% has been prescribed in the law. The Mudaraba is listed on the stock exchange and its share certificates are readily traded. The *Rabb Al-Maal*, though entitled to receive dividends, are not entitled to vote — which lives up to the concept of separation of the management and the fund. The Mudaraba was envisaged as a legal entity to indulge in activities that are not against the tenets of Islamic Shariah and Sunnah, which translates into a multitasking non-banking financial institution. The list of permissible businesses for Mudarabas is endless. They are involved in leasing, project finance, investment banking, housing finance, venture capital, asset management, trading, act as Mutual Fund, act as a special purpose vehicle, and can do basically anything *halal*. Commercial banking is the only activity that the Mudarabas cannot indulge in since that is the domain and activity regulated by the State Bank of Pakistan.

Mudaraba, as a vehicle of financing, is a versatile form of business that does not require being regulated under a multiple licensing regime. The certifying body is the Religious Board comprising a Judge of the High Court and two eminent scholars, who are responsible for certifying that a prospectus of a Mudaraba fulfills and complies with the Shariah. While the nomenclature 'Mudaraba' may be slightly misrepresentative of the activities, it must be appreciated that at the time these IFIs were being conceptualised there were very limited choices in choosing the appropriate title for a company that would finance contemporary businesses on Islamic principles. Since 'Mudaraba' was a term widely used and under-stood, it was the perfect symbol.

One of the main attractions of the Mudaraba as an investment is the tax benefit that can be derived from it. As per the provisions of the law, if 90% of the annual profits are distributed, the Mudaraba is exempt from corporate income tax. These incentives practically drove the market since the promulgation of the law, till 1993 when the Government decided to withdraw the exemption for a short while on the basis of revision of the national tax policy. The implications of the withdrawal of the incentive were very severe resulting in decreasing returns and an equally rapidly diminishing interest in Mudaraba certificates and Mudaraba operations.

Today, the number of Mudarabas has dwindled to 27. The late 1990s and early 2000s saw the erosion of the sector due to reasons explained in the preceding paragraphs. The frail fitness and propriety standards coupled with an overall downturn in the capital market aggravated matters further. A few years later (by 2007), the Pakistani stock market came out of its low levels and emerged as one of the fastest-growing markets in the world. Businesses showed exemplary growth, foreign investors were confident and the stock exchange index broke new records every day. Newly established Islamic funds, Islamic commercial banks, Islamic pension funds, and Takaful companies entered the market. The Mudarabas, too, were reinvigorated and started to perform extremely well but they continued to be misrepresented through market values well below their break-up values. The misplaced image of the Mudaraba sector can, therefore, rightly be blamed on the legal frameworks and financial scandals that surrounded the Mudarabas in the early 1990s. Over the last few years, the Securities and Exchange Commission of Pakistan (SECP) has been striving to uplift the sector to improve market perception. In 2008, the SECP along with the industry association, namely, the Mudaraba Association of Pakistan (MAP) researched and designed new products for the Mudaraba sector to provide a level-playing field with the Islamic commercial banks in terms of their borrowing/lending capabilities. Previously, the Mudarabas were using the following financing agreements while executing transactions with their clients for the business of leasing, purchase, and re-sale of goods through Murabaha and financing through Musharaka arrangement, and so forth:

(1) Vehicle Lease Agreement;
(2) Property/Machinery/Equipment Lease Agreement;
(3) Musharaka Agreement;
(4) Murabaha Agreement;
(5) Sale Agreement; and
(6) Agreement of Tenancy.

These Agreements were approved by the Religious Board for Mudarabas in the late '80s and had become outdated and unacceptable in the market as they could not be modified or developed to keep up with the changing financial environment. Consequently, they lost their competitive edge in the market. Due to the inflexibility of the Agreements, the Mudarabas were facing problems in availing fresh credit lines from the banks/financial institutions and in attracting new customers as they were not as popular as the Agreements developed by the State Bank of Pakistan (SBP) for its Islamic banking companies, thus significantly hampering growth and profitability.

To overcome the dilemma and bring the Mudarabas at a level-playing field with the banking companies, in terms of resource mobilisation and innovation, new modes of financing had to be developed. The SECP and MAP undertook a careful and thorough review of the financing Agreements approved by the SBP for its banking companies. Following extended deliberations with MAP and the stakeholders, 12 new model financing agreements were drafted and presented to the Religious Board for Mudarabas for certification for Shariah compliance which were subsequently vetted. They provide the structure and form of lending/borrowing by the financial institutions. A brief description of the recently approved 12 model Islamic financing agreements vetted by the Religious Board of Mudarabas is as below:

(1) *Ijara* (**Leasing**)

In Ijara, owners hand over the equipment/vehicle to another person for an agreed period at an agreed consideration. After the completion of lease payments, ownership of asset transfers to the client.

(2) *Istisna* (**Progress financing**)

A contract to manufacture goods, assemble or process them, or to build a house or other structure according to exact specifications and a fixed timeline. Payments are made after each stage of work is finished.

(3) *Mudaraba*

Mudaraba is a kind of partnership in which one partner gives money (*Rabb Al-Maal*) to another (*Mudarib*) for investing in commercial enterprises. The investment comes from *Rabb Al-Maal* (Investor) and the management which works having exclusive responsibility of the other, who is called the *Mudarib* (Management). The profits generated are distributed on a predetermined ratio while the loss is assumed by the investor in money terms and management in service provided/effort terms.

(4) *Musawamah*

Musawamah is entered into when it is difficult to determine the cost of a particular good or service, or when the good is comprised of a pool of products. Provided that:

- The underlying asset must be in existence and in the sellers' possession at the time of the sale;
- The sale must occur instantaneously, future sale dates are void; and
- The asset must be of value and usable.

(5) *Musharaka* **(Partnership financing)**

Musharaka means a joint enterprise (Sharing) formed for conducting some business in which all partners share profit according to a specific ratio while the loss is shared according to the ratio of their contribution. It is an ideal alternative for the interest-based financing with far reaching effects on both production and distribution.

(6) *Murabaha* **(Cost-plus financing)**

Murabaha is a kind of sale on cost-plus-profit basis, where the seller specifically declares the cost of the commodity he has incurred, and sells it to another person by adding some profit thereon. Under this agreement, the institution discloses the cost-and-profit margin to the client — it is actually advancing money to the borrower to buy goods from a third party and sell it to the customer on a pre-agreed price. Thus, Murabaha is not a loan given on interest but it is a sale of a commodity for cash/deferred price. In the Islamic financial industry almost 60% of transactions are conducted through Murabaha Financing Agreements.

(7) *Salam* **(Trade finance)**

In Salam, the seller undertakes to supply specific goods to the buyer at a future date in exchange of an advanced price fully paid at the spot. The price is in cash but the supply of purchased goods is deferred. Financial institutions are normally using this for agricultural products and for trade finance business.

(8) *Diminishing Musharaka*

This concept encompasses the joint ownership feature — a financier and his client participate either in the joint ownership of a property or equipment, or in a joint commercial enterprise. The financier's share is divided into a number of units and the client will purchase these units of shares from the financier one by one until the financier's units are totally diminished. As the client owns units, his share in the property increases and on the completion of all payments all units stand transferred to the client eventually deeming him the sole owner of the property, equipment or commercial enterprise, as the case may be.

(9) *Syndicate Mudaraba*

When two or more investors (*Rabb Al-Maal*) contribute their investment to a project run by a management (*Mudarib*). The profits will be distributed on an agreed profit ratio. The loss, if any, will be assumed by the investor in terms of money and by the management company in terms of service provided/effort.

(10) *Syndicate Musharaka*

When two or more parties enter into an agreement to share ownership of property or equipment. Each partner is responsible for his part of investment and profit will be shared on an agreed ratio of all parties.

(11) *Islamic CFS (Continuous Funding System) Murabaha*

Islamic CFS Murabaha is for a credit facility to the client for the purchase of shares through a Master Murabaha Agreement. At the time of investment, the client deposits an agreed margin to buy shares as an agent of Islamic financial institutions from whom he takes credit, the purchased shares are blocked at the central depository account and a lien is marked on them by the IFI. When the sale proceeds are realised and paid to the client, the IFI releases the share. The client is authorised to sell the shares at any time, subject to settlement of the full Murabaha price.

(12) *Sukuk* **(Islamic Bonds)**

Sukuk are the certificates of equal value representing undivided shares in ownership of tangible assets, usufruct and services or (in the ownership of) the assets of particular projects or special investment activity. These certificates establish the claim of the certificate owner over the financial rights and obligations represented by the certificate.

These model financing agreements can be modified to the extent that the substance of the principles of Shariah is not affected.

The Religious Board for Mudarabas has certified the agreements as Shariah-compliant. The financial institutions intending to extend a facility or obtain borrowing can do so only on the specified format of one of the approved financing agreements. These agreements are, in essence, alternatives to the interest-based form of financing.

The new model agreements are expected to change the landscape of the existing Mudaraba sector in Pakistan. The previous agreements had failed to support the complex financial transactions in light of the Shariah and also did not provide the environment to induce innovative and diversified products in the Islamic financial services industry in Pakistan.

Remodelling the Regulatory Environment for a Shariah-Compliant Financial System

The strength of a financial industry is based on the confidence investors have in it. One of the main factors contributing to confidence in a financial centre is its regulatory system, which seeks to promote that very confidence.[4]

So what are the constituents of an effective and ideal regulatory environment for a Shariah-compliant financial system? IFSB's 10-Year Framework is the Master document that simply provides the answer. While the efforts of Islamisation and creating environments for a Shariah-compliant financial system have not lacked any vigour, to bring everything together, the panacea is suggested by IFSB — a regulatory environment that is an interface between a jurisdiction and the IFSB, on the one hand, and among the respective jurisdictions, on the other. This requires a standard holistic legislation that serves as the cornerstone of Islamic financial services

---

[4] H. Bhambra, in *Islamic Finance, The Regulatory Challenge*, edited by Simon Archer and Rifaat Ahmed Abdel Karim.

at the national level, and would also govern the IFIs of a country whether they are regulated by one, two, or more regulators. It would not only essentially provide direction for the Islamic commercial banks and the Islamic non-banking IFIs, but may also cater to the non-financial companies that are interested in gaming 'Shariah-compliant' status. In Malaysia, approximately 87% of all companies listed on Bursa Malaysia are Shariah-compliant. A standard criterion has been used by the Securities Commission, Malaysia to monitor and certify the activities of businesses as Shariah-compliant.[5] Ideally, a unitary Shariah Board should cater to all IFIs in a jurisdiction to maintain uniformity and standardisation. A common regulatory and supervisory framework in all jurisdictions would perpetuate Islamic securities markets all around the world with uniform listing, clearing, settlement, and trading principles thus ensuring minimal regulatory arbitrage.

Pakistan's experience with Islamic finance advocates a strong regulatory environment that encompasses the Shariah and the supervisory aspects *en bloc*. As a first step toward achieving this goal, the SBP and the SECP obtained membership of the IFSB. In 2008, Dr. Shamshad Akhtar, then Governor of SBP, was elected as the Chairperson. In pursuit of remodelling the regulatory environment, the State Bank of Pakistan and the SECP, in 2005, formed the *Joint Forum on Islamic Financial Services*. The objective of the Joint Forum is to develop and strengthen the supervisory framework for Islamic financial services industry for good operational and financial governance in accordance with Shariah as well as recognising the need to establish a joint forum to facilitate mutual and joint cooperation between the regulators in developing and promoting the Islamic financial services industry. The Joint Forum has agreed to cooperate for development of the Islamic financial industry. The Authorities would jointly drive the development to institute a mechanism to coordinate discussions on issues faced by the Islamic financial industry

---

[5] Securities Commission, Malaysia, *Updated List of Shariah-Compliant Securities by SC's Shariah Advisory Council*, Kuala Lumpur, 27 November 2008.

Forum. Discussions on issues requiring a common stance to ensure complete harmony in the regulatory approach of the two regulators, especially the Shariah rulings, are brought to the Joint Forum for discussion and decision. The SBP and SECP collaborate in preparing roll-out plans for guidelines and standards issued by international Islamic financial institutions. One of the main pursuits of the Joint Forum is to explore the possibility of using a common Shariah Board. Also a point on the agenda of the Joint Forum is the development of the Islamic Capital Market. Coordinated efforts are being made to frame rules and regulations for Islamic securities and a Pakistani Islamic capital market. The regulators also work for development of the Takaful sector. To fill the gap existing between the demand for Shariah expertise and availability, the Joint Forum collaborates on intelligence through conferences, workshops symposiums, training programmes, seminars, or any other events relating to Islamic finance to cultivate human capital in both jurisdictions. Regular exchanges of relevant public and privileged intelligence, and other materials necessary for the development of the Islamic financial industry also occur as part of the understanding between the two regulators.

IFSB's 10-Year Framework suggests that two somewhat distinct approaches have been adopted in different jurisdictions to the authorisation of Islamic financial services:

(a) A policy framework approach that requires legal reforms and distinct licensing initiatives; and

(b) A market-driven financial engineering approach that encourages Shariah-compliant products and services within the existing legal and licensing regimes.[6]

In Pakistan, (a) above seems the appropriate choice for remodelling the regulatory environment. In the following paragraphs, a concept

---

[6] *Islamic Financial Services Industry Development 10-Year Framework*, Islamic Financial Services Board and Islamic Development Bank, Jeddah.

has been developed to implement legal reform and distinct licensing initiatives, that is, in the form of regulations/guidelines. A study of the various Islamic financial jurisdictions of the world (referenced jurisdictions as listed at the bibliography), a holistic approach for implementing Shariah compliance, is suggested as a legal framework governing Islamic financial services/non-financial companies structured as follows:

Part I

Preliminary

(1) Short title and commencement should be specific to Shariah compliance, e.g., Regulations for Islamic Financial Services Companies (IFSCs)/Shariah-Compliant Companies (SCCs).

(2) Definitions — a list of the most commonly used terms including those associated with Shariah and Sunnah.

Part II

Registration of Islamic Financial Services' Companies (IFSC)

(3) Eligibility criteria for the establishment of an IFSC — tailored to the respective jurisdictions.

(4) Permission to form an IFSC — a prerequisite in any licensing regime.

(5) Grant of certificate of registration to the IFSC:

    (a) Minimum equity requirement/capital adequacy

    (b) Conversion of conventional business to Islamic business

    (c) Power to impose new restrictions or conditions and to vary or revoke restrictions or conditions imposed on Certificate of Registration

    (d) Cancellation of Certificate of Registration

Part III

Registration of Shariah-Compliant (Nonfinancial) Companies (SCCs)

(6) Eligibility criteria for the establishment of a Shariah Compliance — tailored to the respective jurisdictions.

(7) Permission to form an SSC — a prerequisite in any licensing regime.

(8) Grant of Certificate of Registration to the SSC:

    (a) Minimum equity requirement/capital adequacy

    (b) Conversion of conventional business to Islamic business

    (c) Power to impose new restrictions or conditions and to vary or revoke restrictions or conditions imposed on Certificate of Registration

    (d) Cancellation of Certificate of Registration

Part IV

Shariah Board/Advisors and Shariah Audit

(9) Appointment and functions of Shariah Board/Advisor.

(10) Shariah Audit and Review.

Part V

Fit and Proper Criteria

(11) Fit and Proper Test (Criteria) for Shariah Advisors.

(12) Fit and Proper Test (Criteria) for Chairman/Chief Executive, Board of Directors of an IFSC under these regulations.

(13) Fit and Proper Test (Criteria) for Chairman/Chief Executive, Board of Directors of an SSC under these regulations.

Part VI
Miscellaneous

(14) Conditions applicable to an IFSC/SCC.

(15) Commencement of operations by an IFSC/SSC.

(16) Electronic filing of information documents or returns.

(17) Opening of branches.

(18) Insurance coverage/Takaful premium.

(19) Exchange fluctuation risk.

(20) Submission of Proposals under these regulations.

(21) Documents/Information required.

(22) Eligible persons.

(23) Disclosure requirements.

(24) Constitutional Documents.

(25) Systems and Controls.

(26) Other Regulatory Approvals.

(27) Underwriting.

(28) Accounting, Auditing, and Governance Standards for an IFSC/SCC.

(29) Ownership, Control and Management of IFSC/SSC:

    (a) Prior approval of Regulator for acquisition of substantial interest in IFSC

    (b) Prior approval of Regulator for acquisition of qualifying holdings in a domestic IFSC

    (c) Power of Regulator in respect of contravention of regulations

    (d) Records of transactions and commitments

    (e) Submission of statistics and returns to Regulator

    (f) Reporting of financial difficulties and material events to Regulator

    (g) Penalties on directors and managers

    (h) Offences by directors, employees, and agents

The concept entails that an entity aspiring to become Shariah-compliant, whether it is a financial or a non-financial company, should be licensed by a one-window operation through the approval and vetting of a single Shariah Board. This Authority should oversee all aspects of the licensing and regulation as well as the monitoring of these entities. Parts IV and V of the proposed framework are key — the volatility of the Shariah regulatory environment hinges upon the effectiveness of these components. This would also overcome one of the greatest regulatory challenges and issues of the *Ummah* — standardisation and harmonisation. To achieve harmony, the jurisdictions require conforming to the thought processes of other jurisdictions through the following:

  (i)   Membership of IFSB and participation in its working groups;
 (ii)   Adoption of AAOIFI standards and their implementation;
(iii)   Adherence to the Resolutions and Recommendations of the Council of the Islamic Fiqh Academy;
 (iv)   Adoption of a Code of Corporate governance;
  (v)   International Best practices — to highlight areas that are non-permissible for investment; and
 (vi)   Unilateral and multilateral agreements for information sharing, training needs, and development of the Islamic securities markets.

Islamic Finance and Crisis in the Conventional System

The year 2008 saw the evaporation of billions of dollars in the conventional financial system, to regulatory negligence coupled with overrated debt. The crisis has increased the appeal for Islamic finance. Relatively unscathed by the Subprime mortgage crisis, the IFIs have proven that they are viable and the only alternative replacement of conventional finance. Given the opportunity, IFIs can perform the recovery and provide the stability in the global financial system which is desperately required. Italian economist Loretta Napoleoni, at the October 2008 meeting of "Global Instability: Causes, Consequences and Cures" calls for embracing Islamic finance — what she describes as 'the new economic system'.[7] It is a well-known fact that Muslim funds flow out of the oil-rich countries and into investments abroad. The current scenario is an eye-opener for the Arab magnates and it is a foregone conclusion that the preference to place funds will now be the IFIs. IFIs provide security for non-Muslim funds as well since the Islamic financial system knows no boundaries and is a general code for any financial system. Countries which are facing the adverse affects of the crisis realise Islamic finance can help recover their fallen economies. The future of Islamic financial services is bright. With the appropriate marketing strategy, this industry can become the harbinger of finance. The role of IFSB and other Islamic market infrastructures is integral. The central theme of Islamic finance, that is, asset-backed lending, has to be propagated. It has to be emphasised that Islamic finance could have averted the Subprime and debt crises. Mohammed Mahmud Awan, a scholar at the Malaysia-based International Centre for Education in Islamic Finance (INCEIF), states "A crisis such as the mortgage one would technically be unthinkable in the Islamic capital markets sector because it would be against Shariah principles to sell a debt against a debt".[8]

The conventional financial system has been in existence for many centuries and its overnight exit is unlikely. The Islamic financial system will also not evolve overnight. It is for Islamic finance to mimic the conventional system as far as its products are concerned yet remain within the limits prescribed by Shariah. It is entirely the initiative of the regulators, IFIs, and all stakeholders of the Muslim

---

[7] L. Napoleoni, "Global Instability: Causes, Consequences, and Cures", a lecture series organised by the University of New Mexico, International Studies Institute, USA. Economist and senior partner of G Risk, a London-based risk agency.

[8] A. Glass, "Islamic Finance Could Have Prevented Subprime Crisis", *Arab News*, 24 April 2008.

countries that can determine the success of Islamic finance. As a system which preaches ethical and social responsibility, the acceptance of the principles of Islamic finance cannot be denied (Table 1).

Bibliography

Ainley, M. *et al.* Islamic finance in the UK: Regulation and challenges, *Financial Services Authority*, November 2007.

Archer, S. and Karim, R. Islamic finance: *The Regulatory Challenge*, Singapore: John Wiley & Sons, 2007.

El-Hawry, D. *et al.* Regulating Islamic financial institutions: The nature of the regulated, *World Bank Policy Research Working Paper* 3227, March 2004.

Iqbal, Z. and Tsubota, H. Emerging Islamic capital markets — A quickening pace and new potential, The World Bank.

Mirakhor, A. *General Characteristics of an Islamic Economic System*, Nur Corp., MD, USA, 1989.

Sarker, A. A. Regulation of Islamic banking in Bangladesh: Role of Bangladesh Bank, *International Journal of Islamic Financial Services*, 2(1).

Venardos, A. M. *Islamic Banking and Finance in South-East Asia*, Singapore: World Scientific Publishing Co. Pte. Ltd., 2007.

Documents Reviewed/Analysed for Blueprint of Regulations

  (i) Central Bank of Malaysia — Islamic Banking Act, 1983
 (ii) State Bank of Pakistan — Draft Banking Act, 2006
(iii) Islamic Financial Services Board — Published Standards and Guidelines
 (iv) Central Bank of the Islamic Republic of Iran — The Law for Usury (Interest) Free Banking
  (v) Dubai Financial Services Authority — The DFSA Rule Book — Islamic Financial Business Module (ISF), September 2004
 (vi) Dubai Financial Services Authority — Law Regulating Islamic Financial Business — DIFC Law No. 13 of 2004

(vii) State Bank of Pakistan — Draft Instructions and Guidelines for Shariah Compliance in Islamic Banking Institutions

(viii) Securities Commission Malaysia — Guidelines on the Offering of Islamic Securities

(ix) Central Bank of Bahrain Rulebook — Auditors and Accounting Standards Module

(x) Central Bank of Bahrain Rulebook — Business and Market Conduct Module

(xi) Central Bank of Bahrain Rulebook — Reporting Requirements Module

(xii) Central Bank of Bahrain Rulebook — Capital Adequacy Module

(xiii) Central Bank of Bahrain Rulebook — High-level Control Module

(xiv) Central Bank of Bahrain Rulebook — Public Disclosure Requirements Module

(xv) Securities Commission Malaysia — Shariah-based Unit Trust Funds

(xvi) International Organisation for Securities Commissions — Report of the Islamic Capital Market Task Force of the IOSCO

ISLAMIC STRUCTURED PRODUCTS: ISSUES AND CHALLENGES*

Aznan Hasan

Introduction

Over a period of time, the investment climate has evolved significantly. From a simple and direct exposure to direct typical asset class like real estate, share, fixed income, and money market instrument, the nature of investing has greatly developed into a more demanding and multifaceted instrument. Over the last decade or so, the increase in interest has been seen in the usage of index and a more complex world of derivatives. Instead of having direct exposure to the stock, the investors are now keener toward exposing themselves to the portfolio of structured investment where the risk return profile is improved and more manageable. One of these

---

* The earlier version of this chapter was presented at Muzakarah Pakar-pakar Shariah, Kuala Lumpur Islamic Finance Forum, 2007 (KLIFF 2007) Nikko Hotel, 9 November 2007.

instruments are structured products (SPs).[1] This trend of investing has also infiltrated into the domain of Islamic investment sphere. Having said so, it should duly be noted that the concept of structured products is still very new and discussion on them from Shariah perspective is very rare, if not absent. This chapter intends to explore the complexity of the instrument and to explore some probable Shariah issues surrounding their practices. I must hasten to add here that the real intention of this chapter is to give exposure to the scholars on the concept of SPs and to ignite more discussion on various Shariah issues surrounding its practices. As such, it would not deliberate on the Shariah issues at length, and even in some issues, the Shariah discussion will be quite superficial.

Definition

The most challenging part, I believe, in the discussion on structured products is to give an exact definition and a well-encompassed understanding to the term 'structured products'. This stems from the fact that over the years, structured products have evolved tremendously, covering a very wide range of products and have been extended to a variety of investment instruments. Within this broad ambit, it seems to be very difficult to have a well-encompassed meaning to the term. Wikipedia defines them as: '*synthetic investment* instruments specially created to meet specific needs that cannot be met from the standardised financial instruments available in the markets'.[2] One may easily realise the broad definition of structured products that this definition tries to cover. This broad definition of SPs has been clearly acknowledged by another definition which defines SP as: 'Name covering a broad range of new investment products, many with proprietary names or acronyms, that combine two or more

---

[1] Throughout this chapter, the writer will use Structured Products (plural). Most of the time, the writer will use SPs to denote Structured Products.

[2] en.wikipedia.org/wiki/Structured_product.

financial instruments, at least one of which must be a *Derivative*'.[3] Another Web site defines it as: 'A financial instrument designed to meet specific investor needs by incorporating special, nonstandard features'.[4] The Securities Commission (SC) of Malaysia defines SP in its guidelines on SP as:[5]

> 1.03 For the purposes of these Guidelines:
>
> "(a) 'The term 'structured product' means any investment product that falls within the definition of 'securities' under the SCA, which provides the holder with an economic, legal, or other interest in another asset ('underlying asset') and derives its value by reference to the price or value of the underlying asset;
>
> (b) The term 'underlying asset' means any security, index, currency, commodity, or other assets or combination of such assets".

Recognising the difficulties in providing the well-encompassed definition of SPs, the SC does provide a nonexhaustive list of Structured Products.

Having considered these definitions and alike, it can simply be said that no single definition can certainly cover the wide spectrum of Structured Products. Yet, a thorough study to these definitions and to the various existing structures of SPs allows us to derive some features which are common to SPs, to give us the general understanding to the term. As the name suggests, SPs are structured investment products where no resemblance to any particular asset class, or any standardised financial instrument is to be found.[6] It is

---

[3] http://www.answers.com/topic/structured-product?cat=biz-fin.

[4] www.ashburton.com/XX_Glossary/.

[5] Guidelines on Structured product, para. 1.03.

[6] This has led some investment managers to believe that Structured Products deserve to be considered as a new asset class because they provide return profiles that are distinct from other forms of investment and therefore the products have different risk-and-return characteristics. See for instance: http://www.structured productsonline.com/public/showPage.html?page=321402.

a sophisticated product designed and synthesised to meet specific needs of clients, a feature of which no common financial instruments can serve it. It combines two or more financial instruments, one of which is generally a derivative, to create a single 'structured and packaged product'. As rightly pointed out by some researches, one of the main ingredients for SPs is the use of various techniques involving swaps or options. In most circumstances, if not all, the returns are linked to the performance of an underlying asset or benchmark such as interest rates, equity markets, commodities, corporate credits, foreign exchange markets, real estate, or other financial instrument. For instance, equity-linked notes will have an exposure to the basket of equity or index equity. Instead of having a direct investment to the basket, the strategies employed are by buying options over that equity. In that sense, the exposure of the investors is limited to the option price, whilst at the same time giving them the opportunity to leverage over their position. As will be explained later, the position in Islamic Structured Products, albeit using different structures, does not differ so much from this conventional situation as far as the economic effect is concerned. Yet, the mechanism and contracts employed are different. By doing so, structured products are able to provide the investors with the potential opportunity to earn a higher return, as compared to Fixed Deposit Rates or some other benchmark. For instance, the historical backtesting[7] results for the first Malaysian Islamic Structured Product, Islamic All-Stars Global shows that over 70% of returns are above 7.00% p.a. and over 80% of the time, the returns would have beaten current 5-year Fixed Deposit Rates.[8] More often than not, Structured Products will have the feature of capital protection of some or all of the capital if certain conditions are met. This protection will normally be 'created' by having a strategic portfolio management, and in

---

[7] Historical backtesting is a method for analysing the hypothetical performance of a product using historical market prices of the underlying assets. The testing period was between 1 January 1990 to 11 January 2007.

[8] CIMB Bank 5-year FD 3.95% p.a. as at 15 January 2007.

certain circumstances by providing a guarantee (third-party guarantee or a purchase undertaking in the case of Islamic SPs). In some recent SPs, the situation has been improved further. Besides offering capital protection if held to maturity, some SPs also offer minimum guarantees on the performance of the investment. With all these features, besides some other benefits, SPs have emerged as an additional attractive alternative asset to the traditional asset portfolio as they provide the investors with the flexibility to tailor an investment structure to meet their specific financial objectives.

Advantages of Structured Products

Structured Products are so attractive to various segments of investors, simply because they it provide them with sufficient comfort in investment. As mentioned before, the main feature and benefit of many SPs are the protection of some or all of the invested capital, and as such form an ideal way to link an investment or deposit with the performance of financial markets with little or no capital risk. Generally, SPs can be an attractive addition to investment portfolio as they can give the investor the flexibility to tailor an investment structure to meet their specific financial objectives, taking into consideration factors such as the investors' goals, risk tolerance and time horizon. In some products, especially investment link, these SPs are then wrapped with insurance coverage. This is an extra benefit which will definitely attract even the retail investors.

Types of Conventional Structured Products

Structured Products are by nature not homogeneous — as a large number of derivatives and underlying can be used — but can, however, be classified under the following categories:

- Interest rate-linked notes
- Equity-linked notes

- FX and commodity-linked notes
- Hybrid-linked notes
- Bond-linked notes
- Index-linked notes
- Currency-linked notes
- Commodity (contracts)-linked notes
- Credit-linked notes

Out of these categories, the most applied SPs are equity-linked notes. As far as Islamic SPs are concerned, the bulk of them come in the form of equity-linked Islamic structured notes.

The Building Block in Devising Islamic Structured Products

Although a full exposition of the principles of Islamic commercial law is beyond the scope of this chapter, a brief overview with a particular emphasis on the key elements of SPs is totally essential to this chapter. Since Islamic Commercial Law is largely anchored by the celebrated maxim of 'initial legal ruling is permissibility', the discussion on the permissibility or otherwise any instruments or products is done by observing the well-known 'negative' list of Islamic law and by avoiding their existence in that contract. As such, any product to be devised must be free from any Ribawi elements, no Gharar involved, no gambling features and must be fair and just to the parties to the contract. As has been said by many writings, this notion has provided Islamic law with great flexibility to accommodate various innovations found in the ambit of modern financial environment. Without going any deeper, it must be added further that the needs for Ijtihad in determining the nature and scope of these principles are continuous in nature, for the scope and application of certain principles, like Gharar, are largely influenced by various surrounding and contemporary situations.

Besides that, the devising of Islamic SPs must also observe the nature of the contract to be devised. I must hasten to state at this particular juncture that contrary to conventional modes of financing where the relation is about lending with interest, and what differentiates one contract from another is merely specification, financial products in Islamic Commercial Law are contract driven, rather than specification driven. If the contract to be utilised is a sale-based contract (like Murabaha or Tawarruq), the product to be devised must have features of sale-based contracts. Hence, the knowledge about the parties to the contract, the subject matter and consideration, mode and time of payment, and so forth are of paramount concerns. If the contract to be used is participatory contract like Mudaraba or Musharaka, the nature of contracts and their features must be reflected in the structuring and drafting of the contract. This differentiation will bring about many differences in the features of a particular Islamic SP. For instance, the nature of profit to be generated will differ. In sale-based contracts, the return is in the form of sale price (purchase price plus profit); in lease-based contracts, the return is in the form of rental; and in the case of Musharaka, the return is in the form of profit-sharing ratio. If the relation is structured based on Al-Wakalah Bi Al-Istithmar, then the bank who received the money from the client can decide on certain fixed fees to be paid upfront. This situation is surely not possible if the structures were to use a Mudaraba structure, where in that case the bank as a Mudarib would be entitled to a certain profit-sharing ratio to be distributed according to a certain method. However, this is only possible if the venture (SP) is profitable. All those distinctions must be carefully considered and observed in structuring Islamic SPs.

Since the leverage using conventional instruments like option is not possible, at least from a global perspective, Islamic SPs will have to revise the instrument and offer the Islamic solution which can bring about the same economic implication. So far, promise (Al-Wad) and Urbun (earnest money) are the most used instruments to replicate the conventional option. It is not the intention of this paper to argue for or against the practice of replicating the conventional instrument in Islamic way, and whether this will benefit or damage the Islamic financial practices in the long run. What is intended in this segment is to demonstrate that having the different nature of Urbun and Wad, the structuring of Islamic SPs must really be able to understand these differences and reflect them in their application of any of these instruments. If the structure were to use two unilateral promises (e.g., in the case of SPs offered by Deustche Bank), the designing of these two promises must be made carefully to show the separation of these promises, one from the other.

The protection of capital is another area of concern in SPs. Generally, the 'guarantee provision' in SPs can be achieved by having two methods. In some structures, the protection of the capital is managed via investment strategies (i.e., asset allocation strategy). In this arrangement, the managing of portfolio of the investment will allow for the protection of capital. This will be achieved by using the invested money to buy certain fixed and guaranteed payment, such as by buying and selling commodities or money market instruments. The remaining balance will be used to leverage by investing in a high risk, high return portfolio. If this portfolio performs well, the investors will get a good return from this portfolio besides their entitlement to the portfolio that 'guarantees' the capital. If this portfolio performs badly, the investors will lose their money in this portfolio, but their capital is guaranteed by the first portfolio. This arrangement attracts no Shariah issue so long as the guarantee mechanism is achieved by way of good portfolio management. Another practice is by providing real guarantee to the capital of the investment. If the structure is designed in that manner, various Shariah considerations must be carefully observed. For instance, the appointed manager, be it under the Wakalah or Mudaraba structures, is not allowed to provide the guarantee as it is against Shariah principles in Mudaraba and Wakalah. The guarantee must be provided by a third party. Some scholars go further by stating that this third party must be an entity that does not have any relation to the investment manager. This has been determined by saying that both must not own the other more than 49% of shareholding, or otherwise, they are not considered independent, one from the other.

The brief explanation of this segment intends to enlighten the readers on the unique characters of Islamic financial products and how this uniqueness must be preserved when devising any Structured Products.

Basic Anatomy of Equity-Linked Islamic SPs

As mentioned at the onset of this chapter, it will be very difficult, if not impossible to include all SPs available in the market. Hence, the approach of this segment is by presenting the structure commonly employed in Islamic SPs, where any variation will be discussed within the discussion of that common structure, as and when needs arise. Since the vast majority of Islamic SPs launched to date are capital-guaranteed, equity-linked structures, this segment will use this model as the basic discussion on Islamic SPs.

Figure 1 depicts the most used structure of Islamic SPs. In this structure, the client will channel the capital to the investment manager to be invested in a prescribed investment portfolio. Clients can be institutional investors, where the proceeds come from their own portfolio. The client can also be a bank, where the capital is raised via the offering of this products to its clients.[9] The division of the portfolio and how it is managed will be agreed and be made known upfront. The relation between the client and the manager can be established using either a Mudaraba[10] or Wakalah

---

[9] In this situation, the client (bank) will establish its own relation with its clients, either on Mudaraba or Wakalah.

[10] Like in CIMB Islamic All-Stars Global Restricted Mudaraba Structured Investment-i (Islamic All-Stars Global).

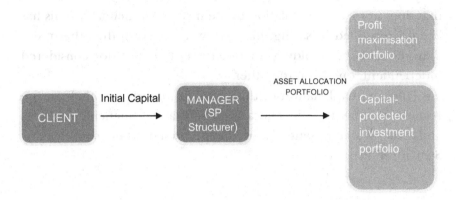

Figure 1 General structure of Islamic SPs.

contract. Though the way the asset allocation portfolio is managed will not differ in both cases, the profit to be distributed to the manager will depend largely on the structure used. If the Wakalah arrangement is applied, the manager can take his fees upfront, notwithstanding whether the portfolio will generate a profit or not. If the structure utilises Mudaraba, the manager is entitled to only the profit-sharing ratio, which can only be distributed if the portfolio manages to generate a return.

Figure 2 depicts the way the portfolio is normally created and distributed as equity-linked SPs. The initial capital invested will be divided into two portfolios. The bigger portfolio will be applied in a relatively secured investment. This is to ensure that the capital invested is protected, even when the leverage side fails to perform as anticipated at maturity date. The most preferable portfolio will be a Murabaha transaction.[11] Some structures use other investment avenues like money market instruments.[12] In commodities Murabaha arrangement, the issuer (or other party) will buy certain metals on

---

[11] This can be seen in various SPs like BNP Paribas's SP like Arboun + Murabaha, Shariah-Compliant CPPI.

[12] For instance, ING Baraka Capital Protected II invest in 3-year Ringgit-denominated Islamic Negotiable Instruments.

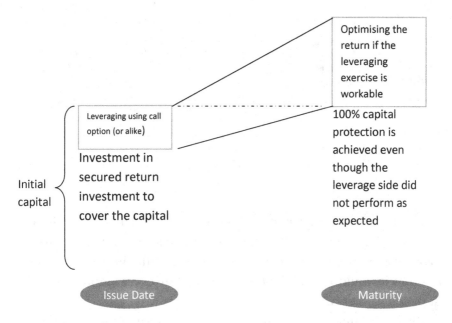

Optimising the return if the leveraging exercise is workable

Leveraging using call option (or alike)

Investment in secured return investment to cover the capital

Initial capital

100% capital protection is achieved even though the leverage side did not perform as expected

Issue Date

Maturity

Figure 2   Asset portfolio allocation.

LME on behaviour of the client (subscribers). Once the commodity settled with the client, the issuer (or other party) will buy the asset from the client at cost plus profit, where the price is to be paid at maturity date. Another portion will be used to buy an Islamic option. This leverage side is meant to optimise the return on investment. It can generate a relatively high profit rate on the capital if it performs well, or otherwise, the investors will lose their money in this portfolio. However, their capital is guaranteed because the performance of commodities Murabaha and alike will cover up the whole capital of the investors.

Though this is the most common structure of Islamic SPs, it is also observed that some Islamic SPs take a different route. Islamic SPs offered by Deutsche Bank and ABN Amro, for instance, invest the whole invested amount into a basket of share from a particular index. After that, two unilateral undertakings (one to purchase and another to sale) to buy and sell the basket at a particular exercise

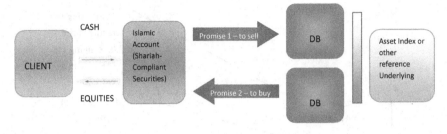

Figure 3

price (benchmarked against a certain index) will be concluded between the issuer and the investors. In this situation, the capital protection of the fund is made by monitoring the index and ensuring that it would not fall below the capital invested amount. This is depicted in Figure 3.

Some Islamic SPs also allow for further leveraging in 'lending portfolio', by allowing the client to 'borrow' money from the issuer to be used for extra investment to take advantage in the upside performance of the fund. This borrowing can take either in the form of interest-free lending (Al-Qard) — or with charged fees, or by having a sort of transaction using Tawarruq (commodities Murabaha) or 'Inah'.

Some Shariah Issues in Islamic SPs

The following are some of the Shariah issues relating to Islamic SPs.

Amalgamation of Contract

Equity-linked Islamic SPs will only be possible if the portfolio of investment is designed to be segregated into two parts. The first part which is the bigger part will be applied to a secured investment, which will generate a profit at least to cover up the initial invested amount. The other part will be used for derivatives purposes. In the case of some Islamic SPs, the whole amount will be applied to a purchase basket of shares in a particular index. Then two unilateral promises will be given and taken between the investors (normally a trustee, or an investment manager will act on their behalf) to sell and purchase the basket of shares at a particular price benchmarked against a certain index. In all circumstances, there will be at least two contracts, which will be executed by the parties. In the former, the bigger part of the amount will be used to purchase commodities Murabaha (where the investors and the issuer will be parties to that contract) and the other part will be used to buy an 'Islamic option', where the issuer is normally appointed as the agent for the investors. Here, several contracts will be executed between the issuer and the client. In the latter, where all the monies will be applied toward purchasing a basket of shares in the index, followed by two unilateral undertaking to sell and purchase and an eventual selling and purchasing of the basket of shares by the client to the issuer, at least two contracts will be executed. Firstly, when the issuer is appointed to purchase the basket, and secondly when the basket of shares is sold to the issuer.

As can be seen from this illustration, at least two contracts will be executed in both structures. This has raised the issue on the amalgamation of two contracts in one deal. The question pertaining to the level of Shariah recognition to the amalgamation of various contracts in a single process is not a new issue. This pre-agreed blending of contracts of diverse forms in a variety of orders and formats has permeated in almost every modern Islamic financial instrument. An easy example could be Murabaha, where the original contract involving the genuine and direct sale of an asset with a disclosed cost price and profit is then coupled with additional features such as a previous order placed by the potential buyer of the asset, an agency to the same party for purchasing and taking possession of the asset on behalf of the bank, a binding promise made by him to purchase the asset from the bank, and so forth. Since a proper treatment of the topic would involve a very lengthy discussion, it can simply be briefed here that opponents regard this practice, at best, as weakening the integrity of the contractual principles involved, and at worst representing a blatant technique for bypassing the Islamic prohibition of usury.[13] They argue that in an environment dominated by conventional banking, such structures could provide Islamic banks with a convenient excuse and means for practising interest-based financing under an Islamic nomenclature. This has led Islamic financial practices to be viewed as nothing but artificial and the underlying practices and effects of Islamic finance are no different from conventional finance at all. It seems that the opponents try to suggest that, in order to minimise the possibilities of Islamic banking mimicking the unhealthy trend of conventional banking, multiple contracts, which, with their collective application, lead to an outcome similar to existing interest-bearing products, should be discouraged, if not banned. Instead, preference should be given to adopt straightforward and uncomplicated Islamic transactional modes, with the parties playing unambiguous roles while bearing the ensuing responsibilities.

On the other hand, scholars also argue that from the Shariah perspective, the merger of contracts need not always cast a doubt on the validity of the product, unless the contracts are made inter-conditional or such amalgamation leads to the overt circumvention of a prohibition or realising a prohibited end. When employed within the necessary limitations and boundaries, and with full consideration given to relevant Shariah guidelines, several contracts taking place concurrently or in close sequence alone would not dictate the invalidity of the process as a whole. Since each contract, in most circumstances is designed to be independent, the perceived amalgamation is allowed and considered as an understanding

---

[13] Tarek El Diwany, 'Travelling the wrong road patiently', in *Banker Middle East*, September 2003, <http://www.islamic-finance.com> viewed on 23 April 2005.

(Muwatah) between the bank and the client to conduct their contractual relationship in a specific manner.

Insofar as this polemic is concerned, the opinion of jurists prevails. Hence, the amalgamation of contracts is allowed as long as the necessary guidelines, as previously mentioned in passing, are well observed.

The Use of Index

An index is a statistical measure of change in an economy or a securities market. In the case of financial markets, an index is an imaginary portfolio of securities representing a particular market or a portion of it. Though anyone can create an index, what sets the big indexes apart is the reputation of the company that creates and manages the index. Each index has its own calculation methodology and is usually expressed in terms of a change from a base value. Thus, the percentage change is more important than the actual numeric value. It helps investors in measuring the performance of the whole stock market or a portion of the overall market. Ideally, a change in the price of an index represents an exactly proportional change in the stocks included in the index. The most well-known indexes are the stock market index and bond market index.

The use of index in Islamic SPs can vary from one SP to another, but this usage can be categorised as below:

(1) An index is used only as a benchmark for pricing. For instance, after obtaining the capital, the investment manager will purchase a Shariah-compliant asset (more often than not, such assets will be shares selected from a certain index, or replicating the whole index). On the leverage side, purchase undertaking, or sale undertaking, or both will be given and taken to buy certain commodities (or shares) at a certain price benchmarked

against a particular index. In this situation, this index is used only as a mechanism to determine the future price of certain commodities to be transacted and the movement of the price to be agreed will depend on the movement of the price of the index.[14] When the sale contract is concluded, the price is certain and fixed. The use of an index in this situation is no different from the use of LIBOR (or the like) to determine the profit rate of a particular transaction. If the use of LIBOR to determine the price is acceptable, there should not be any Shariah issues in using the index in this manner, even if the index is not a Shariah index.[15] There is no issue also on the fixation of a price, because though the price is not known when the undertaking to purchase and/or to sell is given, there would not be any sale contract to be concluded until and unless the price is to be fixed first. So no issues of Gharar is involved here because the uncertainty only relates to the undertaking, not the sale contract.

(2) A promise is made to purchase the whole index or a basket of shares included in the index. Some SPs utilise Urbun to replicate an option to purchase a basket of shares in a particular index, or to purchase the index. If the option is to buy a basket of shares in the index, the issue may not be so contentious, since the sale contract is effected on a certain underlying share. However, the issue may need some elaboration when it comes to an option given to purchase and/or buy an index, especially when the index is calculated based on a free float mechanism and not full market capitalisation.[16] An index is created when

---

[14] Many structured products offered by Deutsche Bank, Goldman Sachs, ABN AMRO, etc. are using this mechanism.

[15] This happens in certain SPs.

[16] The debate still continues as to the most suitable mechanism to be used in establishing an index. Should the stock be calculated based on market capitalisation weighted mechanism (if market cap, should it be full market cap or free float), or price weighted or equally weighted.

the total number of shares which form the index components are made the underlying asset to the instrument. For instance, the S&P 500 represents 500 of the most widely held companies in the United States such as General Electric, Microsoft and Tupperware. The FTSE 100 index holds the top 100 largest companies listed on the London Stock Exchange. So, purchasing an index in fact constitutes the purchasing of proportionate shares making up the index. Based on this opinion, trading in an index is acceptable as long as the underlying assets forming the index are Shariah-compliant. This opinion is based on the understanding that the index is actually representing the underlying asset. Such an opinion, however, met with certain resistance. The opponents argue that since the index is nothing but numbers, trading in an index is like betting over the movement of numbers in the index. No physical delivery will be made as the index is not tangible. As such, trading in an index cannot be equated to trading of a basket of shares. The AAOIFI Shariah Standard has formulated three sub-standards on Index. The AAOIFI Shariah Standard provides:[17]

5/2/3/1: For transaction based in the mere rising and falling of an index — for example, one of the parties say to another that if the index rises to such and such a level, then he is liable to pay the other party such an amount. This is a type of gambling that is prohibited.

5/2/3/2: For option contracts based on the movement of one of the indexes, and this by agreement between the parties to the sale on purchase of the option — for example, if the index rises in this way then 'I will compensate you so much for each point'. In item 5/2/2/, the impermissibility of dealing in options has preceded.

5/2/3/3: For derivatives transactions based upon the movement of the indexes, and this by agreement of the two parties to sell

---

[17] AAOIFI Shariah Standard (No. 20: 5/3/2/(1–3)).

a deferred commodity (for example) for a deferred price. In Item
5/1/2, the impermissibility of dealing in derivatives has preceded.

As clearly observed from the Shariah Standard, Standard no.
5/2/3/1 deals with a real betting on the index, not on the trading of
the index as has been discussed and applied in Islamic SPs. Standard
no. 5/2/3/2 disallows conventional options as provided in Shariah
Standard no. 5.2.2. Moreover, the way the example on how this
option is used also implies the betting mechanism, which is not our
issue. Standard no. 5/2/3/3 disallows the conventional derivatives
as provided in Standard no. 5/1/2.

One may argue that the previous discussion on how the index is
used in Islamic SPs is different from the ones disallowed in
AAOIFI's Shariah Standard, and as such falls out of the ambit of the
Standard.

Issue of Leveraging and Mechanism to Leverage

Two matters are pertinent to this issue.

(1) Some Islamic SPs allow the subscriber to take advantage on the
     upside performance of the fund. This can be achieved by
     channeling some monies to the subscribers on an interest-free
     basis, or a loan with charged fees. This leverage can also be
     achieved by concluding reverse commodities Murabaha con-
     tract or 'Inah' made between the client and the issuer, resulting
     in the client owning certain money and having the responsibility
     to pay back the issuer the selling price at a particular deferred
     period. In this arrangement, instead of giving out the money
     for 'free' the issuer can charge the profit via the commodities
     Murabaha transaction concluded with the client. The question
     that may be asked here: Should the investors be given 'extra
     money' to be invested in the portfolio, especially when this

money comes from the issuer? It may be said that one should only invest using his own money. It is not proper to enter into any investment using borrowed money. Also, is it appropriate for the issuer, as a Mudarib or Wakil, to 'lend' money to the Rabb Al-Maal or principal to be applied for the investment?

It is the conviction of the writer that there should not be any compliance issue on this kind of leverage if a proper mechanism has been used to provide for this leverage. As long as the mechanism to raise extra money is acceptable and compliant with the Shariah principle, the investor should be allowed to gain access to the upside performance of the fund.

(2) The small portion of the invested amount will be used to 'purchase' Islamic option. If the price of the underlying is in favour of the investors, the option held will be exercised by liquidating the Murabaha position and pay the price of the underlying. The shares bought will be sold to the market at premium. If otherwise, the option will be left unexercised. The issue that may be raised in this particular point is the fact that when an 'Islamic option' is bought, the investors do not have enough money to pay the price of the underlying. The payment of this price will only be satisfied by liquidating the Murabaha position. What if the expected payment to be made by the counterparty via commodities Murabaha is not possible? This will affect the performance of the investors in paying the price of the underlying.

The writer believes that this kind of leverage, for several reasons, involves no Shariah issue. Firstly, in most circumstances the expected cashflow from the counterparty in commodities Murabaha is almost certain, especially when the counterparty is the issuer itself. Secondly, as mentioned before, the investors hold the right, but not the obligation to buy. So, if it happens that the expected payment from the issuer (via commodities Murabaha) is not possible, the option will simply be left unexercised. Hence, the fact that the investors do not have money to pay the underlying when they purchased the option does not harm any parties. To continue or not to continue with the option held rests totally with the investors, and the performance will certainly depend on the ability to continue and pay the full price of the underlying.

Islamic Option: Al-Wad vis-á-vis Urbun Concepts

In earlier Islamic SPs arrangement, the return maximisation port-folio will be allocated for direct investment in the equity market, especially into high risk high return portfolio. The later generation of SPs, however, has utilised a more sophisticated instrument by replicating the usage of option in conventional SPs. The instru-ments used are also different from one structure to another. Some Islamic SPs use Urbun,[18] whilst others use Al-Wad[19] to replicate the conventional option. It has to be noted also that at least one SP in Malaysia uses conventional option, instead of the replicated Islamic option.

This section attempts to investigate the usage of Urbun and Wad in Islamic SPs.

---

[18] Like Fortress 5-year (Synergy Islamic Series), offered by SG Bank and Trust which combines Murabaha and Urbun, based on the performance of 5 basket funds (Alfanar Global Health Care A, Alfanar INV Holdings A, Alfanar Europe LTD. A, Alfanar US Capital Value A, Alfanar US Large Cap. LTD. A), or ING Baraka Capital Protected II, where up to 10% of the capital will be invested in SGAM Baraka Option, offered by Societe Generale NV (SGA). This option is devised using Urbun contract.

[19] For instance, Capital Protection Investment Link Fund (CPIL) scheme, offered by Hong Leong Tokio Marine Takaful (HLTM Takaful) and Citibank as the struc-ture provider, using Murabaha and Al-Wad as their instrument. The underlying commodities for Murabaha will be oil, copper and zinc and Al-Wad will be bench-marked against property-related Indices of the European Public Real Estate Index (EPRA) and the Tokyo Stock Exchange REIT Index (TSEREIT).

Urbun

In its Arabic term, Urbun means to pay or receive in advance. Ibnu Qudamah defines it as:

> A transaction whereby the buyer buys a commodity and pays a deposit of one dirham or more on the understanding that the deposit will be considered part of the purchase price if the buyer decided to continue with the contract. If the buyer decided to withdraw from the contract, the seller will forfeit the deposit.

An almost similar definition has been advanced by Al-Ramli. According to him, Urbun is a situation whereby a person buys a commodity and pays some dirhams, with a condition built in the contract that if he continues, the deposit will be considered as part of the purchase price, or otherwise, it is a gift to the seller.

Though most classical jurists tend to define Urbun within the sphere of sale contract only, Imam Malik gives a somewhat more general definition of Urbun. He writes in Al-Muwatta:

> For instance, a man buys a slave or slave-girl or rents an animal and then says to the person whom he bought the slave or leased the animal, 'I will give you a dinar or a dirham or whatever on the condition that if I actually take the goods or hide whatever I have rented from you, then what I have given you already goes towards payment for the goods or hire of the animal. If I do not purchase the goods or hire the animal, then what I have given you is yours without liability on your part'.

The above definition made by Imam Malik shows that Urbun is not only possible in a sale contract, but also in a leasing contract.

Several aspects can be understood from these definitions:

(1) Urbun is paid in lieu of the right given to the buyer to have a waiting period, whether to continue or withdraw from the contract.

(2) This period is undetermined.

(3) The deposit paid will be considered as part of the purchase price if the buyer decides to ratify the contract. If he withdraws, the seller will have the right to keep the deposit. As we may see later, this is the second type of Urbun contract that is disputable among the jurists.

(4) The area in which an Urbun contract can be practised is wide and not limited to the contract of sale only. This is understood from a wider understanding from the scenario that has been advanced by Imam Malik.

Though the jurists are in disagreement on the legality of Urbun, the Islamic Fiqh Academy in Jeddah has resolved that the Urbun contract is allowed provided that the waiting period for Urbun is certain and known to the parties to the contract.

In many Islamic SPs hedge funds and short-selling arrangement to sell stock or to enter into in-kind creation and redemption of Islamic ETF, Urbun has been used to replicate the equivalent conventional products. In SPs, Urbun has been used to replicate the conventional call option. Superficially speaking, a call option looks very similar to Bay Al-Urbun. However, there are some basic differences between call option and Bay Al-Urbun. In Al-Urbun, the deposited price paid in advance to the seller will be counted in as part of the purchase price if the contract is later on ratified. So, if the buyer decides to continue, he will have to pay only the remaining purchase price (original purchase price minus the Urbun price). The situation is different when it comes to call option, where the option premium is not part of the purchase price. So, if the option holder decides to continue with the contract, he will have to pay the full purchase price, as option premium is not counted in as part of the purchase price.

Some other writers attempt to draw another basic economic difference between option and Urbun. They argued that Urbun can be viewed as a 'real option', in which the decision to exercise the option depends on real variables affecting the buyer's payoffs rather than the asset's price. A buyer might pay an Urbun price on a car, say, not to monitor its price, but to have enough time to examine it and see whether it fits his needs and financial capability. On the other hand, a call option is bought to monitor the price of the underlying asset; if it appreciates, the option is exercised; otherwise it will be left unexercised.

Though the use of Urbun to replace conventional option seems easily implementable, there are some Shariah issues that need to be addressed carefully, First, in conventional option, during the call option's holding period, the securities still belong to the securities seller, hence entitling him the dividend generated from the securities during the period. In an Urbun transaction, by virtue of the Urbun contract, the Urbun holder is in fact the owner of the securities. He is entitled to all the dividends gained during that period.[20]

One may answer[21] to this query by highlighting that the issue of dividend is not important, since the seller of the securities may not own the securities when he contracted to sell the securities using the Urbun concept. Though this solves the problem of ownership over the dividend gained during the period, this answer has created a more complicated issue on selling something which one does not own.

As a matter of fact, once the Urbun contract is concluded the right and liability of the subject matter are deemed to have been transferred to the buyer. The parties may agree on who will keep the subject matter during the Urbun period, but the right and liability attached to the subject matter are vested with the buyer already.[22] If the

---

[20] Honestly speaking, the writer has a very limited knowledge on whether this issue has been carefully addressed in all instruments using Urbun to replicate a call option.

[21] This is in fact the answer of a banker, who helped in structuring one Islamic SP.

[22] Some have misunderstood the Urbun contract by saying the contract is not concluded yet when the Urbun contract has been made. For instance, a writer in **Risk Islamic Finance: March 2007** writes: "An Urbun contract lets the investor buy an asset at a fixed price at any point up to the contract's maturity — therefore resembling an options contract. This understanding is wrong because by virtue of concluding Urbun, the parties have entered into a sale contract already. The right owned by the Urbun holder is either to continue with the contract, hence considering the Urbun price as part of the purchase price, or to discontinue with the contract and allowing the seller to forfeit the deposit given by virtue of the Urbun".

subject matter needs to be taken care of, like feeding, and so forth, the expenses will be incurred for his account. When it comes to shares, the right to benefit from the dividend cannot be ignored simply by saying that the ownership of the shares will not be transferred to the buyer because the seller would not own the securities yet when contracting the option; rather he will only buy to deliver the shares when the option holder decides to exercise the option,[23] so no dividends have to be passed to the buyer when contracting. This argument is unacceptable if the opinion of majority scholars and that of AAOIFI which requires ownership of the subject matter before it can be sold to somebody else is to be applied. Because of this reason and others, the writer believes that the structuring of Urbun to replicate the conventional call option is complicated, and if not considered carefully will contradict various Shariah principles relating to ownership and liability in contracts.

Al-Wad

The Islamic law's literature has witnessed the introduction of various new and unprecedented concepts throughout the Muslim history. The usefulness of a particular concept is also relative as the time goes by. A particular concept may be unimportant at a particular time, but very much essential and finds a very wide application at other times. A very good example to support this hypothesis is the utilisation of Wad (promise). The classical jurists though had given some attention to the concept of Wad, but the treatment was relatively very minor. Instead of treating the concept on its own, its marginal practices can be found scattered in various chapters on

---

[23] Even some suggest that instead of buying from the market and delivering them to the buyer, for the buyer to then sell back to the market and benefit from price differences, what really happens is that the seller and the option holder will just agree to offset the difference in price, so the seller will just pay the option holder the difference.

Fiqh. In fact, to find a single, direct and comprehensive definition of Wad in classical writing is not an easy task. The modern practices of Islamic finance, on the other hand, has seen the potential to develop further the concept as it can mitigate various possibilities, such as the performance of contract (as in the case of Murabaha to the purchase orderer), the outcome of the venture (in Mudaraba and Musharaka), ability to pay the rental in Ijarah contract (as in the case of Sukuk Ijara), and so forth. Hence, the issue of Al-Wad, Al-Muwaadah, Al-Muwatah Fi Al-Uqud has been discussed in a relatively lengthy manner.

For reasons of brevity, the issue of whether a promise is binding once given is not a new issue. The majority of jurists uphold that though fulfilling Al-Wad is highly recommended and urged by the Shariah, fulfilling a promise is neither mandatory nor enforceable through the court of law. On the other hand, some jurists, like Samurah Bin Jundub, Umar Ibn Abd Al-Aziz, Ibn Shubrumah, Hassan Al-Basri, Ibn Arabi, and Imam Bukhari, opine that fulfilling a promise is not only morally binding, but also enforceable in the court of law. The middle opinion upheld by the Hanafis and the Malikis looks more toward the effect of such a promise. Hence, the Hanafis maintain that a promise is binding if it is tied up (Muallaq) with the occurrence of a certain/specified condition (Shart). This is to prevent detriment or fraud on the promisee. The opinion of the Malikis states that though a promise is generally not binding,[24] if the promisor had caused the promisee to incur some expense or undertake some labour or liability on the basis of the promise, this promise is mandatory upon him. The court may enforce the promise if sufficient evidence has been provided by the plaintiff that he has suffered losses due to the promise given to him by the defendant.[25]

---

[24] Abu Umar Yusuf Ibn Abdillah Ibn Abd Al-Barr Al-Nimri, Al-Tamhid, Al-Maghrib, Wazarah Umum Al-Awqaf wa Shuun Al-Islamiyyah, 1387H, vol. 3, pp. 208–209.
[25] See for details, Muhammad Taqi Usmani, *An Introduction to Islamic Finance*, 120–126, 87–89, Wahbah Al-Zuhayli, *Al-Fiqh Al-Islami wa Adillatuh*, vol. 4, pp. 2928–2930.

This opinion has been adopted by the Academy Fiqh of Jeddah in one of its resolution, AAOIFI in its Shariah Standard, and has been widely accepted by modern jurists. It is not the intention of this present paper to examine this issue in detail. It suffices to state here that the legality and enforceability of a promise in this manner has been used widely in the structuring of many Islamic financial products.

Insofar as the modern practices are concerned, Al-Wad is said to be able to replicate a conventional call option; however, a close scrutiny to the latter shows some problems in practice.

In brief, the conventional call option gives the holder the right to buy the underlying at a particular date for a certain price.[26] It creates a right to buy on the buyer's side, but an obligation to sell from the seller's side. Whenever the buyer decides to buy, the seller is obliged to sell the underlying. For him to hold the right, the buyer will have to pay a certain percentage of the price of the underlying (called the premium). This premium would be considered as part of the purchase price should he decide to exercise the option and buy the underlying. So, the undertaking is given by the seller, not the buyer, because he is the one who will be obliged to perform the contract, not the buyer. Thus, can we ask the buyer to pay the seller for the undertaking made by the seller? Can this be called Hamish Jiddiyyah (security deposit)? AAOIFI Shariah Standard has discussed the issue of undertaking and security deposit in various occasions relating to Murabaha Ijarah, Istisna, and so forth. In Murabaha for the purchase orderer for instance, the client will approach the bank and give a Wad (promise) to the bank that once the bank purchases the asset (from developer, and so forth.), he will purchase the asset from the bank. To protect the right of the bank, if the client forfeits his promise and discontinues with the contract and as such will cost the bank some losses, the bank is allowed to request for some amount known as Hamish Jiddiyyah (security deposit), for the purpose of

---

[26] A put option, on the other hand, gives the holder the right to sell the underlying at a certain date for a certain price.

Table 1

	Call option (Wad structure)	Al-Wad (in Murabaha)
Promise given by:	Seller	Buyer
'Premium' paid by:	Buyer	Buyer

remedying the bank for possible losses should the client decide not to continue. Here, the undertaking is given by the client and the payment of security deposit is also made by the client. Thus situation is somehow different if Wad is to be used to replicate a call option. The promise to sell will be made by the seller of the option, but the payment of Hamish Jiddiyyah will be made by the buyer of the option, not the seller. This has been summarised in Table 1.

The major enquiry here is 'Can the buyer pay the seller for the undertaking given by the seller to sell the shares whenever he decides to buy?' This is the main problem, I believe, in devising an Islamic call option using Al-Wad principle. Perhaps due to this major unresolved issue, all Islamic options devised thus far are using the Urbun concept and not Al-Wad concept.[27]

The two Islamic SPs that the writer has come across, though using Al-Wad the way it is used, are different. First, the undertaking given involves no payment of premium. Second, instead of having only one unilateral promise, these two structures utilise two unilateral promises.

In LLB Top 20 Middle East Total Return Index issued by ABN Amro Bank N. V., the Trustee grants a unilateral promise ('Wad') to sell to the Issuer the Equities Portfolio at a future date ('Sale Undertaking'), and the Issuer grants a unilateral promise ('Wad') to buy the Equities Portfolio from the Trustee at such a date

---

[27] I must hasten to add here that the Urbun concept is also used to replicate short selling (Shariah Capital). Another concept used is Salam (Al-Fanar). The writer is also aware of the AAOIFI Shariah Standard that disallows Salam on shares, which will definitely disallow short-selling based on Salam.

('Purchase Undertaking'). The Wad price is agreed with reference to the value of the Index Portfolio Return. The proceeds from the Sale and Purchase Undertaking in respect of the Equities Portfolio will be distributed to investors. The same can also be seen in Deutsche Bank's SPs. After the proceeds (capital contribution) have been channelled to an Islamic account, the investment manager will use the money to buy shares (or a basket of shares). At the same time, the investors (represented by the Trustee) undertake to sell the underlying shares held to the investment manager at a certain settlement price. On the other hand, the investment manager will also give an undertaking to the investors (via Trustee) to purchase the underlying shares at an exercise price. The purpose of the two Wad is to overcome the fact that there will be situations where one Wad will be uneconomical to exercise. Having the two Wad will overcome this, as one of the Wad will always be economical to exercise under any circumstances. Though the two unilateral Wad given may be viewed as a bilateral Wad, the argument put forward by the proponent of this structure is that at all times, only one promise will be effective. Moreover, the two Wad are given for two different conditions. As such their independency and detachability are maintained at all times and therefore do not amount to bilateral Wad that may lead to a contractual agreement already.

The purchase and sale undertaking in this situation cannot be said as replicating a call option for two reasons:

(1) It involves no premium; and
(2) The undertaking (obligation) to sell and purchase is made by both parties. Hence its effect is more like a forward, rather than an option.

Since these issuances are not replicating a call option, the writer will not continue further with the discussion on devising call options using Al-Wad. However, the second issue is worth considering. The given of two unilateral promises is argued to be compliant to Shariah because they are independent and unrelated to one another. To extend further the discussion on Al-Wad, the Fiqh Academy of Jeddah in its earlier resolution decided that bilateral promises, if binding on both parties, are not allowed.

The issue of binding promise, if made unilaterally or bilaterally, is treated again in the Fiqh Academy's Resolution No. 157 which reads:[28]

● أولاً:الأصل في

المواعدة من الطرفين أنها ملزمة ديانة، وليســـت ملزمة قضاءً.

● ثانياً: المواعدة من

الطرفين على عقد تحايلاً على الربا، مثل المواطأة على العينة أو المواعدة على بيع سلف ممنوعة شرعاً.

● ثالثاً: في الحالات

التي لا يمكن فيها إنجاز عقد البيع لعدم وجود المبيع في ملك البائع مع وجود حاجة عامة لإلزام كل من الطرفين بإنجاز عقد في المستقبل بحكم القانون أو غيره، أو بحكم الأعراف التجارية الدولية، كما في فتح الاعتماد المستندي لاستيراد البضائع، فإنه يجوز أن تجعل المواعدة ملزمة للطرفين إما بتقنين من الحكومة، وإما باتفاق الطرفين على نصّ في الاتفاقية يجعل المواعدة ملزمة للطرفين.

● رابعاً: إن المواعدة

الملزمة في الحالة المذكورة في البند ثالثاً لا تأخذ حكم البيع المضاف إلى المستقبل، فلا ينتقل بها ملك المبيع إلى المشتري، ولا يصير الثمن ديناً عليه، ولا ينعقد البيع إلا في الموعد المتفق عليه بإيجاب وقبولٍ.

● خامساً: إذا تخلف

أحد طرفي المواعدة، في الحالات المذكورة في البند ثالثاً، عما وعدَ به، فإنه يُجبر قضاءً على إنجـــاز العقد، أو تحمّل الضرر الفعلي الحقيقي الذي لحق الطرف الآخر بسبب تخلفه عن وعده (دون الفرصة الضائعة)

First: In its original rule, bilateral promise creates only religious obligation (Mulzimatun Diyanatan), but not judicial (Qadhaan).

Second: Bilateral promises from both parties to conclude a contract for the purpose of circumventing the prohibition of Riba, like

---

[28] Resolution No. 157, Fiqh Academy of Jeddah, 28 Jamad al-Ula — 2 Jamad Al-Akhirah 1427h (24–28 July 2006), Amman, Jordan.

mutual understanding (Muwataah) to do 'Inah' or bilateral promises (Muwaadah) to do sale and loan contracts is prohibited.

Third: In situations where the execution of sale contract is not possible for reasons such as the fact that the subject matter is not in the possession of the seller, but there are general needs (Wujud Hajah Amah) to oblige both parties to conclude the contract at a later time for various reasons like provisions of law or other reasons, or due to the practice of international trades, like the practice of documentary credits for import practices, hence it is allowed to make bilateral promise to be binding, by way of provisions of law, or by providing a clause in the agreement that binds the parties on their bilateral promise.

Fourth: The bilateral binding promise as mentioned above would not make the contract to be a forward sale. As such, the ownership of the subject matter would not be transferred to the buyer, and the price would not form a debt to be paid by him to the seller, and the sale contract would not be executed except on the agreed date and must be concluded with an offer and acceptance.

Fifth: If one of the parties backs off from performing his promise made in situations that have been mentioned in item No. 3, he will be forced by the court of law to perform the promise, or otherwise he will be forced to remedy the actual loss (Al-Darar Al-Haqiqi) that has been inflicted upon the counterparty due to his non-performance of the promise.

Several issues relating to our discussion have been raised by this resolution. It reinstates the earlier decision that, originally, bilateral promise should not be binding. Only in certain circumstances, when the need (Hajah) arises, bilateral promise can be made binding. This situation is when the subject matter is not yet in the possession of the seller; however, the contract is still important to be concluded (even before the subject matter rests in the possession of the seller).

In this situation, it is allowed for both parties to give bilateral promise to ensure that the contract will be concluded as expected later. In some Islamic SPs, even though the basket of shares is in the owner-ship of the investors already when the promises are given, the two promises are important to ensure that both parties will conclude the contract as projected. Can we consider this as a need to allow for the practice of bilateral promise? Or, is the resolution meant to be applied only to situations when the subject matter is not in the possession of the seller and not on other situations? A point to ponder.

Nevertheless, the argument in allowing these structured prod-ucts is not based on permissibility of bilateral promise.[29] Rather, the argument is built on the premise that these structured products do not employ bilateral promise; instead two unilateral promises have been used.

Al-Muwaadah may be defined as a bilateral promise given by both parties, one to another to undertake a certain particular task or job like Al-Muwaadah to sell and purchase certain specific shares. How to differentiate a bilateral promise with two unilateral promises? It is said that promises to sell and purchase the specific asset are con-sidered to be bilateral if made contingent one to another and/or based on the same condition (e.g., the seller said to the buyer: "If thing A happens, I will sell asset B at price C", and the buyer also said: "if thing A happens, I will buy asset B at price C"). On the other hand, two promises are considered unilateral if the condition for their fulfillment and/or the prices are different. (e.g., (1) the seller said to the buyer: "If thing A happens, I will sell asset B at price C", and the buyer said to the seller: "If thing D happens, I will buy asset B at price C". (2) The seller said to the buyer: "If thing A happens, I will sell asset B at price C", and the buyer said to the seller: "If thing A happens, I will sell asset B at price D".)

---

[29] Maybe because the endorsement on these Structured Products were done before the Fiqh Academy of Jeddah convened for their 17th Conference in 2006, where the resolution on bilateral promise was made.

Tawarruq structures in commodity Murabah

There are so many discussions on Tawarruq Fiqhi and Tawarruq Masrafi. This chapter has no intention to make a thorough investigation into this matter. For the sake of brevity, it can be said that though most jurists are agreeable to Tawarruq Fiqhi, some jurists at least have some reservations in allowing the modern Tawarruq. As commodity Murabaha structure lies at the centre of some SPs, the illegality of this instrument (if this opinion is to be considered) will certainly affect the authenticity of Islamic SPs. As some Shariah rulings have made it clear that the practice of modern Tawarruq structure may not be Shariah-compliant, the alternative structure may be needed to replace the commodity Murabah structure to provide the capital guarantee mechanism. In some structures, the money market instruments and fixed income securities have been utilised. For instance, Equity-Linked Ringgit Structured Investment (ELRSI-i) offered by OCBC Bank (Malaysia) Berhad uses fixed income securities, like Negotiable Debt Certificate-i to provide the capital protected mechanism. The HSBC Islamic Equity Structured Product and CIMB Islamic All-Stars Restricted Mudarabah Structured Investment-i are also using Islamic fixed income and debt instrument for their capital protected investment portfolio. It should be noted at this particular juncture that two issues may be at the centre of this application. First, there must be availability of money market instruments to cater to the needs for SPs, if the swift is to be made from Murabaha to money market products. The surge in the offering of SPs means a huge number of money markets instruments is needed to cater for this. Second, the acceptability of Islamic money market instruments is also varied. Only limited numbers of money market instruments are acceptable according to an international standard. Even at an international level, not all money market instruments are tradable. Sukuk Al-Salam instrument, for instance, is not tradable. The only available instrument is Sukuk Al-Ijara. But, do we have enough Sukuk Ijara to be used for SPs?

The purchase undertaking made by the parent to the investors
(where the investment manager is a subsidiary of the parent
and the guarantee made by the parent on the payment of
purchase price to be made by third party to the investors)

In some practices of Islamic SPs, a contract will be concluded between the investors and the issuer (SPV incorporated by the parent company), where the issuer is appointed either as an agent or a Mudarib to enter into a series of deferred payment in Murabaha transactions with third party[30] on a scheduled Murabaha date. The payment of these Murabaha will be benchmarked against a certain index. In certain practices, this third party may be another subsidiary of the parent, or a related company. The parent then will give a purchase undertaking to the investors to purchase the certificate at par at the scheduled maturity date should the total payment to be generated falls below the initial capital invested. At the same time, the parent will also become guarantor to the third party in paying the deferred price to be paid to the issuer under each Murabaha transaction.

Two issues need our attention on this practice:

(1) Is it allowed for the parent to give a purchase undertaking to purchase back the certificate at par value? There is no direct standard in AAOIFI Shariah Standard on that. In fact, there is no direct provision on the purchase undertaking given by the issuer (SPV) to buy back the certificate from the investors. However, a related standard can be found in Musharaka standard. In the Musharakah standard, it is stipulated that it is not permissible for the partner to buy back the assets of the Shariah on the basis of face value as this constitutes the guarantee over the capital which is against the principle of Musharaka.[31] It may

---

[30] In some practices, this third party may be another subsidiary of the parent, or a related company.
[31] AAOIFI Shariah Standard, Standard No. 12, item No. 3/1/6/2.

be argued that since both Musharaka and Mudaraba are trust-based contracts (Uqud Al-Amanah) and both are classified under participatory contracts (Uqud Al-Sharikah), they should share the same ruling on this issue. If this line of argument is acceptable, the Mudarib cannot give a purchase undertaking to buy back the certificate at par value as this is tantamount to guarantee of the capital provided by Rabb Al-Maal. However, the purchase undertaking in this case is provided by the parent, not the SPV itself. Can we consider the parent as third party as they have their own separate legal entities or the parent does not qualify as third party as they are related to one another? Though there is no definition on third party in purchase undertaking, the definition of third party for guarantee purposes is provided indirectly in the standard relating to the guarantee provided in Musharaka contracts. Hence, the standard defines 'third party' as: '…(c) The third-party guarantor should not own more than a half of the capital in the entity to be guaranteed, and (d) the guaranteed entity should not own more than a half of the capital in the entity that undertakes to provide guarantee… .'[32] If an analogy is possible to be made in this case, we have to admit that the act of the parent giving a purchase undertaking to the investor might bear the same result of giving a guarantee by the parent to the subsidiary, which has been ruled to be impermissible. But if we consider the purchase undertaking given by the parent is in no way similar to the guarantee provided by the parent to the subsidiary, or if we agree that the separate legal entity acquired by both of them entitles them to be considered as foreign, one to another, the purchase undertaking given in this situation bears no Shariah issue at all.

---

[32] Part of the standard provided in: AAOIFI Shariah Standard, Standard No. 12, item No. 3/1/4/3.

(2) Guarantee provided by the parent over the deferred payment
     obligation to be made by the third party, in the case where the
     third party is also a related party to the parent (be it subsidiary,
     associate or investment company). The writer believes that
     this practice should not cause any Shariah issue, because the
     guarantee is provided in lieu of payment of the purchase price.
     The guarantee over payment of purchase price to the seller can
     be made even by a related party.

Al-Wakalah Bi Al-Istithmar *vis-á-vis* Mudaraba

The relation between investment manager and investors is either
based on Al-Wakalah Bi Al-Istithmar or Mudarabah. Structurally
speaking, there is no difference between the two in terms of managing the investment. The difference lies in the fees and profit
sharing ratio. Though both contracts establishing trust relationship (Aqd Al-Amanah), thus precluding the investment manager
from any liability should the investment fail to achieve the
expected capital protection mechanism and/or expected profit, in
Wakalah Bi Al-Istithmar, the investment manager entitles for a
fixed fee for the efforts that he has spent in managing the fund,
disregarding whether the fund is profitable or not, whilst in
Mudharaba, as a Mudarib, the investment manager entitles for a
share of profit based on an agreed ratio, once the investment has
realised a profit. There are pros and cons to both arrangements.
In Wakalah structure, the investment manager can deduct from the
capital certain fees payable for his work. As such, his management
fees are secured, no matter how the SPs turn out to be later. Whilst
he can protect his 'right' in case of nonperformance of the fund, he
cannot take advantage on the good performance of the fund. This
advantage can be achieved via Mudaraba arrangement. Though
there is a risk that the investment manager would not be getting

any return over the efforts that he has spent in case of nonperformance of the Islamic SPs, he has the advantage to benefit more if the fund performs well, because what he will get is a profit sharing ratio which may give him a higher amount of profit, if the fund performs well.

Conventional Option Contract

In some Islamic SPs, like the HSBC Amanah Islamic Equity-Linked Structured Investment-i, a ringgit-denominated Islamic-Structured Investment linked to a basket of shares in the index, the profit maximisation portfolio utilises the conventional option. This may raise Shariah issues since the use of conventional option is not acceptable according to the AAOIFI Shariah Standard. In Malaysia, though there is no direct ruling in allowing conventional option, the ruling allowing call warrants and Transferable Subscription Right (TSR) can be used as the basis in supporting the permissibility of conventional call option.

Limitation on Withdrawal

In most Islamic SPs, the capital protection mechanism is only achieved (or promised) if the capital is held to maturity. If the capital is withdrawn before the maturity of the investment, there is no guarantee that the investor will get a return over the investment, or even the capital. In certain SPs, the investors are not allowed to withdraw their capital except at certain intervals. (These intervals may be semiquarterly, quarterly, annually, or on other arrangement.) Though classical writing jurists classified Mudaraba or Wakalah as nonbinding contracts (Uqud Ghayr Lazimah), thus allowing the Rabb Al-Maal or Al-Muwakkil to withdraw their funds and terminate the contracts at all times, the modern deliberation on the matter has decided that the parties can agree that the withdrawal of funds and termination of contract by both parties (Rabb Al-Maal or Al-Muwakkil) and Mudarib (or Al-Wakil) can only be done at certain particular intervals to avoid any harm from the other party. The AAOIFI Shariah Standard on this matter reads: 'The general principle is that a Mudaraba contract is not binding, that is, each of the contracting parties may terminate it unilaterally except in two cases:[33]

(a) When the Mudarib has already commenced the business, in which case the Mudaraba contract becomes binding up to the date of actual or constructive liquidation.
(b) When the contracting parties agree to determine a duration for which the contract will remain in operation. In this case, the contract cannot be terminated prior to the end of the designated duration, except by mutual agreement of the contracting parties.

The Ceiling for Investment Profit Rate

Though previous discussion highlighted the advantages and disadvantages for applying Wakalah or Mudaraba contracts, the practice of putting a ceiling over the expected return to the investor has rendered the upside performance of the fund for the advantage of the investment manager. In this arrangement, the investment manager has indicated upfront to the investor on the indicative (expected) profit rate. It would be agreed upon by all parties that in the case where the investment manager managed to generate a higher profit rate, the remaining (over and above expected profit rate) will be given to the investment manager as an incentive over his good management of the fund. As such, the

---

[33] AAOIFI Shariah Standard, Standard No. 13 (mudaraba), item No. 4/3.

manager will take advantage on the upside performance of the fund. The AAOIFI Shariah Standard has allowed for such an arrangement provided that it is agreeable between the parties to the contract.[34]

Currency Exchange Rate

In some SPs, though the proceeds is raised using one currency, the investment will be made in another currency. For instance, in ING Baraka Capital Protected, up to 10% of the investment portfolio will be invested in SGAM Al-Baraka Option, denominated in US Dollar'. Hence, the conversion to and from US Dollars must be Shariah-compliant. If the hedging were to be made to protect the currency fluctuation, like forward currency contract, it is desirable that the forward currency contract utilise the Islamic version of forward currency contract. This will be dealt with later in the coming section.

Hedging Using Conventional Hedging Mechanism

In some structures, especially when the performance of the SP relies on the performance of an index, there may be a need to hedge the SPs' position. Should the hedging mechanism utilise Islamic instruments only, or can the fund utilise the conventional hedging instruments as well? It must be emphasised at this particular juncture that it is certainly highly recommended that the hedging mechanism utilises only Islamic instruments. Nevertheless, can the fund utilise the conventional hedging mechanism, and will that affect its compliance to Shariah? The writer will not consider the

---

[34] AAOIFI Shariah Standard, Standard No. 12 (Musharaka) item No. 3/1/5/9.

situation of necessity (Dharurah) or needs (Hajiyat),[35] because these two situations will have their own rules and regulations which are beyond the scope of this study. On this particular issue, the jurists rule that the conventional hedging mechanism is not allowed if it runs against Shariah principles. However, the 'unislamicity' of this hedging, if exercised, would not affect the compliance of the fund, as this is seen to be external to and separate from the fund's activities.

Conclusion

It is the intention of this short chapter to shed light over the practice of various Islamic SPs. As one may observe, in most circumstances, the Shariah issues involved in devising Islamic SPs as discussed in this chapter are only raised, but not treated deeply as far as Shariah rulings are concerned. As has already been mentioned, this manner of discussion is intentional since each one of these issues, if they were to be discussed thoroughly, requires a lot of space which may not be able to be covered by this chapter. However, it is highly hoped that this short discussion is able to raise some Shariah concerns over the practice of Islamic SPs.

---

[35] Generally, the jurists whilst discussing the validity or otherwise a particular ruling (Hukm) will consider two situations. In a normal situation, the ruling will be given in its general application (Hukm Al-Asl Al-Amm), where the application of law will affect every situation and individual. However, in certain exceptional circumstances (Al-Awarid), where the general application of rules of law is not possible, certain flexibilities may be granted in case of necessity (Dharurah) or needs (Hajah). However, these exceptional circumstances must be discussed on a case-to-case basis, and, if certain flexibilities are granted, will subject to certain scope, framework, and limitation.

ISLAMIC BANKS: RESILIENCE AND STABILITY — NOT IMMUNE FROM CRISIS

Shamshad Akhtar

Background

Deepening of financial market turmoil has triggered a debate on how Islamic banks (IB) have weathered the unfolding global crisis relative to the conventional finance industry. At one level, this debate has credibility as Islamic finance (IF), despite performing similar role and functions of promoting financial intermediation like conventional finance and differs in both appearance and substance from the conventional finance industry. At another level, this debate seems superfluous as cyclicality does affect financial markets depending on their exposure to vulnerable regions, sectors and market and risk management capabilities, regardless of their specific characteristics.

Islamic finance, shaped by the rich core principles of Islamic jurisprudence, allows IBs the flexibility to structure a variety of transactions and products both on the asset and liabilities side. Islamic finance has elements which promote conservatism by prohibiting a range of instruments and transactions including those structured around *riba* (interest rates) or involving uncertainty and speculation features. Transactions and modalities backed by a range of participation structures carry different risks relative to the conventional products depending on how they are structured. While IF may have inbuilt risk safeguards, it brings with it newer exposures which can complicate or magnify risk. Proponents have underscored that safeguards within IF tend to augment the financial resilience and stability of IBs. Critics would however contend that while this may be true, Islamic industry lags behind in maturity and sophistication, which has exposed the conventional banks to esoteric products with deeper risks and vulnerabilities.

This chapter advocates that proper understanding and appreciation as well as oversight and management of balance sheet risks are critical to the resilience and stability of IBs. This chapter highlights the:

- Strong growth momentum of IF and acknowledges that the industry has weathered the crisis well thus far, but given its severity and magnitude, IBs are likely to come under stress.
- Islamic industry strengths and inbuilt safeguards, which augur well for its resilience and stability.
- Differences and complexity of IB's balance sheet and off-balance-sheet exposures, and recognises that these institutions do face a range of risks, which vary in specifics and substance.
- Lack of development of an Islamic money market that has compounded the liquidity risks facing IB relative to conventional banking; while some countries have introduced few instruments for

liquidity management, constraints and shortages of short-term paper that hurt the industry's risk management and earning capabilities.

Growth and Steady Diversification Persist,
but IF is not Immune from Global Crises

An age-old system, IF has grown uninterruptedly over the last few years. Rejuvenated by a Muslim-dominated geographical belt and supported by the West, IF has its distinct theoretical and ideological discipline whose foundation lies in Islamic jurisprudence. The richness of its ethical framework and the wide range of trade, exchange and business practices have catalysed a real breakthrough, and renewed commitment and fervour in the IF industry. These are supported by the:

(i) Accumulation of sovereign wealth and excess liquidity in oil-producing countries, dominated by Muslim population, with an appetite for alternative asset classes;

(ii) Rising demand for *Shariah*-compliant products and services; and

(iii) Acceleration of economic and infrastructural development in some Muslim countries using oil revenue surpluses generated.

These drivers of change triggered exponential growth in IB. The industry grew in the range of 20–40% per annum during 2000–2006, backed by Islamic capital and benefitting from strong global economies. The industry nurtured itself behind the dynamism of the global financial markets. Catalysing the growth of industry was a rise in global savings and investments. These trends benefitted from internal revenue generated by oil surplus economies, whose strong fundamentals attracted foreign capital flows.

Now IBs are facing their first full-blown crisis. The present crisis is global, multidimensional and severe in its depth, breadth, and intensity. Not only is the recession deep and widespread, but also its impact has been felt across the continents. The magnitude of global economic and financial losses is unprecedented and policy responses, including rescue packages, are to cost the global economy trillions of dollars. In this setting to argue that IBs would go unscathed would be naïve.

Analysts' reports[1] have extensively evaluated the impact of the global crisis on the IBs industry. Broae, which is at best preliminary as the crisis is still unfolding, does concur that IBs are weathering the crisis reasonably well. The first round impact of the crisis was subdued as the Islamic industry, given its conservatism and prohibitions, did not have exposure to the subprime mortgage market. In the second round, from mid-2008, stress started to appear, and there is evidence in that at the introductory level, the Islamic banking has shown a degree of resilience and stability because it is less leveraged and does not have exposure to credit derivative products (not acceptable under IF) or most securitised financial instruments. The industry exhibited greater reliance on customers and retail business, avoided the abuse of underwriting standards, and maintained high-lending standards. Strong asset quality and high provisions for nonperforming loans (particularly for Gulf-based banks) served as additional layers of protection against the emerging risks. Advances to total assets ratios continued to grow in double digits and IBs benefitted from issuance of tier 2 capital, enhancing their funding profile and regulatory capital ratios.

Notwithstanding these encouraging factors, IF markets and institutions did show strains during 2008, businesses and product

---

[1] These include: Moody's Investor Service: *Gulf Islamic Banks Resilient Amid Global Credit Woes*. Global Banking, Special Comment. November 2008; Merrill Lynch: *Let the Dust Settle*. Middle East and North Africa. Article dated 6 November 2008.

issuance, including Sukuk, slowed down by the end of 2008. Islamic banks' high real estate and construction exposure, as a proportion of lending rose (in the range of 25–33% or so for Gulf-based Islamic banks), are now hurting the banks. Declining oil revenues will have consequences for economic and infrastructure activity and shrinking liquidity is raising the cost of funding and magnifying the short-term liquidity gaps. Overextended IBs are either re-positioning or adopting appropriate measures, including capital injections, to restore confidence and avoid adverse spillover to other institutions. Potential challenges facing the industry are multiple but can be resolved through proper oversight, both at the regulator and institutional levels, and adequate funding buffers built up with oil surpluses will help rescue banks.

Regulators are bound to be adopting a tougher stance on prudential guidelines for real estate and consumer lending guidelines, while steepening the supervision and enforcement. This should be good for the long-term sustainability of the industry.

Balance Sheet and Off-Balance Sheet (OBS) Risks for IBs

Islamic banks are well integrated and do not operate in isolation; therefore, they are likely to be impacted by the global recessionary trends and changing market fundamentals. Generally, financial institutions, be they conventional or Islamic, thrive well as long as they have proper access to both retail and corporate funding on the liabilities side and they are able to maintain adequate risk management and diversification on the asset side to preserve profitability and financial soundness. Managing the balance sheet's risks, whether for an Islamic or conventional bank, requires proper recognition of industry and individual transaction-specific risks, well-developed alternate avenues of investments and money market instruments. This helps the bank build an investment portfolio that is diversified across asset classes, geography, issuers, and currencies, and one that is more liquid than its credit exposures and more profitable than its interbank liquidity management.

Banks further face underlying market imperfections, typically moral hazard, asymmetric information, and externalities that become significant with the rising stress in the real economy and downswings in asset prices. Under this scenario, banks often become either over-competitive or risk-averse, both with associated negative consequences. These factors compound when there is panic and/or growing market illiquidity that may trigger market failures and high volatility, which tests the resilience of financial markets and institutions.

In a number of ways, IBs operate on similar lines as conventional banks in terms of raising cash flow resources and re-cycling them to a range of investments and assets dominated by credit exposures. In this regard, IBs face the same risks as conventional banks including credit risks, maturity and currency risk, solvency risks, market risks, and operational risks.

An Islamic bank, if practised in letter and spirit, however, has structural features that nurture the conservative business approaches and transactions and promote profit sharing. Together, if properly applied, these features help foster resilience and stability. Among other features:

- Structurally Islamic finance's 'exclusion principles', which ban certain types of transactions and activities, such as prohibitions on interest–based, speculative (*maysir*), *gharar* (uncertainty), and *haram* products, do keep IBs' risks contained.
- 'Inclusive elements', such as the option to structure the profit and loss-sharing (PLS) modality and backed by assets, offer IBs an opportunity for balancing risks; and, if a bank has appropriate capacity, it can manage and monitor risks associated with underlying assets. The ability to structure PLS accounts allows shifting of part of the transaction's credit risk from the IB's balance sheet

to the borrower, proportionate to the agreed formula for risk-sharing, though this has other consequences as discussed later.

- Emphasis in IB on trading of goods and services and its advocacy for PLS in businesses supported through a variety of partnership arrangements (in sharp contrast to loan-based financing in conventional banks) offer diverse and prudent financing options, be they asset-backed or equity-based.

- The *Shariah*-based model of corporate governance can reinforce standard principles and legal frameworks for corporate governance. Islamic banks' corporate governance framework focuses on a faith-based approach. It mandates business conduct in accordance with *Shariah* principles, and underscores that no party of any contract or exchange be exploited. Islamic finance recognises profit motive and the PLS conceptual framework accompanied by the need for maximisation of shareholder wealth and creating adequate safeguards for customers/depositors, respectively. Some of these elements may be in conflict with each other but then corporate governance framework for IBs has to treat these tensions effectively, while providing an enabling framework that allows opportunities for growth and strengthening of the system. Elaborate contracts and legal framework are a way to ensure the risk-sharing arrangements are defined properly.

- Large-scale development of blended instruments, while creating risk management complexities, illustrates IBs' flexibility to allow for apportioning risks in different ways among the participants. Successful application and integration of Islamic instruments with conventional financing have helped in this area and facilitated closure of large and complex multisource financing deals. Project financing backed by asset and equity and structured using combination of Ijara, Istisna, Sukuk, Musharaka, and other modalities has offered opportunities for risk diversification, and avenues for resource mobilisation, revenue-sharing and ensuring performance of services between contractual parties. These deals have illustrated how conventional and Islamic financing can blend and coexist under common legal and regulatory arrangements.

Finally, supported by a deeper economic and ideological base and with recognised potential for financial engineering and innovation, Islamic economic and financial architecture has now achieved broader appeal and depth that go beyond Muslim countries. The Islamic economic system offers perspectives on allocation of resources, production and exchange of goods and services, and distribution of wealth as well as offering ethical and socially sustainable approaches to development finance. Islamic finance further recognises the right to property supported by stakeholders' obligations, principles, and rules of conduct; a contracting system and institutional framework; and procedures for enforcement of rules that all together lay the foundation for Islamic business and financial architecture. The core of these relationships, backed by solid principles of rights and obligations of parties to contractual arrangements, offers a rich array of opportunities for risk diversification. Together these elements help strengthen IBs' resilience and stability to withstand crises.

Depending on the nature and structure of transactions, IBs do face some different risks that vary in specifics and substance. It is therefore critical that the industry determines, recognises, and addresses all types of risks facing the industry on a timely basis. These risks emanate from certain types of permissible and innovative products and businesses, and from the lack of supportive regulatory and supervisory infrastructure. Central banks need to launch aggressive efforts to recognise IF risks and advocate appropriate corrective actions and implementation of prudential regulations.

Islamic bank liabilities, when structured along Islamic principles, have a different risk profile and such risks could be higher than those in conventional banks depending on how a given product or transaction is structured. Typically, on the liabilities side Islamic banks can carry:

(i) *Qard-Al-Hasana* and *Murabaha* products — both of which are largely short-term placements — could potentially be no different from customer deposits in conventional banks. However, Murabaha structured with a simultaneous commodity buy and sell entails transaction costs, counterparty credit risk, and potentially price, market, and exchange rate risks. Murabaha also poses liquidity risks. In contrast, conventional banks borrow liquidity funds directly from customers or other institutions without any underlying exchange of commodities.

(ii) Investment deposits' capital value and rates of return are variable and not guaranteed. As such, they inadvertently carry an incentive for risk-taking and moral hazard and could cause a problem for banks if not adequately cushioned by capital.

(iii) PLS accounts, if appropriately structured, can be a source of strength as they allow flexibility to pass the losses of poorly performing assets to account holders and thus help lower the risks of banks. While there may be possibility of transferring risks to customers and parties associated with the transactions, in practice, IBs have not been exercising this option due to perceived reputational or redemption threat as depositors prefer or are used to certainty of returns. If banks opt not to share losses, they end up with 'displaced commercial risk' as equity holders must fund payments to investors. Islamic banks facing low profitability would in general be less inclined to fund such transactions, or losses. Even if they fund such transactions, it would have implications for bank capital.

In recent years, IBs have exhibited strong growth and margins. However, if competition among IBs grows or there is a change of depositor sentiments, for example, a preference for conventional banking or larger banks in risky times, IBs may not have the ability to offer competing returns. On the other hand, the depositors for IBs are likely to be sticky and loyal as driven by explicit preference and faith they opted for this discipline.

The asset side of IB balance sheets versus conventional banks' reveals varying risk profiles depending on the product offered and the state of the development of industry. To the advantage of IBs, the prohibition of interest-based debt finance helps discourage leveraging, while IBs' close association with asset-based transactions allow them an opportunity to monitor the underlying assets. This undoubtedly gives an inherent edge and resilience to IBs. While IBs may thrive on such complex structuring of transactions, with hindsight the industry has to realise the dangers of excessive leveraging without adequate safeguards. Conventional banks that span off their assets to multiple institutions and special purpose vehicles may have removed the risky assets off balance sheets. Over-leveraging, while helping generate additional business space and opportunities for conventional banks, did not absolve them from the risks and destabilised the system, ending up with defaults, a liquidity crunch and in some cases insolvency.

Islamic banks' flexibility to structure a diversified set of products with different risk-sharing mechanisms generally augurs well for their stability. However, there are some key challenges that IBs face:

(i)   Few Shariah-compliant products result in practical issues and risk concentration. Loans and advances, concentrated on the asset-based investments, entail credit risks. Such transactions are complex and costly, while involving bank risk exposure to the underlying tangible assets as all transactions and trade are backed by commodity, real estate, and immovable property placements.

(ii) Equity participation, mainly of Shariah-compliant companies, could involve selection bias as it precludes cherry picking.

(iii) Greater exposure to properties and real estate (which are typical to asset-based structures) directly, or indirectly under different structures of *Sukuk*, have registered a slow down.

(iv) PLS financing provides an option to diffuse some degree of credit risk from the banks' balance sheets. Depending on how they are structured, PLS arrangements could result in 'commercially displaced risks' for equity investors rather than straight vanilla loan, where the borrower alone bears risk.

(v) Islamic finance does not provide for hedging of risk, though IBs are making some inroads in this area.

(vi) Lack of standardisation of products has encouraged IBs to innovate, but the probability of getting exposing banks to high costs of structuring products and/or exposing themselves to unrecognised risks at the formative stage has the potential to create moral hazards.

(vii) Legal and operational risks are quite significant for IBs. The industry has to enter into complex contractual arrangements to avert criticism that they are emulating conventional finance businesses and instruments. The motivation for IBs to do so is also customer-driven: to comfort them with familiar arrangements and processes and to enable effective benchmarking of returns thereby competing with conventional finance that has an edge from its long presence and tradition. Notwithstanding these considerations, IBs enter into complex legal paperwork to mitigate the potential risks relating to litigation too since most products and transaction call for risk-sharing by banks.

Evidence further suggests that despite attempt to diversify their asset base, IBs exhibit high dependence on a few products such as Murabaha *and* Ijara. Aggressive institutions, however, succeeded in a degree of product diversification by exploiting Sukuk, Musharaka, and other PLS variants. Reliance of such instruments on riskier and volatile assets has its own challenges. For instance, structuring the short-term interbank commodity Murabaha and other placements involve spot buy and sell transactions with several counterparties, who then enter into transactions with brokers entails multiple layers of risks. *Sukuk* structures, backed by properties, real estate and projects, involve varying quality of assets and their associated risks. Musharaka portfolios tend to have exposure to the equity of private companies. Confining to Shariah-compliant firms for equity participation means higher exposure to unlisted and newer companies. Almost all IBs also face Shariah-compliant risks that are subject to different interpretation depending on the Islamic jurisprudence followed.

Internal safeguards limit off-balance-sheet (OBS) exposures in IBs. IBs may have certain OBS-specific exposures, such as to their PLS or joint ventures transactions (where the IB acts as a principal with associated operational, credit, and counterparty risks) but proper capital requirements cushion these risks. Conventional banks, on the other hand, may have an unlimited and ever-expanding range of OBS exposures. Complex derivates and speculative products can represent not only material risks, but the risks are also difficult to assess and track. Furthermore, IBs have lower exposure to interest rates than conventional banks due to the prohibition of *riba*. Any exposures they do have is harder to hedge, while the benchmark for pricing many IF products remains the London Interbank Offered Rate (LIBOR), which is tied to financial assets and there may be a mismatch between IBs pricing and performance — being tied to real assets. Nevertheless, the Shariah restriction to transact on real assets in the economy reduces leverage, which in turn reduces downside risk in a financial crisis. Conventional banks lack equivalent OBS safeguards, which proponents point to as a clear advantage of IF.

Liquidity Management Risks

As the history of failure of financial institutions would corroborate, liquidity risk has proven to be an Achilles' heel for banks. The ability to access or dispose off excess liquidity by flexible buy and sell off liquidity instruments with varying tenors is critical for regulators and financial market participants who have worked together actively to develop, manage, and monitor the liquidity frameworks. The recent episode of a severe liquidity crunch in developed markets has illustrated that a failure to supplement liquidity can convert solvent banks to insolvency.

The requirement that IBs back all transactions with tangible assets precludes IBs reliance on conventional tools and options for liquidity management such as repos and reverse repos options, and so forth. In absence of Shariah-compliant instruments and markets, IBs face liquidity risks that include:

- Funding risks as IBs are unable to fund their asset portfolio at appropriate maturities and rates;
- Market risks as IBs are unable to liquidate a position in a timely manner at reasonable prices; and
- Maturity mismatch risks as liabilities are short-term, while assets are relatively longer in tenure.

As a result, IBs may not be able to meet their obligations on a timely basis or may incur losses in doing so, with associated consequences for their earnings and capital.

Liquidity risks could also stem from either macroeconomic adversities that are exogenous to the bank and/or from the nature of the banking business and internal financing and operational policies. Islamic banks can therefore face one risk or a combination of risks such as:

- Incorrect judgement or a complacent attitude toward the timing of the bank's cash in- and out-flows;
- An unanticipated change in the cost of capital or availability of funding;
- Abnormal behaviour of financial markets under stress and accordingly an inappropriate range of assumptions used in predicting the cash flows;

- Risk activation by secondary sources such as failure of business strategy, corporate governance, merger and acquisitions policy;
- A breakdown in the payments and settlements system;
- Complex contractual forms;
- Shariah restrictions on the sale of debt; and
- A deficiency in financial infrastructure.

Among others, the last three sources are particular to IBs.

Islamic finance products, transactions, and contracts have their industry-specific liquidity risks too. For example, Murabaha receivables are debt payable to maturity, not saleable at a price difference from the face value in a secondary market. This is a source of liquidity risk for the bank, particularly if the average maturity of deposits is shorter than the average maturity of Murabaha contracts or if the deposits are sensitive to market returns. Liquidity risk in Murabaha contracts can also arise when business and other risks associated with these contracts affect the liquidity. Likewise, in the case of Salam if the need for cash arises, the bank is unable to exit the contract by selling it to a third party before maturity because of Shariah restriction: "do not sell what is not in your possession". This precludes the existence of a secondary market for trade in Salam contracts. In Istisna contracts, the primary liquidity risk arises in the same way as in Salam contracts, since debt cannot be sold, though risk in Istisna is lower because the bank can provide funds in installments or even defer the whole amount to a future date thus maintaining its liquid assets within the duration of the contract. In Ijara contracts, liquidity risk arises when the bank has to pay the price of the asset upfront to acquire the asset before it can lease to its customer. The liquidity risk depends upon whether or not the asset is readily resell-able in the market.

In recognising liquidity risks in Islamic banking contracts, there have been efforts to develop Islamic money markets and Shariah-compliant instruments. Development of liquidity management frameworks and instruments is underway but efforts are fragmented and there is no conformity in solutions. Some IBs rely on transactions among IF institutions, and special arrangements with conventional banks. In many countries, this takes the form of interbank mutual financing facilities within a profit-sharing framework. In some cases, interbank transactions have been structured between conventional and Islamic counterparties based on commodity Murabaha contracts, or special arrangements for holding compensating non-interest-bearing deposits with each other. The reliance on central banks for liquidity management is still low as most short-term borrowing facilities from central banks have not been adapted to accommodate the Shariah.

A range of strategies, options, and techniques is under discussion to address the liquidity issues and constraints. For one, IBs have the option to choose relatively less illiquid instruments such as relying on interbank loans using short-term Mudaraba contracts and through Salam and Ijara Sukuk. Islamic banks can arrange financing with prospective entrepreneurs for Murabaha and other transactions and then advertise for new investment deposits to ensure that they can smoothly pay a reasonable return to their depositors. Islamic banks can maintain reserves to ensure against liquidity risk, albeit at a cost that might be restrictive in certain cases. While most of Sukuk issuance has been of medium- to longer-term in nature, short-term Sukuk can serve as money market instruments for liquidity management. Similar to conventional interbank lending, short-term Sukuk, mostly commodity Murabaha, have been used for liquidity management in some countries.

Among Islamic countries, some developments are noteworthy. Sudan uses a variety of Sukuk for monetary policy operations. Bahrain Central Bank has issued, since 2001, short-term Sukuk with maturities of 3 or 6 months. Pakistan's public sector companies were allowed to issue statutory liquidity reserve-eligible Sukuk certificates and this has been complemented by a government-structured Ijara

Sukuk that are being sold via competitive auctions among primary dealers held by the central bank. Instruments, issued at face value, carry an initial maturity period of 3 years and *are* tradable and transferable in the secondary markets. They can serve as collateral in money market transactions, promoting interbank lending activities between IBs. In Malaysia, Government Investment Issues and Malaysia Islamic treasury bills, eligible for statutory liquidity reserve requirements, allow IBs to hold liquid paper.

While some critical developments are emerging, short-term liquidity instruments are management purposes through outright sament of secondary market and insufficient supply of these instruments market operations by central banks. The volume of Islamic money market instruments is relatively secondary to operations by central banks. While some of these instruments are negotiable in secondary markets, IBs hold the security, complicating price determination and eligibility for resale. Once the volume of these instruments gains a critical mass, overall market liquidity and its management practices will be strengthened.

Since the market is dominated by Mudaraba- or Murabaha-type contracts, investors are exposed to volatile returns and commodity markets, respectively. Islamic money markets, whether involving a concentration of transactions between IBs or special arrangements with conventional banks, suffer from segmentation. Development of Islamic money markets on a cross-border basis has been further constrained by the differing interpretations of Shariah rulings on financial matters. Multiple contract requirements to structure issuance of Islamic securities, their Shariah endorsement, and tax rulings increase the cost of issuance of Islamic securities compared to conventional issues. A lack of clarity regarding the arrangements for, or the complete absence of an effective lender of last resort facility for IBs in many jurisdictions further complicates matters for IBs, compelling these institutions to maintain a very high level of excess reserves.

Conclusion

The Islamic banking industry has thrived over the last few years. Transformation has been remarkable, moving from an 'embryonic stage' to being an 'emerging force'.[2] This is confirmed by the robust growth in terms of rise in its businesses and proliferation of IF institutions and their spanning off partnerships and strategic alliances.

Islamic banks have demonstrated their resilience and stability supported by Islamic injunctions and ethical principles that nurtured conservatism and prudence and benefitted from confining their strategic alliances to the region. Credit portfolios being essentially domestic and concentrated in the retail sector have served to insulate IBs. The asset quality of IBs is largely intact and higher provisions will cushion non-performing loans. Banks have adequate capital and operate in environments with ample core liquidity.

However, IBs do face wide-ranging industry-specific risks that emanate at the product and transaction levels on both the liabilities and asset sides. A better assessment of the strengths and weaknesses of the Islamic industry requires a better understanding of aggregate transaction level risks at the bank level more effectively. A review of a typical IB balance sheet does confirm that aside from conventional bank risks, IBs face a range of different types of risks associated with underlying assets. These risks are not observed in conventional banks in their straightforward fund-raising and borrowings, whereas IBs' internal safeguards do materially reduce off-balance-sheet exposures. Of concern are however IBs' fiduciary and reputational risks that stem from lack of clarity of risk-sharing arrangements for underlying transactions as well as operational, Shariah-compliant, and liquidity risks.

---

[2] McKinsey & Company: *Navigating Through Troubled Waters* — The World Islamic Banking **Competitiveness Report**, November 2008.

Recognising these risks, IBs have launched efforts to develop a liquidity management framework and to apply different types of risk mitigation approaches.[3] Aside from changes in the design of product structures, to mitigate risks, IBs rely on special purpose vehicles, service and procurement agency contracts, third-party insurance, etc. This helps limit the bank's risk exposure related to assets or trade to clearly define and attribute the institutions risks *vis-à-vis* other parties.

As the crisis unfolded and worsened, it has become quite evident that, like other countries, most of the jurisdiction with a substantial IB presence are indeed affected by the global crisis, some more than others. Growth forecasts for 2009 in these countries have been lowered frequently. Equity market downturns are significant and real estate and properties have taken a hit too. These trends are raising concerns.

Prospects for the industry remain bright because of its edge and niche, though the industry cannot be immune from the scale and magnitude of the unfolding global economic and financial crisis. Unfolding events have taught us that complacency is not advisable when the tidal wave is high. The Islamic banking industry should draw lessons from this crisis. Adoption of the Islamic Financial Service Board (IFSB) prudential regulation and supervision standards now in place is critical. In addition, there is a need to develop standardised legal contracts and products to resolve extreme differences in interpretation that currently stand in the way of achieving harmonisation and setting standards. Furthermore, industry needs to gear itself for the next phase of development by moving from the current focus on replicating the conventional products to product innovation, industry consolidation, and strengthening the operational efficiency. Such steps should augur well for sustaining the growth momentum of the industry.

---

[3] Monetary Authority of Singapore: *Risks and Regulation of Islamic banks: A Perspective from a non-Islamic Jurisdiction.* MAS Staff Paper No. 49, December 2008.

Glossary

Amana	Deposits held at the bank for safekeeping purpose. Capital value guaranteed but earn no return.	Source
Diminishing Musharaka	Diminishing Musharaka is a form of partnership in which one of the partners promises to buy the equity share of the other partner gradually until the title to the equity is completely transferred to the buying partner. The transaction starts with the formation of a partnership, after which buying and selling of the other partner's equity take place at market value or the price agreed upon at the time of entering into the contract. The 'buying and selling' is independent of the partnership contract and should not be stipulated in the partnership contract since the buying partner is only allowed to give only a promise to buy. It is also not permitted that one contract be entered into as a condition for concluding the other.	International Financial Services Board (IFSB), 2008, Technical Note on Strengthening Liquidity Management.
Profit Equalisation Reserve	Profit equalisation reserve (PER) is the amount appropriated by the IIFS out of the Mudaraba income, before allocating the *Mudarib's* share, to maintain a certain level of return on	IFSB, 2008, Technical Note on Strengthening Liquidity Management.

	investment for IAH and to increase owners' equity.	
Gharar	Literally, it means deception, danger, risk, and uncertainty. Technically, it means exposing oneself to excessive risks and danger in a business transaction as a result of uncertainty about the price, the quality, and the quantity of the counter-value, the date of delivery, the ability of either the buyer or the seller to fulfill his or her commitment, or ambiguity of the terms of the deal, thereby exposing either of the two parties to unnecessary risks.	IFSB, 2007, Compilation Guide on Prudential and Structural Islamic Finance Indicators.
Haram	Prohibited	IFSB, 2007, Compilation Guide on Prudential and Structural Islamic Finance Indicators.
Ijara	An Ijara contract refers to an agreement made by IIFS to lease to a customer an asset specified by the customer for an agreed period against specified installments of lease rental. An Ijara contract commences with a promise to lease that is binding on the part of the potential lessee prior to entering the Ijara contract.	IFSB, 2008, Technical Note on Strengthening Liquidity Management.
Ijara *Muntahiyah*	An Ijara *Muntahiyah Bittamlik* (or Ijara *wa Iqtina*) is a form of	IFSB, 2008, Technical

Bittamlik	lease contract that offers the lessee an option to own the asset at the end of the lease period either by purchase of the asset through a token consideration or payment of the market value, or by means of a gift contract.	Note on Strengthening Liquidity Management.
Istisna	An Istisna contract refers to an agreement to sell to a customer a non-existent asset, which is to be manufactured or built according to the buyer's specifications and is to be delivered on a specified future date at a predetermined selling price.	IFSB, 2008, Technical Note on Strengthening Liquidity Management.
Juala (*/Joalah*)	A party pays another a specified amount of money as a fee for rendering a specific service in accordance with the terms of the contract stipulated between the two parties. This mode usually applies to transactions such as consultations and professional services, fund placements, and trust services.	IMF Working Paper, 2008, Islamic Banks and Financial Stability: An Empirical Analysis.
Kafala	*Kafalah* is a contract in which a third party becomes surety that provides guarantee for the payment of debt on behalf of the debtor. It is a pledge given by a third party to a creditor to the effect that if the debtor defaults in payment of the debt, it will be paid by such third party as *Kafeel*, i.e., Surety.	State Bank of Pakistan, IBD Circular No. 02 dated 25 March 2008.

Maysir	The Quranic expression is *maysir* (2:119, 5:90), but the term often used in Islamic law is *qimar*. All activities involving betting for money or property or undue speculation are prohibited in Islamic law. Most juristic discussions focus on defining precisely which activities are unduly speculative and hence unlawful.	The Oxford Dictionary of Islam, available online at www.oxford-islamic-studies.com.
Mudaraba	A Mudaraba is a contract between the capital provider and a skilled entrepreneur whereby the capital provider would contribute capital to an enterprise or activity, which is to be managed by the entrepreneur as the *Mudarib* (or labour provider). Profits generated by that enterprise or activity are shared in accordance with the terms of the Mudaraba agreement whilst losses are to be borne solely by the capital provider unless the losses are due to the *Mudarib's* misconduct, negligence or breach of contracted terms.	IFSB, 2008, Technical Note on Strengthening Liquidity Management.
Murabaha (*/Murabah*)	A Murabaha contract refers to a sale contract whereby the IIFS sells to a customer at an agreed profit margin plus cost (selling price), a specified kind of asset that is already in their possession.	IFSB, 2008, Technical Note on Strengthening Liquidity Management.

Musharaka	A Musharaka is a contract between the IIFS and a customer to contribute capital to an enterprise, whether existing or new, or to ownership of a real estate or moveable asset, either on a temporary or permanent basis. Profits generated by that enterprise or real estate/asset are shared in accordance with the terms of the Musharaka agreement whilst losses are shared in proportion to each partner's share of capital.	IFSB, 2008, Technical Note on Strengthening Liquidity Management.
Mutajara	A placement with the central bank, acting as a fixed-income portfolio for liquidity purposes.	Standard and Poor's, Islamic Finance Outlook 2006.
Qard	*Qard* is a contract of loan between two parties in which the borrower is required to pay back only the principal amount borrowed. The *Qard* shall be repayable on demand.	State Bank of Pakistan, IBD Circular No. 02 dated 25 March 2008.
Qard Al-Hasana	Financing extended without interest or any other compensation from the borrower. The lender expects a reward only from God.	IFSB, 2007, Compilation Guide on Prudential and Structural Islamic Finance Indicators.
Riba	Literally, increase or addition or growth. Technically, it refers to the 'premium' that must be paid	IFSB, 2007, Compilation Guide on

	by the borrower to the lender along with the principal amount as a condition for the loan or an extension in its maturity. Interest as commonly known today is regarded by a predominant majority of *Fuqaha* to be equivalent to *Riba.*	Prudential and Structural Islamic Finance Indicators.
Salam	Refers to an agreement to purchase, at a predetermined price, a specified kind of commodity not available with the seller, which is to be delivered on a specified future date in a specified quantity and quality. Buyers make full payment of the purchase price upon execution of a *Salam* contract. The commodity may or may not be traded over the counter or on an exchange.	IFSB, 2008, Technical Note on Strengthening Liquidity Management.
Shariah	Refers to the *corpus* of Islamic law based on Divine guidance as given by the *Quran* and the *Sunnah,* which embodies all aspects of the Islamic faith, including beliefs and practices.	IFSB, 2007, Compilation Guide on Prudential and Structural Islamic Finance Indicators.
Sukuk	*Sukuk* are certificates that represent the holder's proportionate ownership in an undivided part of an underlying asset, where the holder assumes all rights and obligations to such asset.	IFSB, 2008, Technical Note on Strengthening Liquidity Management.

Takaful	*Takaful* is derived from an Arabic word which means solidarity, whereby a group of participants agree among themselves to support one another jointly against a specified loss. In a Takaful arrangement, the participants contribute a sum of money as *Tabarru* (donation) into a common fund, which will be held as security.	IFSB, 2008, Technical Note on Strengthening Liquidity Management.
Tawarruq	*Tawarruq* literally means to liquidate. In the *fiqhi* term, it is to sell a commodity at spot after its purchase on deferred basis. In practice, *Tawarruq* is an arrangement in which one party sells a commodity to the other party on deferred payment at cost plus profit. The other party, namely, the buyer, then sells the commodity to a third party on cash with a purpose of having access to liquidity.	State Bank of Pakistan, IBD Circular No. 02 dated 25 March 2008.
Wakalah (/*Wikalah*)	*Wakalah* is a contract of agency in which one person appoints another person to perform a certain task on his behalf on agreed terms and conditions, usually against a certain fee. A contract of *Wakalah* can take place only in respect of such acts, which the principal is competent to perform himself, provided such an act can be performed by the agent.	State Bank of Pakistan, IBD Circular No. 02 dated 25 March 2008.

| *Zakat* | The amount payable by a Muslim on his or her net worth as part of his or her religious obligations, mainly for the benefit of the poor and the needy. Paying *Zakat* is an obligatory duty for every adult Muslim, whose wealth exceeds a certain threshold. | IFSB, 2007, Compilation Guide on Prudential and Structural Islamic Finance Indicators. |

ISLAMIC CAPITAL MARKETS: A GROWING AREA FOR INVESTMENTS

Michael Mahlknecht

Introduction

Islamic finance has expanded strongly all over the world during the past few years and is demonstrating significant product innovation and sophistication. This includes a broad range of investment products, which are not limited to the total replication of conventional (i.e., non-Islamic) fixed-income instruments, derivatives, and fund structures. Shariah-compliant products have proven to be attractive also to non-Muslim investors and offer many opportunities even for non-Islamic Institutions. Firstly, this is attributable to the fact that up to 50% of the total savings of the Muslim population worldwide are projected to have been invested in a Shariah-compliant way within the next decade, making it an extremely fast-growing business worldwide. Secondly, the current supply of attractive Islamic products is still far smaller than the existing demand of Islamic banks, insurances ('Takaful') and other Islamic institutions, which further fuels its global market growth. Thirdly, Islamic instruments are highly useful alternative investments for the diversification of portfolios, as they have a low correlation to other market segments, allow the selective underweighting of particular sectors and they seem to be relatively independent even from market turbulences like the Subprime crisis. As a consequence, the increasing standardisation for derivatives and Sukuk (Islamic bonds) as well as the growing liquidity and organisation of the Islamic capital market offer many opportunities to innovative investors.

Islamic Derivatives and Hedging

Islamic finance is based on the prohibition of interest ('Riba'), excessive uncertainty ('Gharar'), and gambling ('Maysir' or 'Qimar'). From these foundations, it is deduced that conventional financial products, such as interest-bearing instruments, options, forwards, futures, and insurances, as well as conventional practices like short-selling and leveraging, cannot be regarded as compliant with Islamic law ('Shariah'). Nevertheless, the Islamic finance industry has made considerable efforts to create products and solutions of the same value, in many instances by replicating conventional structures in a Shariah-compliant manner. This has led to discussions between scholars and practitioners, as some scholars regard specific replication techniques merely as ploys and ruses. While no definite answer can be given yet concerning the question of Shariah compliance for every single instrument, clearly some trends are emerging in this dynamic market. Islamic hedging products are essential for asset management and risk management in any Islamic context, and provide answers to many of the investors' needs.

Current Trends in Standardisation

The high importance of Islamic derivatives and hedging techniques in practice is proven, first, by the fact that the majority of Islamic institutions are actively using them in various ways, and that an increasingly large number of treasury departments are offering Shariah-compliant derivatives and Structured Products to their clients. Secondly, the strong acceptance of these instruments is highlighted by the trend toward their worldwide standardisation, which can be currently observed in the market. One example of this was the creation of Islamic Profit Rate Swaps (IPRS) by the Malaysian CIMB Bank in 2004, which was an Islamic replication of conventional interest-rate swaps (IRS) through an Islamic Swap Master Agreement that mirrored the ISDA Master Agreement for IRS in a fully Shariah-compliant way. In September 2006, the ISDA and the International Islamic Financial Market (IIFM) signed a Memorandum of Understanding as a basis for developing a Master Agreement for over-the-counter (OTC) Shariah-compliant derivatives. This ISDA/IIFM Ta-Hawutt (Hedging) Master Agreement will be based on the ISDA Master, which is being adapted to take account of Shariah requirements with the assistance of the IIFM Council of Shariah Advisors. Key topics of discussion have been compensation provisions, payment and delivery obligations, representations, governing law and arbitration, default and termination events, as well as the provisions on inconsistency and single agreements. With respect to the governing law and arbitration, the group concluded that agreements should be governed by English or NY law (without cross-referencing to Shariah law, since Shariah compliance is regarded as being a starting threshold condition for entering into the relevant transactions), and that parties may choose arbitration, in which case they have to select an arbitration body and a number of arbitrators. Furthermore, each party should be required to represent its satisfaction as to the Shariah compliance of the transaction entered into, without relying on the other party in this context. Ideally, each party should be required to provide evidence of its satisfaction with respect to the issue, such as showing a copy of a relevant fatwa.

Since it turned out to be a particularly complicated issue resolving a Shariah-compliant close-out mechanism across a universal product range, it was proposed to finalise, first, an agreement to cover Murabaha-based transactions and to widen the scope in a following step. One problem here was that the requirements for certainty implicate that the Murabaha transactions must be entered into in succession. In order to bring those future trades into account, the parties must give an undertaking to purchase designated assets at an index-based value, which is analogous to the conventional mark-to-market value, in a very similar way to selling a (physically settled) put option. On a close-out, the unmatured Murabaha transactions are valued, and the party, which is in-the-money with regard to future Murabaha transactions, can require the other party to purchase the assets at a price that amounts to their market value plus the amount that it is in the money.

Innovative Instruments and Methods

Generally speaking, derivatives and hedging mechanisms employed in Islamic finance can be broadly categorised into three groups: standardised hedging products, like the aforementioned 'Ta-Hawutt' Murabaha transactions; accepted traditional Islamic financing modes or methods, such as Salam ('Islamic forward'), Arbun (prepayment, sometimes used to replicate option-type payoffs), and Khiyar (contract options in Islamic law), which can directly be used for hedging in a way similar to derivatives; and, finally, hedging mechanisms frequently used by practitioners that make free use of combinations of Shariah-compliant contracts in a way sometimes criticised by Islamic scholars. It should be noted that the latter two categories also form the basis for future product standardisation.

Taking a closer look at the last category above, i.e., hedging mechanisms created by practitioners, these usually draw on well-known vanilla instruments like Salam, Arbun, Ijara, Qard, Murabaha, as well as unilateral binding promises (Wad). For instance, swap transactions can be easily arranged by combining cash and Murabaha-based commodity trades, or through the exchange of Qard (benevolent loans). Foreign exchange risks can be hedged, for instance, using Murabaha-based platinum trades, or through Wad promises.

Potentially, also other conventional instruments can be mimicked in a Shariah-compliant way. For instance, standard forward contracts can be totally replicated using Salam, Murabaha, and cash trades. This can be proven by imagining four parties: the party with the forward long position ('F-long'), the short forward party ('F-short'), a third party undertaking Murabaha transactions in an asset X independent from the intended forward ('Mur'), and a fourth one undertaking cash transactions in that asset ('Cash').

F-long is long a Salam on the desired asset with F-short and long a Murabaha on X with Mur, and sells X in a cash transaction to Cash. As a result of that, his net position on exchanged assets and money in the present is zero, while, at maturity, he receives the desired asset from F-short and pays the price (to Mur) — just as in a conventional forward contract. The same is true for F-short: This party receives and pays nothing at the start of the transactions; while at maturity it delivers the relevant asset to F-long and receives the money for it (from Mur). Again, this result is 1:1 equivalent to a typical forward short position. The third party, Mur, is simultaneously conducting two Murabaha trades on the same asset X (which can be chosen arbitrarily) with the same mark-up and price, which results in zero loss or gains. Party Cash, finally, purchases the asset X from F-long and sells it on at the same price to F-short on cash. All transactions undertaken by Mur and Cash are merely auxiliary services for F-long and F-short and may therefore imply some amount of fees. In a similar manner, forward contracts may also be replicated through Istisna or Joala contracts.

In conventional finance, futures contracts complement forwards to reduce the counterparty risks. However, standard futures contracts are usually deemed not Shariah-compliant. Besides the obvious derivative-type aspect, this is mostly owing to the fact that futures are priced mark-to-market (MtM) and require regular margin calls from out-of-the-money parties, without any real transfer of the underlying asset. A Shariah-compliant variant could be to marginally adjust periodic repayment amounts within a real Shariah-compliant contract like Ijara, linked to changes in the value of the underlying asset. By this, even though no true replication of standard futures would be attained, forward positions can be made possible, which help in limiting an investor's exposure to counterparty risks.

By making use of Islamic forwards and call options (Arbun), also put option-like positions might be derived in a fully Shariah-compliant way, thanks to standard put-call parity: $F = C - P$. In case that Islamic sufficient call options are not available (e.g., due to limited standardisation of derivatives, or to a restricted permissibility of Arbun-based transactions), the same payoff profiles as for calls and puts may be replicated through dynamic trading of the underlying asset. In practice, however, this may be complicated by a lack of tradable Islamic instruments in the market, the fact that no Gamma or Vega trading will be feasible, and that transaction costs for such a strategy are usually high.

On the other hand, as explained above, employing *de facto* Islamic derivative structures in practice is an important prerequisite for a later acceptance and standardisation of the Islamically replicated instruments. Shariah scholars and jurists may hence be convinced to allow some derivatives usage, and a subsequent standardisation of the instruments helps in significantly lowering the transaction costs. In fact, a survey conducted by Delta Hedge among 34 financial institutions in EMEA and Asia between

June and July 2008 shows that more than half of the participating companies regard a further standardisation of Islamic derivatives as very important, and more than 1 out of 3 interviewed experts as important.

Islamic Structured Products

There has been some demand from investors for Shariah-compliant-Structured Products over the past few years. Islamic Structured Products are being sold mostly OTC, while there is still a low level of liquidity on the DIFX TraX, where both conventional and Islamic Structured Products can be traded. It is worth mentioning that Islamic Structured Products are not solely attractive to Islamic investors, as they are potentially appealing also to conventional investors worldwide. As the results of the recent 'Global Structured Products Survey' conducted by Delta Hedge show, 63.5% of the interviewed 143 financial institutions from 29 countries stated that Structured Products will become more multifaceted, explicitly mentioning Islamic products as an increasingly interesting segment.

Islamic Replication of Conventional Certificates

There are various ways to structure such instruments in a Shariah-compliant way. One possibility is to use roll-over Murabaha contracts, the mark-ups of which are being fixed depending on the previous performance of defined benchmarks or market rates. It is well-known that the mark-up in Murabaha contracts can be freely set depending on benchmark market rates also derived from non-Islamic markets. The most common example for such a benchmark rate is certainly the London Interbank Offered Rate (LIBOR), which is frequently being used for this purpose. However, the use of benchmark rates from conventional finance is not limited to

LIBOR. It is equally possible to link a Murabaha mark-up to quite different benchmarks, as long as the Shariah requirements on Murabaha are fulfilled.

A broad range of conventional Structured Products can be readily replicated in this manner, including, but not limited to currency range accruals, interest rate range accruals, commodities range accruals, and capital-protected investments linked to equity indices. A cutting-edge application, for instance, could be a 2-year Shariah-compliant currency wedding cake, which combines the following Murabaha transactions: first, one Murabaha commodity trade (with 3 months maturity), with mark-up LIBOR + ×% p.a.; and afterwards, 7 commodity trades (each one for 3 months again) for each trade being based on the USD/EUR rate remaining within one of the predefined currency ranges (wide/middle/narrow) for that whole time.

Other structuring techniques rely on standard mechanisms used for conventional products, and simply 'Islamise' them. For instance, many types of Structured Products can be implemented by relying on the conventional bond + call strategy, using Murabaha contracts (instead of zero-coupon bonds) and Arbun (instead of conventional financial options). In a similar way to bond + call strategies, capital-guaranteed investments can be structured using Constant Proportion Portfolio Insurance (CPPI) techniques. Thereby, many types of capital-guaranteed funds linked to Equity markets, as well as sophisticated Structured Products like Stellars can readily be accessed in a Shariah-compliant form.

A relatively recent innovation is the extensive use of Wad (promises) for structuring Islamic products. Wad might be used for the creation of FX forward instruments and of Shariah-compliant total return swaps. These total return swaps can be used to create complex Structured Products, whose payoff may be linked even to non-Islamic assets. In practice, a Wad-based total return swap assumes a fully Shariah-compliant asset pool, where Islamic investors can invest their money. However, the investors promise (Wad) the issuer to sell their shares in this Shariah-compliant asset pool to the issuer at maturity for a price that will be calculated depending on the achieved performance of another instrument (or pool of instruments) during the product's lifetime. At the same time, the issuer promises the investors to purchase all their shares from the Shariah-compliant asset pool at that exact price at maturity. Although this economically equals a Total Return Swap to be executed at maturity, the two promises are formally independent from each other (unilateral promises) and are thus binding from the Shariah point of view. The price calculation (i.e., the final payoff at maturity) can depend on the performance of any asset whatsoever, explicitly including non-Islamic instruments (or pool of instruments), such as hedge funds.

Note, however, that this does not mean in practice that Islamic product development is really totally independent from Shariah. First, Shariah compliance may not be looked at only from a formal point of view, but at a product level it can equally be relevant to judge the compliance of a product in substance. Second, issuers of complex products usually have to hedge these in order to manage their own risks arising from those products, and hedging possibilities may be significantly limited for Islamic financial institutions due to the ethical constraints in Islamic finance.

At last, it is questionable whether an excessively free use of Wad will be accepted by all Islamic scholars or Islamic customers in the future. For instance, retail customers may be sceptical towards such instruments, as the author has found out talking with Muslim organisations in various EMEA countries. When such formally compliant structures are regarded as ploys or ruses, this could furthermore entail potentially significant reputation risks for the respective institution and for the Islamic financial industry in general.

Islamic scholars, on the other hand, can bring forward various arguments against the "Shariah conversion technology" represented by the Islamic TRS. One is by making recourse to the concept of 'Sadd Al-Dharai', which is the instrument in Islamic jurisprudence that blocks ostensibly legitimate means when these are employed for illegitimate ends.

Another criticism could be that those Shariah scholars, who have approved such products, failed to consider the purpose of the transaction, the movement of the cash and, most importantly, the ramifications for the Islamic financial industry as a whole. The reason for these failings, from this point of view, would be that those scholars had not discerned the difference between using the Libor as a benchmark for pricing and using non-Shariah-compliant assets as a determinant for returns. By means of Islamic total return swaps, the investor actually participates in the non-Shariah-compliant investments, however indirectly, and the money paid will most certainly be used to finance those other investments. The attempt to draw a legal analogy (Qiyas) between the use of Libor for pricing and the use of the performance of non-Shariah-compliant assets for pricing could therefore be regarded as inaccurate and misleading. From such a perspective, there would be no need to resort to Sadd Al-Dharai, since the transaction would be prohibited outright.

Moving Forward: Structured Products Based on Khiyar

Islamic law offers other, more specific possibilities to structure a variety of products, which have not been fully exploited thus far. This is especially true for embedded contract options, which are standard elements of Islamic sales contracts, such as Khiyar Al-Tayeen and Khiyar Al-Shart. Khiyar Al-Tayeen implies the option to choose an object of sale out of multiple varieties of a given article, while Khiyar Al-Shart is a stipulation that any of the parties has the option to rescind the sale within a predefined period. Whilst Rainbow options are usually not considered to be Shariah-compliant, Khiyar Al-Tayeen gives the investor the right to choose the best-performing investment alternative (*ex post*), and to the seller the right to sell the worst-performing asset at maturity. In the easiest application, an issuer may simply hold two portfolios (which, for the purpose of contracts entailing Khiyar Al-Tayeen, may be viewed as similar base portfolios to choose from) and sell both a best-of and a worst-of-type Structured Product to its clients. In more complex cases, splitting up an institution's investments in various assets into products with differing, customer-oriented risk/return profiles can involve complex hedging mechanisms, or even the need to hold a certain part of the associated risks with the issuing company itself. Such structures can allow investors, for instance, to choose *ex post* between a combined Equity/Commodity market portfolio (weighted 70:30), and another one, weighted 30:70.

An especially interesting application of Khiyar Al-Shart is the so-called Istijrar mechanism, which to date has mostly been used for project financing. It enables, for instance, a financial institution and an investor to fix a certain (average) price for a forward trans-action, provided that no upper and lower price barrier is being exceeded by the underlying asset. If one of these thresholds has been broken, the parties can choose to exercise their options. In that case, another pre-defined settlement price is used to settle the contract, allowing an investor to choose between the average price and a provisional (predefined) price and to effectively guard himself against extreme volatilities. Thus, Istijrar contains an interesting combination of implicit Asian and Barrier options, which make it an attractive tool for a flexible and efficient fund management, as well as for the design of innovative Structured Products.

Islamic Structured Products are still a relatively recent product innovation, which will certainly be further developed within the next few months and years. Nevertheless, as the results of the survey conducted by Delta Hedge show, already today a significant number of market players regard the future standardisation as important (41.2%), or even as very important (32.4%) for the industry.

Islamic Bonds: Sukuk Certificates

A Low-Correlation Asset Class

Though comparatively young, the market for Sukuk certificates is growing worldwide at a fast pace. Sukuk are often thought to be an Islamic equivalent of conventional bonds, constructed in a way similar to asset-backed securities (ABS). In contrast to bonds, they represent ownership stakes in existing or well-defined Shariah-compliant assets. While this view captures many important characteristics of Sukuk, it is important to understand the specifics of these instruments, and how Sukuk are viewed (and often criticised) by Islamic scholars. At the beginning of 2008, statements issued by the standard-setting Accounting and Auditing Organisation for Islamic Financial Institutions (AAOIFI) and by members of its Shariah board about the noncompliance of most existing Sukuk structures seemed to bring into question the acceptance of Sukuk by the investment community. Furthermore, the Subprime crisis seemed to affect all major segments of the international financial markets, and it could in fact be observed that Sukuk issuance significantly slumped in 2008 compared to 2007.

However, a comparison of Sukuk market data with traditional bonds shows firstly that the relative performance of Sukuk against conventional bonds has been positive over the past few years. For example, the HSBC/DIFX US Dollar Sukuk Index, which consists of USD/GBP/JPY/EUR-denominated fixed- or floating-rate vanilla Sukuk, has generally outperformed bond indices, such as the Barclays Capital Aggregate Bond Index (formerly, Lehman Aggregate Bond Index), since its inception at the end of 2004. During this period, Sukuk have been exhibiting very low volatility and correlation to global fixed-income, equity, and alternative market indices. Secondly, it is equally true that Sukuk are gaining a market share worldwide. While in 2005, Sukuk issuance in the Middle-East and North Africa (MENA) amounted only to approximately 10% of conventional bonds in this region, this number rose to 50% in 2007 and almost 70% in 2008. In Malaysia, the world's largest domestic Sukuk market, such numbers have already been achieved in previous years, with the Sukuk issuance reaching 250% of bonds issuance in 2005. The development of the Sukuk market also seems to be relatively stable and independent from the Subprime turbulences: in the second half of 2007, sales of Sukuk increased 27% to 10 billion USD, in contrast to US corporate debt, where sales slumped by 200 billion USD in the same period.

The Sukuk market has grown more than 15-fold in the space of 10 years, and it is expected that this favourable trend is going to persist. Latest news in the global Islamic capital market include the issue of the first Japanese Sukuk by Mizuho Corporate Bank, while the governments of Japan and the United Kingdom are consulting on the issuance of sovereign Sukuk, and the South-Asian financial hub Singapore is developing a facility to make Sovereign-rated Sukuk available to investors. Various Islamic markets (especially Dubai, Bahrain, and Malaysia) have aspirations to become global or, at least, regional centres of Islamic finance, while London is equally active in this field. Also the Third Market in Vienna does enable trading of a first Sukuk certificate, which has been issued by a US-based company.

Structural Trends: The Path Toward Standardisation

The criticism made by the AAOIFI with regard to Sukuk, on the other hand, does not appear to have any detrimental influence on the development of the international market for these instruments. In a paper released in February 2008, Sheikh Muhammad Taqi Usmani, president of the AAOIFI Shariah Council, questioned various mechanisms commonly employed in Sukuk structures, which have the purpose to distinguish Islamic Sukuk with the same characteristics as conventional bonds, such as regular distributions to the holders of the instruments, and as guaranteeing the return of principal at maturity. He found that these mechanisms did not conform to Islamic law, specifically referring to two Equity-linked types of Sukuk that began to gain importance in 2006: Sukuk based on Musharaka (i.e., 'Islamic partnership/joint venture'), and Sukuk based on Mudaraba (trust) transactions.

The AAOIFI decision, which followed Mr. Usmani's paper, however, impacts on neither existing Sukuk nor plain-vanilla Sukuk structures based on Ijara (i.e., the Islamic form of leasing), which were the most popular on the market for several years. Therefore, as the results of the survey conducted by Delta Hedge show, about 3 out of 5 analysts accept the AAOIFI's statement as a step toward increased standardisation, leading to the use of Ijara for fixed-income-type Sukuk certificates, and of Mudaraba and Musharaka for Equity-linked securities. It should be noted that the AAOIFI defines 14 types of Sukuk, the main ones being based on Ijara, Salam (deferred commodity delivery), Istisna (manufacturing or project finance), Mudaraba, Musharaka, and on Murabaha. Furthermore, there are variations such as hybrid Sukuk, which are based on different Islamic financing modes, and convertible Sukuk, which are convertible into equity. Sukuk certificates are thus extremely flexible from a structural point of view and can deliver manifold risk/return profiles to their investors. Sukuk shares can be readily employed both in fund management and as structural components in the design of Islamic Structured Products.

Islamic Fund Management

Outperforming the Conventional Indices

Shariah-compliant investing has sometimes been perceived as systematically underperforming the conventional investment market. Empirical research, however, proves that this is certainly not the case. Islamic investing is surely not the 'poorer cousin' of its conventional counterpart. If one compares, for instance, the FTSE Global Islamic Index with the conventional FTSE All-World Index, it can be discovered that the index values moved in an almost fully parallel way between the establishment of the Islamic index variant in 1994 and the year 2005. The Islamic index values exhibited only a slightly higher standard deviation (18%, compared to 16% of the conventional index) and higher index values in the time between 1996 and 2001. After the emergence of the Subprime crisis, Islamic indices have even clearly outperformed conventional indexes. Good examples for this are the Shariah-compliant versions of the renowned indices MSCI World, MSCI USA, and MSCI Emerging Markets, which have outperformed their conventional counterparts by almost 10% on average in May 2007. The same trend could be observed for other indices, e.g., the Dow Jones Islamic World Developed Index, since mid-2007.

This striking degree of outperformance is largely due to the fact that almost all companies from the financial services sector are excluded from Islamic indices. In fact, about 98% of financial institutions are usually left out of the indices due to the prohibition of Riba. Furthermore, 3 out of 4 companies from the consumer goods sector are typically deleted from the indices, while on average only 1 out of 5 companies from other industries is being considered not to be Shariah-compliant. Islamic investments, thus, cannot only be considered as ethical investments, but are also valuable to investors who want to underweight, for instance, the financial sector in their portfolios. Moreover, Shariah-compliant filter criteria result in a clear preference for enterprises with very low levels of debt/low debt-to-market capitalisation ratios.

New Types of Islamic Funds

It should be noted that there is a variety of Islamic fund types that are accessible to investors. Besides vanilla investment funds (which permit investment in Shariah-compliant equities, Sukuk, Islamic

Structured Products, and so forth), there is also an increasing supply of Islamic hedge funds, a nascent venture capital and private equity industry, and a new generation of Islamic REITs. Islamic private equity is still a largely untapped asset class, but private equity investments in MENA have risen from a mere US$316 million in 2004 to US$5.19 billion in 2006, with an increasing part structured under Islamic supervision. This boost comes as no surprise, as Islamic finance is strongly geared toward real-economy, equity investments, which can be effectively performed through the traditional financing modes Mudaraba and Musharaka. The viability of Islamic REITS is complicated owing to Shariah precepts that restrict the investment universe. However, at the end of 2005 the Securities Commission in Malaysia issued guidelines for Islamic REITS, which led to the first launch of Islamic REITs in 2006. According to these criteria, Islamic REITs have access to a wide range of permissible investments, ranging from real estate to real estate-related assets, Islamic ABS, Shariah-compliant liquid assets, as well as the investment in private companies whose principal assets comprise real estate. Currently, the first Islamic REIT investing entirely on shopping malls in China is being issued. Keeping in mind that pork — which is forbidden in Islam — is a traditional ingredient of the Chinese cuisine, and that the pig is a cultural symbol for prosperity in much of China, this shows how flexible Islamic REITs can be and, thus, appealing also to non-Islamic investors.

A True Islamic Shorting Approach

The issue of Islamic hedge funds practices deserves special attention, as techniques like leveraging and short-selling, which are central to many conventional hedge fund concepts, are not Shariah-compliant. Nevertheless, more and more Islamic institutions and hedge funds claim to offer Shariah-compliant shorting solutions, which are often presented as if they represent a major breakthrough for Islamic finance. In reality, basically every contract can be 'Islamised' using concepts from modern financial engineering; the question is rather how high the transaction costs are and whether the investment community regards such mechanics as Shariah-compliant or as just an undesirable ploy.

Furthermore, typical strategies for 'Islamic shorting' rely on standard Islamic instruments like Salam and Arbun. While both enable to cash in on declining markets, none of them is equivalent to conventional shorting, since they do not truly entail borrowing an asset from another investor. A genuine replication of shorting can be attained using binding unilateral promises (Wad) in combination with Murabaha (deferred-payment) transactions. For this purpose, party A first purchases an asset from party B through a Murabaha (for the Murabaha price X) and then sells it on to another party for the spot market price. In addition to that, party B gives a unilateral promise to party A to buy back the asset at some future date at a pre-agreed price Y. Conversely, party A promises to sell the asset to party B at that date for that price Y.

Such a combination of two (unilateral) promises is equivalent to a forward position on the asset. Now, if the price Y is set equal to the Murabaha price X, the combined payoff of the Murabaha transaction and the forward position at maturity is zero. Only the 'borrowed' asset is 'given back' (which party A must purchase on the market, at some indefinite future date before, or at maturity), making the whole structure an exact Islamic replication of short-selling. In practice, the forward price Y agreed on, would be lower than the Murabaha price X to create an incentive for the counterparty, and to realistically account for expected dividend yields, brokerage fees, and other borrowing costs.

As for conventional short-selling, with such an approach, important issues have to be considered. For instance, if the Murabaha (and the forward repurchase through Wad) is carried out with the owner of the asset directly, it is necessary that this party is holding a sufficient amount of the required asset, and that it does not want to retain flexibility with regard to the time when it sells its assets in the future (as the transaction is fixed-term for the borrower). In this case, Wakala fees would have to be paid by the shorting party to its broker, who has arranged the transactions on behalf of this party. If, however, the Murabaha (and the forward repurchase through Wad) takes place with the shorting party's prime-broker (who does not own the asset himself), the broker himself must get into transactions with one of his other clients, who owns a sufficient amount of the needed asset. In that case, the remuneration for the broker would increase and be the difference between price X and price Y. Such an approach requires extremely careful structuring, in order for the broker to avoid undesirable market risks. If all parts of the structure (the Murabaha transaction, as well as the Wad promises) are conducted with merely one counterparty, the whole process may be regarded as constructing a dummy transaction with the only purpose being to enable Shariah-non-compliant short-selling. Lastly, the fact that this kind of Wad-based short-selling solution is fixed-term for the lending party may increase transaction costs and shorten the length of the transaction, compared to conventional short-selling mechanisms. An important advantage of such an approach is that procedural complexity is left with the prime-broker, while fund managers do not have to care about formal requirements. Hereby, experienced conventional fund managers can easily be mandated to manage Islamic funds, without being familiar with the specifics of Salam or Arbun contracts.

Quantitative Issues

An efficient pricing of Islamic instruments and the quantification of risks are associated with increased complexities compared to a standard products pricing, hedging, and risk management. This is caused, firstly, by the higher transaction costs that arise in many cases where conventional products are replicated to ensure

Shariah compliance. These transaction costs need to be considered explicitly in pricing and in hedging methods, as well as for the purpose of precise potential loss analyses in risk management. Secondly, Islamic capital market instruments are often structured and complex by their very nature, which create major challenges for software systems. Thirdly, Islamic finance carries several intrinsic risks, which differ from conventional finance in many aspects, including, but not limited to, specific operational risks (Shariah-compliant risk), business risks, commodity and inventory price risks, mark-up risks, liquidity risks, and counterparty credit risks. Fourthly, a realistic risk assessment is often methodologically difficult to achieve owing to patchy data and missing time-series for many Islamic market segments.

Transaction costs are obviously of special relevance for the analysis of complex Islamic products, such as Sukuk, Structured Products, and derivatives that have been replicated in a Shariah-compliant way at the price of high transaction costs. Whilst in some cases, standard models can be easily extended to account for these transaction costs, often extensive simulations will have to be performed. As such tasks can be computationally very intensive, high-performance software systems should be employed for this purpose. A high performance and flexibility of systems should also be imperative due to the fact that Islamic products are often structured by their very nature. For such instruments, each single structural component has to be carefully analysed on its own, as well as concerning their interdependency with other constituents of the structure. Hereby, all risks associated with a given product can be discovered and explicitly be modelled.

In general, mark-up risks affect all kinds of structures containing Murabaha, Ijara, and Istisna contracts, while commodity risks are present in Murabaha, Salam, and Istisna contracts, and business risks exist in Mudaraba and Musharaka contracts. Counterparty risks, liquidity risks, as well as FX risks (which arise in Islamic instruments in a mostly analogous way compared to conventional products) can be expected to exist in any type of structure. Furthermore, the risk of second-guessed Shariah compliance *ex post* can lead to financial losses, caused by the uncertain outcome in a Shariah court and an insufficient legal enforceability, as well as to diminishing liquidity of the relevant transaction due to lacking acceptance of the product in the market. It is thus an operational risk type specific to Islamic instruments. All these risks have to be analysed in detail, since they can adversely affect the individual types of instruments in quite different ways.

Finally, risk assessment methodologies have to be fine-tuned to account for the peculiarities of Islamic financial instruments and for the specific data situation. This is equally true for the estimation of input parameters, such as volatilities and correlations, or default probabilities and expected losses. For instance, to establish credit rating estimates, it is often not possible to simply apply standard logit or probit regression techniques; owing to incomplete historical data, or structural models, the viability of which requires the existence of liquid public equity markets. A stochastic financial modelling of firm values, based on a Monte–Carlo simulation of relevant value drivers, can help in solving this problem. Analogously, an adequate risk modelling of Islamic hedge funds must consider the trading specifics of these funds, such as Islamic shorting techniques, and may be limited in regard to style-based risk analysis. It is, in any case, absolutely necessary to define all Islamic instrument details in pricing and risk analysis systems, as rough approximations (e.g., using conventional methods) can heavily distort results and be very dangerous and harmful.

Outlook

The Islamic financial industry offers a broad range of attractive investment opportunities that are suitable also for conventional investor portfolios. Major strengths are a high stability of markets, a low degree of correlation with traditional and alternative investments, and an increasingly sophisticated range of standard and tailor-made financial solutions. Conventional products and techniques, such as short-selling, Structured Products and funds, can be replicated in a Shariah-compliant way, while Islamic specifics like contract optionalities and equity financing modes are highly flexible to create new investment opportunities in Asia, MENA, and other regions worldwide.

Standardisation is rapidly evolving for derivatives, hedging and *de facto* for Islamic bonds (Sukuk), and it may soon also include Structured Products and relevant fund management practices. Whilst more and more products are being created for the purpose of risk management, it must be emphasised that Islamic finance carries specific risks largely due to the real transactions taking place as its foundations. As a consequence, credit risks, market risks, operational risks, and specific counterparty risks have to be analysed in detail when planning investments in Islamic products.

SHORT-SELLING REPLICATION IN ISLAMIC FINANCE: INNOVATION AND DEBATE IN MALAYSIA AND BEYOND

Ryan Calder[1,2]

Introduction

The short-selling of stocks has long been considered impossible in Islamic finance. This chapter begins by reviewing why. It then moves on to the search to develop Islamic alternatives to conventional short-selling. Several systems have recently come on the market that aim to replicate short-selling in Shariah-compliant ways. This includes one being developed by Bursa Malaysia and the Malaysia Securities

---

[1] Please address correspondence to Ryan Calder at *rcalder@berkeley.edu*.

[2] Author's Note: I thank the following people for their time, advice, and support: Maia Sieverding, Dato Dr. Nik Norzrul Thani, Dr. Aida Othman, Dr. Megat Hizaini Hassan, Zalina Ahmad Ramli, Dr. Angelo Venardos, Juliet Lee, Asharul Huzairi Mohd. Mansor, Prof. Dr. Engku Rabiah Adawiah Engku Ali, Roslan Abdul Razak, Prof. Dr. Mohammad Hashim Kamali, Dr. Mercy Kuo, Dr. Md. Nurdin Ngadimon, Zainol bin Ali, Bindesh P. Shah, and the staff of the IBFIM Knowledge Management Centre in Kuala Lumpur. All errors are mine alone.

Commission that replicates stock borrowing and lending using Wad
(unilateral promise). Other industry players have endorsed short-
sale replication systems that use the Salam contract, the Arbun
contract, or Wad in a different way. Hedge funds and other institutional investors seeking to be Shariah-compliant are keen to adopt
an Islamic alternative to short-selling, but each method has advantages and disadvantages, with its proponents and detractors. This
chapter guides the reader through different structures Islamic
institutions are using to replicate short-selling, the state of the
nascent market for short-sale replication, and the outlook for the
future.

What Is Short-Selling?

Investors engage in short-selling in order to turn a profit from a
decline in the price of a security. In a conventional short sale, an
investor (with the help of a prime broker) will borrow a security
from someone else, sell it immediately, wait until the price of the
security goes down, buy the security back from the market, and then
return it to the lender. This allows the investor to earn a profit on
the security's decline in price.

United States law defines a short sale as the "sale of a security
which the seller does not own or any sale which is consummated by
the delivery of a security borrowed by, or for the account of, the
seller" (United States C.F.R. 2009). Short-selling, also known as
"shorting" or "going short", is thus the opposite of "going long", which
is simply the act of buying and holding a security in the expectation
that its price will increase.

Who Engages in Short-Selling, and Why?

People engage in short-selling for various reasons. Some people short-
sell a security because they expect its price to fall. The simplest reasons

to expect a price drop are because a company appears overvalued or market conditions are worsening. Alternatively, investors may expect a share-price decline because they anticipate imminent merger or acquisition activity. This leads them to use short-selling in a practice known as merger arbitrage ("merge-arb" for short). In merger arbitrage, an arbitrageur will buy the target company's stock after the terms of an acquisition are announced in the assumption that it will rise when the acquisition is completed. The arbitrageur simultaneously shorts the acquirer's stock, which he expects to fall because the acquirer will issue its own shares to exchange for the target's shares, diluting the acquirer's shares.

However, betting against one company's securities is often not the rationale behind short-selling. A large portion of short-sellers are in fact employing strategies not predicated on a particular outlook for the company whose securities they are shorting (Clunie and Ying 2006:6). Instead, they seek to take advantage of relative movements between different securities. For example, in a market-neutral strategy, a portfolio manager takes both long and short positions on securities expected to behave similarly so as to reduce the volatility in his or her portfolio while exploiting market inefficiencies. In convertible arbitrage, a buyer of convertible bonds hedges his position by shorting the underlying security. In index arbitrage, a trader might buy the index while shorting the individual stocks that compose it, again exploiting minor market inefficiencies. Likewise, an investor practicing index futures arbitrage or index options arbitrage might go long in index futures or index options respectively while shorting the individual stocks that make up the index — a strategy driven by deviations in futures and options prices from their theoretical values (Fung and Fung 1997; Lo and MacKinlay 2001:347–368). These types of approaches are usually not based on the expectation that one particular stock is overvalued; they instead seek to take advantage of exposure to the price

movements of related securities. Hedge funds are avid practitioners of such strategies.

Problems with Conventional Short-Selling as Viewed
from the Islamic Perspective

People have long maintained that the short-selling of stocks is unacceptable in Islamic finance (Khan 1983:95; Zaky 1992:81; Zaher and
M. Kabir Hassan 2001:191; Archer and Karim 2002:22; Al-Alwani
2005:151; Venardos 2006:43; Iqbal and Mirakhor 2007:176; Ayub
2007:75; Schoon 2009:23–28). Those who argue that Islamic finance
is fundamentally more conservative than conventional finance often
cite the ban on short-selling as an example of this guarded approach.
So why is the short-selling of stocks Haram? Here, I review some of
the Islamic objections to conventional short-selling.

Selling an Item Without Owning It

First, many Shariah scholars frown on selling an item before it is
owned. One of the most frequently cited Ahadith[3] in Islamic commercial jurisprudence (Fiqh Al-muamalat) reads:

لا تبع ما ليس عندك

Lā tabiᶜ mā laysa ᶜindaka

"Do not sell what is not with you" or "Do not sell what you do not have"
or "Do not sell what you do not own" (depending on translation).

This Hadith would seem to make a *prima facie* case against short-
selling, since a short-seller sells a security that she has borrowed but
does not own.

---

[3] Ahadith is the plural of Hadith.

Case closed? It depends whom you ask. Mohammad Hashim Kamali, for example, has noted (in a context unrelated to short-selling[4]) that issues have been raised regarding this Hadith (Kamali 2000:110–116). There may be weakness in its authenticity: it appears in the collections of Abu Daud and Al-Tirmidhi, but not in those of Al-Bukhari and Muslim Ibn Al-Hajjaj (ibid.: 110). Even scholars who acknowledge the Hadith as authentic disagree as to its exact chain of transmission (*Isnad*) (ibid.: 110, 111). Moreover, Kamali asserts that there is "room for interpretation regarding the precise legal value" of this Hadith: he feels it may not be entirely clear "whether it conveys a total ban (*Tahrim*), or abomination (*Karahiyyah*), or even mere guidance and advice of no legal import" (ibid.: 111).

Let us assume, however, that we accept this Hadith as both authentic and binding. The issue of interpretation then arises: What exactly does this Hadith mean? *Fuqaha* (scholars of Islamic jurisprudence) have debated this for centuries.

The Arabic preposition *inda*, which appears in this Hadith, is one of the sources of ambiguity. One of the most common words in the Arabic language, *inda* can refer in different contexts to "having" in the most general sense, or to ownership, or possession, or access, or proximity in time or place.[5] As a result, scholars have disagreed for centuries about what exactly this Hadith prohibits.

Its simplest interpretation, adopted by many *fuqaha* past and present, is that a seller must own an item outright when she sells it.[6] Along the same lines, the Shariah board of the Accounting and Auditing Organization for Islamic Financial Institutions (AAOIFI)

---

[4] It is important to note that Kamali's discussion of this Hadith was part of a book arguing that commodity futures and commodity options should be considered Halal, and was not part of a discussion about the short-selling of securities. Kamali does not discuss the short-selling of securities in the book.

[5] Karin C. Ryding summarises the meanings of inda in her excellent book *A Reference Grammar of Modern Standard Arabic* (Ryding 2005:399, 400). She also notes that inda is actually not a true Arabic preposition but rather a "semi-preposition".

[6] For a good summary of the positions of classical scholars from different schools of jurisprudence on this question, see Al-Islambuli (2005).

has ruled explicitly that "it is not permitted to sell shares that the seller does not own", adding that "the promise of a broker to lend these at the time of delivery is of no consequence". AAOIFI's rationale is that "the sale of something that is not within the liability of the seller nor in his ownership" is "prohibited according to the Shari'a" (AAOIFI 2007b:390).

However, other *Fuqaha* have taken a more liberal stance, arguing that certain types of objects may be sold before ownership is established. Imam Al-Shafii (150 A.H.–204 A.H./767 C.E.–820 C.E.), who founded the Shafii *madhhab* (school of jurisprudence) that is dominant today in Southeast Asia, maintained that "one may sell what is not with one provided that it is not a specific object, for the delivery of a specific object cannot be guaranteed if the seller does not own it" (Al-Shafii 1940:337; in Kamali 2000:113). Following this line of reasoning, it would be unacceptable to sell a house or a piece of land without owning it, because those are unique objects with highly specific attributes; but it might be acceptable to sell a unit of a highly fungible commodity, such as a bushel of a particular kind of wheat, that could be replaced with an identical quantity of the same good to facilitate future delivery.

Ibn Taymiyah (661 A.H.–728 A.H./1263 C.E.–1328 C.E.) and Ibn Qayyim Al-Jawziyah (691 A.H.–751 A.H./1292 C.E.–1350 C.E.), both of the Hanbali school, also take a liberal perspective on this question, though a slightly different one. They argue that this Hadith prohibits "the sale of what is not present and which the seller is unable to deliver" (Kamali 2000:113, 114). Like Imam Al-Shafii, they emphasise the ability of the seller to say confidently that she will be able to present the item at the agreed future date of delivery.[7]

---

[7] Following the perspective of Ibn Taymiyah and Ibn Qayyim Al-Jawziyah, the *Salam* contract — which many jurists view as an *exception* to the rule that "one may not sell what one does not have" — is in fact not an exception, but rather an *extension of the same underlying logic*: that of seeking to ensure that the seller will be able to present the good as promised at the agreed future date of delivery. (I thank Prof. Dr. Engku Rabiah Adawiah Engku Ali for bringing this to my attention.)

The upshot is that one *might* find it acceptable to sell shares without owning them depending on (a) which schools of jurisprudence one adheres to and which jurists' opinions one finds most compelling, (b) whether one considers shares to be fungible commodities, and (c) whether the sale of shares without owning them does not run afoul of other injunctions, such as the ban on dealing in Riba (this would clearly contravene the sale of shares in conventional banks, for example).

Stock Borrowing and Lending (SBL)

Aside from the issue of selling something that one does not own, the short-selling of stocks as practiced in conventional finance is potentially problematic for a second reason: many Shariah scholars consider it impermissible to borrow and lend shares.

Different scholars take different views on what kind of good may be the subject of a loan contract. Many jurists feel that "a loan contract can be validly concluded with regard to every property on which Salam is valid" (although some scholars, especially from the Hanafi Madhhab, take a more restrictive view) (Dusuki 2008:206).

A Salam contract, or forward-sale contract, is one in which a buyer pays in full now for a product that the seller will deliver to him later. In the case of Salam, there is scholarly consensus that the goods need not be in the seller's possession, or even in existence at all, to be the subject of a sale. This makes sense when one considers that traditionally, Salam sales often financed agriculture, as when a farmer required capital to purchase seeds or other inputs in advance of planting and harvesting (Cuno 2006; Doumani 2006).

There are specific conditions as to how a Salam may be transacted — including the types of goods that may be traded with it. Scholars agree that goods can only be the subject of a Salam sale if they can be "precisely determined in terms of quality and quantity", yet "not particularised to a specific unit" (Ayub 2007:244; see also

Thomas *et al.* 2005:94). For example, a specified type, quality, and quantity of corn may be the subject of Salam (and may therefore be the subject of a loan contract), but a particular ear of corn may not. Such rules aim to eliminate uncertainty (Gharar) as to: (a) exactly what was lent, (b) whether equivalent goods will be available on the market at the time of delivery in the event that the borrower cannot produce the goods himself, and (c) whether the delivered goods are precisely equivalent to what was promised.

As technologies and economies of production have evolved through history, the kinds of goods that scholars have considered sufficiently standardised to serve as the subject of a Salam sale have changed. During the classical age of Islamic jurisprudence (1st–7th centuries A.H./7th–13th centuries C.E.), jurists debated whether items as diverse as cane, bread, honey, cheese, precious stones, musk, carpets, perfumes, shoes, bowls, fish, leopards, and even trained dogs were sufficiently standardised to be the subject matter of Salam (Ayub 2007:244). On occasion, scholars even argued that one kind of wheat was "Salam-able" but another not: Jurists ruled that Iraq wheat, Khorasan wheat, or Ferghana wheat could be sold through Salam because they came from regions that regularly produced wheat in sufficient quantities to supply markets reliably; but they averred that the wheat of Herat, which came only from that one city, could not be the subject of a Salam sale because it was not produced in sufficient quantity to ensure guaranteed circulation (Johansen 2006).

Today, however, mass production and the technologies of modern markets have made it easier to specify the characteristics of standardised goods with great certainty and to predict reliably that they will be available at a future date. Commodities of many types are accepted with a high degree of consensus as the subject of valid Salam contracts today. Indeed, the AAOIFI's standard for acceptable subject matter (Al-Muslam Fihi) of Salam includes not only "fungible goods (such as wheat and other cereals)", but "also … items of material value (such as livestock)" (AAOIFI 2007a:165), and even "the general usufruct of a particular asset, such as ... having the use of an aircraft or a ship for certain period". Nevertheless, the AAOIFI still rules out Salam on "anything for which the seller may not be held responsible, like land, buildings, or trees" and on "articles whose values change according to subjective assessment, like jewellery and antiques" (AAOIFI 2007a:165). Thus while the items that are "Salamable" have changed through history, the principles underlying their permissibility or impermissibility have remained static.

We now return to our original question: Can stocks be the subject of a loan contract? Some scholars argue yes, contending that different shares[8] in a corporation are fungible goods — that is, goods with homogeneous (Mithli) properties that make them freely exchangeable or replaceable (Dusuki 2008:206,207). This means they can be the subject matter of a Salam contract, and therefore of a loan contract as well.

Others say no. This includes the AAOIFI Shariah board, whose ruling focuses less on whether different shares are fungible items and more on the equivalence of shares compared over time — that is, whether a share in a company today can be considered equivalent to a share in the same company tomorrow. In ruling that it is impermissible to lend shares, the AAOIFI's Shariah board states:

> The basis for the impermissibility of lending the shares of corporations is that the share at the time of repayment — in consideration of what it represents — does not represent the same thing that it did at the time of lending due to the constant change in the assets of the corporation. (AAOIFI 2007b:390)

In the end, we face the question of just what a share of a corporation is. Is one share in a corporation fungible with another? And is a share

---

[8] By "different shares", I refer to shares of the same type, but merely with, say, different serial numbers. I am *not* referring to different types of common stock, or of common stock versus preferred stock, etc.

in January equivalent to a share in June? The ontology of shares is at issue here: do we conceive of a share as something uniform, standardised, fungible, and existing in the abstract universe of a traded market — in short, first and foremost as a *financial security*? Or do we conceive of it as a unique bundle of contractual rights that vest the shareholder with the ability to make decisions affecting a concrete, complex, and dynamic business operation with real assets and real employees — in other words, as a *participatory ownership stake*? "Western" securities law is generally untroubled by the Janus-faced nature of shares, but Islamic commercial jurisprudence must grapple with it.

Ontological dilemmas aside, however, the reality on the ground is that a large and relatively stable majority of prominent Shariah scholars active in Islamic finance today find stock lending — as practiced in conventional finance — to be problematic. For the time being, this makes its commercial adoption by Islamic financial institutions untenable.

Entanglement with Riba

A third potential problem with conventional short-selling as viewed from the Islamic perspective is that interest typically gets involved in the process. In a conventional short sale, when an investor borrows stock and then sells it, he or she must leave the full market value of the sold stock in a margin account with his or her broker, plus an additional margin requirement (under United States law, this is initially at least 50% of the short-sale value). The brokerage house will then use the money in this account to earn interest for itself. (Of course, if the brokerage house were willing to invest the money in the margin account in a Shariah-compliant way — e.g., by investing in Murabaha instead of in interest-bearing instruments — this problem could be avoided.)

Form versus Substance

A fourth potential problem with short-selling — whether conventional short-selling or *any* system that claims to replicate or approximate it in a Shariah-compliant way — is the meta-issue of "form versus substance". A few observers of Islamic finance argue that some, if not all, of the Islamic-finance industry's operations today are misguided because they simply reflect adherence to the letter of Islamic law at the expense of fulfilling its spirit (El-Gamal 2006a; see also Habil 2007 for a discussion of the tension within Islamic finance on this topic).

Mahmoud El-Gamal is an ardent expositor of this view, and he sees efforts to replicate short-selling as an example of what is wrong with Islamic finance today. In his view, Islam prohibits short-selling — not merely in form, but in substance. El-Gamal argues that while it may be easy to synthesise short sales from "Islamic" instruments, doing so makes "a mockery of Islam". He writes:

> *Every* contract can be 'Islamized' in the age of financial engineering [italics original]… It is a silly game. The distinction between contracts that are "now allowed in Islam" and those that aren't is only a function of who is willing to pay sufficient fees for the rent-a-jurists to certify an engineered product, and how high are the transaction costs of the reengineering. (El-Gamal 2006b)

Not surprisingly, El-Gamal's views raise the ire of many practitioners and Shariah scholars involved in the Islamic-finance industry. But while they may bristle at El-Gamal's strident language, they remain cognizant of the broader issue of form versus substance, which is the core of many legal debates — not only in Shariah and Fiqh, but in the history of Western law as well (Kennedy 1976).

Those in the industry have several responses to the argument that much of Islamic finance is founded on mere mechanical adherence to the letter of the law. Some assert that Islamic finance is a work in progress, and that taking imperfect steps in the direction of a holistic Islamic financial system is better than nothing. Others argue that Islamic financial institutions must offer products and services — like replicated short-selling — comparable to those their conventional counterparts offer, or else they will lose all but their most loyal customers. That, they argue, would render Islamic financial institutions unprofitable and bring the project of Islamic finance grinding to a halt. Still others contend that replicating short-selling is acceptable because that which Islam does not prohibit is permitted, and that Shariah is intended to make life easier, not to bring hardship. Still others contend that short-selling brings benefit to society by smoothing out speculative asset-price increases and imparting useful price information to the market.

Efforts to Construct a Shariah-Compliant Short Sale

So far, I have reviewed the many arguments made against allowing conventional short-selling in Islamic finance. Indeed, the vast majority of Shariah scholars interested in Islamic finance today consider conventional short-selling to be Haram.

The Market for An Islamic Alternative to Short-Selling: Islamic Hedge Funds and Islamic ETFs

However, demand for an Islamic alternative has grown in recent years, driven by the prospect of Islamic hedge funds and Islamic exchange-traded funds (ETFs). Why do hedge funds and ETFs need to short-sell? Hedge funds frequently engage in short-selling as part of long-short strategies and other market-neutral strategies. As hedge funds have become heavyweights of the conventional financial universe — with total global hedge-fund assets under management tripling between 2000 and 2007, reaching US$1.7 trillion by mid-2007

(Farrell *et al.* 2007:24) — Islamic-finance practitioners and investors have begun to envision Islamic hedge funds. Since 2006, a handful have launched. Islamic ETFs are proliferating as well: financial institutions from around the world have listed them on stock exchanges in Kuala Lumpur, Singapore, London, Zurich, Istanbul, and Abu Dhabi, with more sites on the way (Abu Bakar 2008). Islamic ETFs are keen to find an Islamic alternative to short-selling because conventional ETFs rely on short selling as an integral part of the creation and redemption of ETF creation units and shares (since the original stock shares deposited in a trust to form the ETF's underlying asset base are borrowed shares).

History of Efforts to Construct a Shariah-Compliant Short Sale

The history of efforts to implement Shariah-compliant shorting has been a back-and-forth one. At the end of 1995, Malaysia first introduced conventional regulated[9] short-selling using securities borrowing and lending (SBL). Shortly thereafter, the Malaysia Securities Commission began exploring Shariah-compliant means of shorting. Through the mid-1990s, it worked with Shariah scholars to develop an alternative based on Ijara (lease), which I discuss further below. Just as the Malaysia Securities Commission had come close to finalising its Ijara-based platform, however, the Asian financial

---

[9] "Regulated" means, among other things, that "naked" short selling is not allowed. A naked short sale is one in which the short-seller, before having borrowed the security or perhaps even ascertaining for sure that he can borrow it, commits to selling it. (The opposite of a naked short sale is a "covered" short sale — one in which the short-seller has already secured access to the security when he commits to selling it.) Most national regulatory authorities prohibit naked short-selling, although many — including for some years the U.S. Securities and Exchange Commission (SEC) — have had difficulty enforcing the ban in practice (Bris *et al.* 2004). In addition to prohibiting naked short sales, the Malaysia Securities Commission also imposes other regulatory requirements on short sales, such as limiting short-selling to specified stocks that meet liquidity requirements.

crisis struck. Facing a volatile stock market and capital flight, the
government of Prime Minister Mahathir Mohamad suspended all
short-selling at the end of 1997. Nevertheless, the Securities
Commission's Shariah board officially endorsed an Ijara-based form
of SBL in March 1998, despite the fact that it would not be implemented because all forms of SBL had been banned.

Through the 2000s, Islamic finance boomed worldwide.
Innovation proceeded apace as high oil prices and economic
growth channeled capital to Muslims in the Gulf, Southeast Asia,
and elsewhere. Liberalising national financial markets and the
emergence of an international Islamic-finance infrastructure also
bolstered double-digit annual increases in Shariah-compliant assets
(Warde 2010).

Inspired by the success of conventional hedge funds and
undaunted by the fact that many Shariah scholars frowned on the
idea, a few people began envisioning Islamic hedge funds. In 2001,
hedge-fund manager Eric Meyer met in the United States with
Shariah scholar Shaykh Yusuf Talal DeLorenzo and discussed the
possibility of an Islamic hedge fund. Out of this conversation
emerged Shariah Capital, a company of which Meyer is CEO and
DeLorenzo is chief Shariah officer and an executive director.
Shariah Capital provides technologies and advisory services to support hedge funds and other financial institutions seeking to be
Shariah-compliant. In 2008, Shariah Capital, together with prime
broker Barclays Capital, launched the Al Safi Trust Platform for
hedge funds. Adopted the same year by several Dubai-based funds,
the Al Safi platform employs an Arbun-based short-selling structure
that Shaykh DeLorenzo has endorsed. At the same time, other players have also been targeting the market for Islamic hedge funds.
Fimat, the prime-brokerage arm of France's Société Générale,
launched some of the earliest Islamic hedge funds at the end of
2006, employing a Salam-based short-selling structure (*Hedgeweek*
2008). And in 2009, Amiri Capital introduced a short-selling replication mechanism based on Wad as part of a push to establish

Shariah-compliant long-short equity funds and prime-brokerage services.

Meanwhile, the issue of short-selling had arisen yet again in Malaysia. In March 2006, the country's Securities Commission reintroduced conventional short-selling after a hiatus of more than eight years. Shortly thereafter, Bursa Malaysia (formerly the Kuala Lumpur Stock Exchange) began developing a Wad-based short-selling platform with the support of the Securities Commission and the approval of the Securities Commission's Shariah board, led by Aznan Hasan. Demand from Islamic ETFs was the strongest motivation, although Islamic hedge funds were an important driver as well. As of 2009, this platform is under development, with Bursa Malaysia chief executive Yusli Mohamed Yusoff publicly endorsing the project to the press (Liau 2009).

Based on this brief but eventful history of the "Islamic short sale", we can make two observations. First, it is clear that demand has been strong enough to elicit a number of very different approaches from industry players. Each has advantages and disadvantages relative to the others, as I discuss below. Second, it is worth noting that the impetus behind innovation differs in different parts of the world. While Islamic hedge funds have been driving short-selling innovation in the Gulf market, which has a high concentration of ultra-high-net-worth Islamic investors, Islamic ETFs have been the driver in Malaysia, where there are fewer ultra-high-net-worth investors but a solid and growing base of increasingly sophisticated small and medium-sized Islamic investors as well as a national government and regulatory authority committed to shepherding a robust Islamic financial architecture into being (Thani and Hassan 2009).

Attempts to Construct a Shariah-Compliant Short Sale

There are a number of ways to replicate a short sale with instruments already being used in the Islamic-finance industry. After reviewing how a conventional short sale works, this section describes potential and existing alternatives and evaluates advantages and disadvantages of each.

Conventional Short Sale

First, let us review how a conventional short sale works. (For simplicity's sake, the examples below leave out brokerage fees and other ancillary expenses.) Assume a hypothetical investor named Sharif wants to short-sell 100 shares of stock in XYZ Company. He currently owns no XYZ stock. Leila, another hypothetical investor, owns the stock. Leila, through a prime broker, lends 100 shares of XYZ stock to Sharif. Sharif immediately sells the stock, which is currently trading at RM40, receiving RM4,000 for the sale. Two weeks later, after XYZ has fallen to RM35 per share, he buys back 100 shares from the market and returns them to Leila, realising a profit of RM500.

Ijara-Based Structure

As early as the mid-1990s, the Malaysia Securities Commission looked to Ijara (Islamic lease[10]) as the basis for a Shariah-compliant alternative to conventional SBL. The mechanics of an Ijara-based short sale are simple: instead of Sharif borrowing a stock from Leila, he leases it from her. Sharif's rental payments to Leila compensate her for the privilege of using her stock. Just as in conventional SBL, Sharif returns the stock to Leila at the end of the lease term.

---

[10] More specifically, Ijara is the hiring or renting of an asset, a commodity, or labor to benefit from its usufruct (Ayub 2007:279). Ijara can also be thought of as a contract to purchase the usufruct that derives, over a specified period of time, from the asset, commodity, or labor (Abu Ghuddah n.d.).

The advantage of an Ijara-based short-sale system is that from a mechanical standpoint, it works just like conventional SBL. This makes it relatively easy to adapt an existing conventional SBL system into an Ijara-based one.

The stark disadvantage, however, is that Ijara-based short selling is very controversial from a Shariah perspective. At least two points of controversy arise. First, many scholars disapprove of the idea that Sharif may sell to a third party the stock that he is leasing from Leila. One of the defining characteristics of an Ijara is that "the leasing agency [in our case, Leila] must own the leased object for the duration of the lease" (Iqbal and Mirakhor 2007:84). As we have seen earlier, it is highly problematic to sell an asset owned by someone else. Moreover, "the Ijara contract is intended for utilization of the asset and not for consumption of the asset" (ibid.:85). Second, many jurists frown on allowing a financial asset to be the subject of an Ijara contract. Property and capital assets that can be utilised without being consumed — such as land, machinery, and houses — are common subjects of Ijara. The labor of, say, a doctor or a carpenter may also be the subject of Ijara (Ayub 2007:280). However, leasing "financial and monetary" assets raises eyebrows.

Nevertheless, the Malaysia Securities Commission's Shariah Advisory Council (SAC) approved Ijara on stocks in 1998 as a basis for the implementation of SBL. The SAC justified this through the principle of Istihsan (application of discretion in a legal decision) based on Maslahah (that which serves welfare) (Securities Commission Malaysia 2007:74). It argued that an exception should be made to allow the lessee ("Sharif") to sell the leased shares to a third party without nullifying the Ijara contract because this was not only beneficial to the original shareholder ("Leila") but also because it could "provide liquidity to the share market". In other words, making an exception to the normal rules of Ijara was acceptable because the outcome was good for the market.

Critics argued that turning thus to Istihsan and Maslahah established a slippery slope. If selling leased stocks was acceptable because it provided market liquidity, what else might be justified in the name of market liquidity?

Ironically, this debate remained essentially a legal and philosophical one, because SBL using Ijara never gained traction. Between 1997 and 2006, all SBL was suspended in Malaysia anyway. After 2006, regulated short-selling with SBL resumed, but Bursa Malaysia and the Malaysia Securities Commission began development of the Wad-based short-selling system shortly thereafter. The Ijara short-selling question faded into the background. For its part, Bank Negara Malaysia, the central bank, stated in 2009 in a draft of its Shariah parameters that shares of a company may not be the subject of Ijara (Bank Negara Malaysia 2009:9, Item 34).

Salam-Based Structure

The Salam sale, or Bay Al-Salam, is a forward sale. The basic concept of a Salam is to pay now and take delivery later. The buyer is required to pay in full at the time the contract is established.[11] At that time, the buyer and seller also fix the terms of delivery, such as the quantity and quality of goods, the mode of delivery, and the date of delivery. As discussed above, Salam is only applicable to certain goods, and has a long history of being used to finance agriculture as well as the production of other items — such as textiles (Cuno 2006; Doumani 2006) — in which it is useful to provide capital up front before production has occurred.

Earlier, I noted that Shariah scholars disagree about whether a share of a company may be the subject of a Salam contract. If one

---

[11] Some Shariah scholars consider it permissible, in some cases, to allow the buyer a brief window of time after the agreement of a *Salam* contract in which to pay the seller. AAOIFI, for example, writes: "The capital in a salam contract must be paid immediately at the place where the contract is concluded. However, as an exception to this ruling, payment may be delayed for two or three days at most" (AAOIFI 2007a:165).

does assume that a Salam sale on a share is valid, then it is easy to use Salam to approximate a short sale.

The most basic Salam-based alternative is even simpler than the conventional version in that no lending or borrowing takes place. Our hypothetical short-seller Sharif simply enters into a Salam contract to sell 100 shares of XYZ stock to Leila for future delivery. Leila gives Sharif RM4,000 today, paying the current market price of RM40 per share. Sharif agrees to deliver the 100 shares to Leila in two weeks. In two weeks, the price has fallen to RM35 per share. Sharif buys 100 shares of XYZ from the market and gives them to Leila. He realises a profit of RM500.

One advantage of a Salam-based alternative to conventional short-selling is that no securities borrowing and lending (SBL) is involved. If a streamlined Salam-based system were developed for matching stock users and stock suppliers, this could potentially give Salam-based shorting a technical advantage over SBL. At the moment, no such system has appeared on the market, but it is not impossible to envision. However, Salam-based shorting seems unlikely to enjoy a significant Shariah-compliance advantage over SBL. This is because, as discussed earlier, those scholars who consider stocks to be "Salam-able" are also likely to consider stocks valid for lending, while those who do not consider stocks to be Salam-able will probably not consider stocks valid for lending.

Salam-based shorting has at least two major disadvantages relative to other Shariah-compliant possibilities for replicating short-selling. First, as discussed, many scholars — including the members of AAOIFI's Shariah board — do not accept stocks as the basis of a Salam contract. However, some scholars do, such as the Shariah Advisory Council of the Malaysia Securities Commission (Securities Commission Malaysia 2009).[12] Yet even aside from the Shariah-compliance question,

---

[12] The Shariah Advisory Council (SAC) of the Malaysia Securities Commission ruled that trading shares under the Salam contract is permissible as long as: (a) the shares are not considered to be too specific (Muayyan) an item; (b) the category, type, and amount of the shares can be determined; and (c) the shares' date of delivery can be ascertained. (Securities Commission Malaysia 2009:2).

there is a major practical obstacle to widespread Salam-based short-ing, especially in stock exchanges. Note that in the example above, Leila (the stock supplier) had to pay Sharif (the short-seller) *up front* at the time the Salam contract was agreed. This is very different from a conventional short sale, in which Leila pays Sharif nothing. Even if one were somehow to avoid requiring a cash outlay by Leila, such as by having Leila enter into a simultaneous Salam with some middleman (e.g., a broker), the fact remains that someone (e.g., the broker) must pay Sharif RM4,000[13] up front when the Salam is written. While this does not necessarily rule out a Salam-based alter-native to conventional short-selling, it might pose a challenge to its widespread adoption on stock exchanges. Market participants may not be used to such a model, and existing IT systems and regulatory frameworks might have trouble adapting to it.

Nevertheless, financial institutions have found ways to offer Salam-based short-selling. Newedge (formerly Fimat), a joint ven-ture between French banking giants Société Générale and Calyon, launched a platform for Shariah-compliant hedge funds in 2005 incorporating Salam-based short-selling. A number of hedge funds based in Europe and the United States have signed up to use the platform. Newedge's global head of prime brokerage maintained that "although different solutions seem more acceptable for differ-ent regions, many Saudi scholars prefer the Salam contract for equities" (Davidson 2008). Permal has also managed a long/short Islamic hedge fund called Alfanar employing a Salam-based short-selling system. (It is important to note that Newedge and other

---

[13] In actuality, Leila (or the broker) would probably end up paying Sharif *less* than the full market value of RM4,000. When a Salam contract is written on a commod-ity (e.g., wheat), the Salam sales price is typically lower than the spot price for the same commodity because the seller (Sharif) receives payment up front but does not have to deliver until later. In the case of a Salam on stocks, this discount could serve as compensation to the stock supplier (i.e., Leila and/or her broker), akin to the fees that stock lenders receive in conventional short-selling.

institutions offering Salam-based short selling may or may not use the structure described above.)

Wad-Based Structures

At least two industry players have proposed structures that aim to replicate short-selling by using Wad (unilateral promise). The first is London-based Amiri Capital, which is launching the Amiri Equity Alternative Strategies Fund (AEAS), an Islamic fund of long-short equity fund managers. Newedge Group is the fund's prime broker, and Dar Al Istithmar its Shariah advisor. The Dar Al Isithmar Shariah board, which approved the AEAS Fund, includes Sheikh Hussain Hamid Hassan (chair), Ali Al Qaradaghi, Abdul Sattar Abu Ghuddah, Daud Bakar, and Aznan Hasan.

The AEAS Fund's short-sale replication mechanism involves two parties — AEAS and some counterparty — each entering into a Wad with the other to buy or sell stock in the event that the stock price moves in one direction or the other. Only one of the promised transactions will be exercised, since the price will either go up or down relative to the starting price, but not both. The mechanism is thus analogous to what conventional financiers call a synthetic short sale: buying a put option and writing (i.e., selling) a call option.

Meanwhile, Bursa Malaysia (the Malaysian stock exchange), with the oversight of the Malaysia Securities Commission, is developing (as of late 2009) a different mechanism to replicate short-selling using Wad. Although the initial impetus for development was demand from Islamic ETFs, the system may attract Islamic hedge funds as well.

There are two cornerstones of the system. The first cornerstone is that no lending and borrowing will take place. Instead, the "supplier" of stock (comparable to the stock lender in the conventional scenario) will actually sell the stock to a central facilitation agency

(CFA), which will then sell it on to the "user" of the stock (who is comparable to the "borrower" in the conventional scenario). Later, the user will sell the stock back to the CFA, which will then sell it back to the supplier. The Wad agreements serve to ensure that the user will sell the stock back to the CFA, and that the supplier will then buy the stock back from the CFA at prices and terms specified in advance.

The second cornerstone of the Bursa Malaysia system is that the Bursa itself will act as the CFA, and thus the counterparty, for all transactions. It will establish and manage the constantly changing database of the pool of stocks that suppliers are willing to offer, and then will operate a real-time bid-ask system to match these with the stocks that users request.

Let us revisit our hypothetical scenario. Sharif wants to short 100 shares of XYZ stock, which currently trades at RM40 per share. He puts in an electronic request to Bursa Malaysia's CFA system, which scans its database of potential suppliers and locates Leila, who is willing to supply 100 shares of XYZ. The CFA confirms the deal, automatically establishes the necessary Wad agreements, and begins executing the trade. First, Leila sells 100 shares to the CFA (Bay 1).[14] Delivery is immediate, but settlement is deferred, with the CFA paying Leila in monthly installments.[15] Next, the CFA sells the 100 shares on to Sharif (Bay 2). Again, delivery is immediate, but settlement is deferred into monthly payments. Both Bay 1 and Bay 2 are true sales that transfer ownership.[16] They are both executed at the price of

---

[14] Bay means "sale" in Arabic.

[15] These monthly installments are not equal monthly installments. Rather, they fluctuate based on the changing value of the stock's market price. Also, they depend on the maximum period over which the user may use the stock, which will be determined in advance by Bursa Malaysia and may be in the range of 18 months, 24 months, or some comparable period.

[16] In this sense, the Wad-based short sale is somewhat similar to a conventional repo (repurchase) agreement, in which a (usually fixed-income) security serves as collateral for a cash loan, with the security actually changing ownership rather than simply being lent.

RM40 per share, but in Bay 1, the CFA pays Leila a pre-determined markup (x%) that is distributed across the installments to compensate her for making shares available; and in Bay 2, Sharif pays the CFA a slightly higher markup (x% + ε%). The CFA retains the difference (ε%) as compensation for running the system. Sharif then sells the shares on the market for RM40 per share. All of the above happens virtually instantaneously.

Two weeks later, assume XYZ shares are trading at RM35. Sharif decides to cover his short position. He buys 100 shares of XYZ stock back from the market and notifies the CFA. As Wad 1 requires him to do, Sharif now sells the 100 shares back to the CFA at the price of RM40. As Wad 2 requires her to do, Leila now buys the 100 shares back from CFA, also at RM40. The transaction is complete.

An advantage of a Wad-based system is that while it does not involve stock borrowing and lending, it operates in a way similar enough to conventional SBL that it can be adapted from a conventional SBL system, as Bursa Malaysia is doing. Pricing under the Wad-based system at Bursa Malaysia, for example, will likely be the same as pricing for the conventional short-selling system.

One possible disadvantage is that not everyone agrees whether a Wad can be binding. In the Bursa Malaysia system, each Wad is a Wad Mulzim (binding unilateral promise): Wad *1* is Sharif's promise to sell XYZ shares back to the CFA when he is done with his short sale, and Wad *2* is Leila's promise to buy the shares from the CFA when the CFA wants to sell them back to her.

There are three main perspectives in the debate over whether Wad can be binding:

- The "non-binding view": Fulfillment of a unilateral promise, though commendable, is neither mandatory (Wajib) nor legally enforceable. Classical jurists endorsing this view include Imām Abu Hanifah (founder of the Hanifi school of jurisprudence), Imam Al-Shafii (founder of the Shafii school of jurisprudence), Imam Ahmad Ibn Hanbal (founder of the Hanbal school of jurisprudence), and several Maliki jurists (Uberoi *et al.* 2009a:1). A number of contemporary jurists echo this view; see Saudi scholar Rafic Yunus Al-Masri's clear exposition of it (Al-Masri 2002).

- The "binding view": Fulfillment of a unilateral promise is mandatory (Wajib) and incurs both moral and legal obligation, making it enforceable in court. This was the view of only a minority of classical jurists, but among their number were notable figures such as Samrah bin Jundab (a Companion of the Prophet), Umar Ibn Abd Al-Aziz (one of the most respected Umayyad caliphs), Hasan Al-Basri, Imam Bukhari (compiler of one of the great Hadith collections), and Ibn Arabi (the great medieval Iberian polymath).

- The "conditionally binding view": Although not normally binding, a unilateral promise becomes binding and potentially enforceable in court if it has caused the promisee to incur liabilities. The Islamic Fiqh Academy issued a Fatwa taking this position in December 1998, and many of the Fuqaha most prominent in the Islamic finance community today endorse this stance (Uberoi *et al.* 2009b).

The direction this debate takes will have a major impact on innovation strategies in Islamic finance. The binding view and the conditionally binding view make the Wad-based short sale possible, but the non-binding view rules it out.

Beyond just short-selling, the question of whether Wad can be binding has generated much discussion as Islamic financial institutions increasingly employ Wad as a structuring tool — in Murabaha products, Musharakah Mutanaqisah (diminishing partnership), Sukuk, cross-currency swaps, and Islamic derivatives. In one usage that garnered attention in Islamic finance circles, Deutsche Bank used Wad in 2007 to construct what is in effect a total return swap: clients invest in liquid Shariah-compliant assets whose returns are swapped for the returns on non-Shariah-compliant assets such as a hedge fund. The Shariah board that approved the structure was a

Who's Who of Islamic-finance luminaries: Hussain Hamed Hassan (chair), Ali Al Qaradaghi, Abdul Sattar Abu Ghuddah, Mohamed Elgari, and Daud Bakar. However, another prominent Shariah scholar, Shaykh Yusuf Talal DeLorenzo, directly questioned the product's authenticity in a public paper, arguing that while Wad itself may be "widely seen to comply with Shariah norms," "products that use a Wad to deliver returns from non-compliant investments" are unacceptable (DeLorenzo 2007). It is clear that the various uses of Wad continue to foster debate.

Although it is too early to say definitively how this debate will play out and whether Wad Mulzim (binding unilateral promise) will gain complete acceptance across the world of Islamic finance, the fact that Bursa Malaysia received no major Shariah-related objections from the international Shariah scholars at a 2008 International Islamic Capital Market Forum in Kuala Lumpur where it presented its plans to develop the Wad-based short sale is anecdotal evidence that the Islamic finance community may be heading toward acceptance.

Arbun-Based Structure

In addition to Salam and Wad, the Arbun (down payment, also known as "earnest money") sale is also being used to structure Islamic alternatives to short-selling. In an Arbun sale, a buyer makes a down payment when a sale is agreed, and is committed to pay the remainder later if and when he decides to take the goods. If the buyer decides not to take the goods, then he forfeits the down payment and must return the goods. In this regard, Arbun is similar to a conventional option contract. (See Billah 2003:72–83 for a discussion of the contract and the positions taken on it through history by jurists and schools of jurisprudence.)

In 2008, Shariah Capital, together with prime broker Barclays Capital, launched the Al Safi platform for hedge funds. Al Safi employs an Arbun-based short-selling structure that Shariah

Capital's chief Shariah officer Shaykh Yusuf Talal DeLorenzo has endorsed.

Shaykh DeLorenzo explains Shariah Capital's "Arboon Short Sale" in a white paper entitled "A Shariah Compliant Alternative to Selling Short with Borrowed Securities" (DeLorenzo 2008). Based on Shaykh DeLorenzo's explanation, it appears that in the Arboon Short Sale, the prime broker agrees to sell stock to the short-seller (an investment manager) at the quoted market price. The short-seller makes a down payment to the prime broker that is equal to the margin-account deposit that would have been made in a conventional short sale. As stipulated in a "Master Securities Arboon Sale Agreement", this down payment transfers ownership of the stocks to the short-seller. Now that he has ownership, the short-seller sells the stocks (through the prime broker) to some third party in the market at the market price. Then, at some time in the future, the short-seller decides to close out the transaction. He buys back the required number of shares from the market (again through his prime broker) and then returns them to the prime broker, who retains the down payment.

Since the specifics of Shariah Capital's Shariah-compliant short sale are not public and are based on a proprietary model, its mechanics may well differ from the theoretical Arbun-based structure outlined above. Indeed, the devil is often in the details when it comes to developing a Shariah-compliant short-sale alternative, particularly because of the challenge of simultaneously meeting Shariah requirements and government regulatory requirements. Shariah Capital CEO Eric Meyer has commented that while achieving Shariah compliance required "a great deal of intellectual capital", "the most demanding part" of bringing the Arboon Sale to market "was reconciling Shariah principles and precepts with the realities of U.S. Securities and Exchange Commission regulations that are based on the Securities Act of 1934 and the Investment Company Act of 1940" (Meyer 2006).

In general, an advantage of Arbun-based short-selling is that its mechanics are similar to those of a conventional short sale. For example, a parallel exists (albeit not an exact one) between the down payment in an Arbun sale and the margin deposit in a conventional short sale. And unlike in a Salam-based structure, the stocks in an Arbun-based structure can move in the same way as in a conventional short sale: first from the prime broker to the short-seller, then on to the market, and then from the market back to the short-seller and to the prime broker. These similarities may make an Arbun-based structure easier to understand for both clients and service providers and may render it more adaptable to the platforms that prime brokers already use for short sales.

Yet like the other structures discussed, Arbun-based short-selling may be potentially controversial from a Shariah perspective — depending whom you ask. Classical Fiqh is particularly critical of the Arbun sale. Through the history of jurisprudence, most scholars from the Maliki, Hanafi, and Shafii schools have held that Arbun is invalid. They refer to a Hadith included in Al-Muwatta', the monumental Hadith collection of Maliki school founder Imam Malik bin Anas, that reads

رسول الله صلى الله عليه وسلم نهى عن بيع العربان

Rasūl allāh ṣallá allāhu ʿalayhi wa-sallam nahá ʿan baÿ al-ʿurbān

The Messenger of God, peace be upon him, forbade ʿurban[17] sale (Malik Ibn Anas 1986).

Different scholars have taken different approaches to this Hadith, which is also recorded in the Sunan of Abu Daud and the Sunan of Ibn Majah, two of the other Hadith collections considered most important by Sunni Muslims (Abu Daud Sulayman Ibn Al-Ash'ath Al-Sijistani 1996; Ibn Majah 1998). Some have questioned its

---

[17] Urban, Arban, and Urbun are different Arabic spellings of the same word.

authenticity. A minority of classical scholars — largely Hanbalis, including Hanbali school founder Imam Ahmad Ibn Hanbal — have relied on a conflicting report saying that Umar bin al-Khattab (one of the Prophet's companions and the most powerful of the four Rashidun caliphs) himself practiced Arbun sale, and that Umar's son validated it (Kamali 2000:201). However, the historicity of that account has been questioned too.

In the face of conflicting historiographies, some prominent contemporary Fuqaha argue that Arbun sale should be accepted because they feel it can benefit people in the modern era. Among them is Yūsuf Al-Qaradawi, who asserts that the best course is to apply reason to present circumstances and permit Arbun so as to remove hardship and bring benefit to people (Kamali 2000:202; Al-Amine 2008:239). Another is Mustafá Al-Zarqa', who stresses the utility of Arbun to modern commerce (Al-Amine 2008:239).

Modern scholars and financial institutions have responded to some classical objections. One criticism of Arbun over the centuries has been that it may harbour Gharar (uncertainty) if it includes no time limit for contract cancellation. The Islamic Fiqh Academy addressed this issue by stipulating that every Arbun contract include a time limit for cancellation (Majis Majma Al-Fiqh Al-Islami Al-Duwali 1993) — a possibility that some classical Hanbali jurists raised (El-Gamal 2006a:91). The Fiqh Academy's decision has lent Arbun credibility. Indeed, Shaykh DeLorenzo cites the Fiqh Academy's 1993 decision accepting the use of Arbun by "modern Islamic banks and investment houses" (DeLorenzo 2008). However, some object that Arbun still contains Gharar because the seller does not know whether the buyer will conclude the sale (El-Gamal 2006a:91) — a questioning of the Shariah validity of the option concept itself.

Another potential issue with using Arbun to replicate a short sale as described above is that it is not in accord with the traditional usage of Arbun as a down payment. In the theoretical Arbun-based short sale above, if the short-seller is actually planning to complete the short sale, then he knows in advance that he will not be "keeping" the stocks on which he has made a down payment. He knows from the beginning that he will be returning them to the prime broker, forfeiting his deposit as the cost of making a short sale. He does not enter into the Arbun thinking that he probably — or even maybe — will later complete the transaction and buy the goods in full after making his initial down payment, but rather enters the contract knowing in advance that he will not accept the goods.

Conclusion

Efforts to develop Shariah-compliant short-selling alternatives are part of an ongoing wave of innovation in the Islamic finance industry that gained pace in the mid-2000s. This innovation wave, which we might call the "post-Sukuk" wave, has had multiple causes: high oil prices, deregulation, the internationalization of finance, the evolution of more robust national and international standard-setting frameworks for Islamic finance, and an increase in the number of scholars versed in both Fiqh and finance (Kahf 2004; Warde 2010). In addition to short-selling alternatives, it has encompassed efforts to develop Islamic derivatives and hedging techniques (e.g., profit-rate swaps, Islamic currency swaps and forwards, Islamic options), new types of Shariah-compliant securities (e.g., securities referenced to commodities, equities, funds, and baskets), Islamic credit cards, Islamic mortgages, and novel project-finance and trade-finance structures — to name a few.

What is the Status of the Market?

For the moment, the market for Shariah-compliant alternatives to short-selling is nascent but growing fast. As this chapter has discussed, several offerings are available. Most target Islamic hedge funds as their primary client base: these offerings include Amiri Capital's Wad-based structure, Newedge's Salam-based structure, and Shariah Capital's Arbun-based structure. Meanwhile, Bursa Malaysia, the Malaysian stock exchange, is targeting Islamic ETFs using a Wad-based structure incorporated into the workings of the exchange itself.

Thus the fledgling market for short-sale replication is somewhat bifurcated by both client base and geography. On one side are the players targeting Islamic hedge funds. They are based in the United Kingdom (Amiri Capital), continental Europe (Newedge), and the United States (Shariah Capital). Their clients are primarily headquartered (though not necessarily domiciled) in the United States and the United Kingdom, for that is where the majority of Islamic hedge funds are based at the moment. These funds' investors reside largely in the GCC, although some come from Southeast Asia and elsewhere in the Islamic world. Meanwhile, on the other side of the market for short-sale replication is Bursa Malaysia, the lone exchange-based contender, which will target Islamic ETFs in particular.

What should Potential Customers Keep in Mind?

Investors and fund managers choosing a short-selling platform must realise that their options are not mere variations on a single theme, as competing financial products often are, but that they differ in structurally fundamental ways. Even though all have been developed with the oversight and active involvement of some of the world's most prominent Shariah scholars, not all will necessarily be popular with every Shariah expert. That said, it would be difficult to argue that one of the structures described above is clearly more universally accepted than the others; differences of opinion arise on a product-by-product, scholar-by-scholar, and Madhhab-by-Madhhab basis. Therefore, investors and fund managers should take the time to understand each structure well and consider whose opinions — past and present — are most important to them.

Beyond Shariah considerations, investors and fund managers should evaluate which options are best suited to the legal enviroment in which they do business. Developers of Shariah-compliant platforms to replicate short-selling attest that while the basic structures they employ — as shown above — may be simple, harmonising Shariah requirements with securities law adds tremendous complexity. It is therefore critical that investors and fund managers "do their home-work" to make sure the platform they choose will function properly in the jurisdictions in which they are domiciled and do business.

In particular, investors and fund managers should explore what contingencies are built into the platform for unexpected mishaps. Platforms replicating short-selling, like other complex legal structures, prove their mettle under extreme or unusual market conditions. Aware of this, platform developers expend great effort ensuring that they have Shariah-compliant, legally sound structures to deal with infrequent but potentially critical situations. Amiri Capital, for example, spent an entire year of its two-and-a-half-year product-development process developing a netting structure for its short-sale replication mechanism that could complete the physical transfer of assets required by Shariah even in the event that one of the counterparties to the transaction went bankrupt (Shah 2009). Other players likewise incorporate contingency plans for unlikely events into their platforms.

Where is the Market Headed?

Prognosticating about finance is treacherous. Nevertheless, I hazard some thoughts about the future of Shariah-compliant alternatives to short selling. First, the broad trend among Shariah scholars toward gradual acceptance of techniques to replicate short selling is more likely to continue than not. None of the replication techniques

I have discussed has the acceptance of *every* Shariah scholar, but this has not kept replicated short-selling from going from being a pipe dream to being increasingly accepted in half a decade. This is due in part to providers' efforts to integrate leading scholars into their product-development processes. But is also due to an increase in the visibility of Islamic finance and a proliferation of training and certification programs in the past few years. This trends have made Shariah scholars in general more familiar and more comfortable with complex financial transactions and instruments. In other words, as the intellectual enterprises of Fiqh and financial structuring have spent more time brewing together in the cauldrons of Islamic financial institutions, new techniques like Islamic short-sale replication have bubbled to the surface.

A second and contrasting point, however, is that a ruling against short-sale replication by one or two leading Shariah scholars could dampen the market's prospects considerably. In 2007, Sheikh Taqi Usmani presented a paper at the meeting of the AAOIFI Shariah council that suggested the structures employed by about 85 percent of Sukuk are un-Islamic (Usmani 2007). This threw the Sukuk industry into turmoil and sent prices tumbling. The possibility exists that a prominent jurist could rule similarly against some of the short-sale replication techniques discussed above, or even against the idea of Shariah-compliant short-sale replication *tout court.*

Yet while that may sound like a nightmare scenario to providers of short-sale replication, such an event could prove beneficial in the long run. Nothing would focus more energy and attention on developing novel structures, and on improving existing ones, than an unexpected jolt to the business of short-sale replication.

Third, the vitality of the market for replicated short-selling will depend on macroeconomic health in the GCC and Southeast Asia. In the GCC, the global financial crisis that began in 2008 popped speculative bubbles in property and equity markets. The capital pouring into Islamic investment vehicles, including the nascent Islamic hedge-fund sector, slowed to a trickle. If global recovery from the present crisis is robust and global oil demand is sustained in the medium term, GCC investors are likely to regain confidence and feel warmer about Islamic hedge funds. That would strengthen demand for Shariah-compliant short-sale alternatives.

In Southeast Asia — which has not been struck as hard by the global crisis as North America, Europe, and the Gulf — sustained stable growth over the 2010–2015 horizon is also the formula most likely to attract investors to Islamic hedge funds and Islamic ETFs. Moreover, unless Southeast Asia experiences an economic meltdown worse than the 1997–1998 crisis, governments are unlikely to halt short-selling (Islamic or otherwise) the way Prime Minister Mahathir Mohamad's administration did in Malaysia in 1997. In Malaysia in particular, the state now views Islamic finance as a lever of economic growth and has been an enthusiastic champion of Islamic-finance infrastructure and innovation (Muhyiddin 2009), making another government "crackdown" on conventional short-selling or replicated short-selling unlikely.

Fourth, while it is possible that the market for Islamic short-selling alternatives could converge toward a single standardised structure, convergence appears unlikely in the short or medium term. Competitors' claims aside, there is no single replication structure that is clearly superior to the others along one dimension or other, whether that be Shariah compliance, regulatory harmonisation, tax considerations, or economic efficiency. This contrasts with the case of Sukuk, for example, in which some structures — like Sukuk Al-Ijara — are frequently described as more "orthodox" and less controversial than others.

The fact that short-selling can be replicated in a number of different ways also suggests that the market for it will continue to grow. Replicating short-selling using Islamic contracts and instruments is not difficult from a theoretical perspective (see, for example, Hassan and Lewis 2007:90–95). The challenge stems from the need to harmonise Shariah with regulatory requirements, tax considerations, and legal contingency plans. Seeing multiple avenues open in front

of them, new competitors are likely to continue bringing new structures onto the market in the next decade as the Islamic finance
industry grows.

Meanwhile, as new players enter, existing players will expand
their offerings into new markets. Bursa Malaysia, for example, will
be well positioned to offer its exchange-based short-sale replication
system to other stock exchanges if the system succeeds in Kuala
Lumpur. (In this regard, Bursa Malaysia will enjoy an advantage relative to other exchanges that would seek to develop their own
in-house Islamic short-sale replication system because it has bene-
fited from strong government support and significant coordination
among Bursa Malaysia, Securities Commission Malaysia, and the
central bank, Bank Negara Malaysia.) In short, innovation in this
field is just beginning, and Islamic short-selling alternatives will
likely become more widespread in the next decade.

Is All This a Good Thing?

The question may long remain, however, whether Islamic short-sale
replication is in line with Maqasid Al-Shariah — the objectives of
Islamic law. It is one thing to say that a technique used to replicate
short-selling complies with the letter of Islamic commercial law
(Fiqh Al-Muamalat), but it is another thing to show that the benefits
(Masalih) it engenders outweigh the evils (Mafasid). The hope is
that complying with the letter of the law — however interpreted —
does indeed lead to social good and to outcomes consonant with
Maqasid Al-Shariah. However, when the letter of the law comes to us
via juristic interpretations formulated in the classical age of Islamic
jurisprudence but the substantive impact of financial instruments is
felt in a twenty-first-century economy, the possibility arises that
adherence with the letter of the law and with its spirit may not necessarily guarantee each other. In a globalised economic system
founded on complex and intertwined financial markets behaving in

unpredictable ways, it may be rash to assume that adhering to classical juristic rules insures us against the deleterious effects that even "Shariah-compliant" financial structures could have, whether at the individual level or the systemic.

Ultimately, we may have to wait and see what kinds of effects Islamic short-sale replication has. The history of conventional short-selling is instructive here. On one hand, short-sellers have been vilified for centuries as vultures who undermine market confidence, being blamed as early as the 17th century for financial crises (De Marchi and Harrison 1994; Ferguson 2008). On the other hand, many economists insist that short-sellers provide information that helps smooth out markets, acting as one of the few safety valves to relieve upward price pressure driven by "irrational exuberance" during speculative asset bubbles (see, inter alia, Figlewski 1981; Jones and Lamont 2002).

What about Islamic short-sale alternatives? Do they have positive, neutral, or negative effects on the individuals that use them and the markets and societies in which they are used? What criteria should be used to evaluate them? Do Shariah experts have the breadth of knowledge necessary to evaluate them, or is a wider dialogue needed (Siddiqi 2007)? What can religious texts, and their classical and contemporary interpretations, reveal about how to achieve the Maqasid Al-Shariah as societies, markets, and technologies change? After all, debates over what is Haram and what is Halal have always been linked to changes in societies, markets, and technologies — as the history of the Salam contract shows, for example. We should not be surprised if debates over Islamic short-sale replication continue.

References

AAOIFI (2007a). Shari'a standard no. 10: Salam and parallel salam. In *Shari'a Standards*, pp. 161–176. Manama, Bahrain: Accounting and Auditing Organization for Islamic Financial Institutions.

AAOIFI (2007b). Shari'a standard no. 21: Financial paper (shares and bonds). In *Shari'a Standards*, pp. 375–395. Manama, Bahrain: Accounting and Auditing Organization for Islamic Financial Institutions.

Abu Bakar, D (2008). More Islamic ETFs in the works. *Islamic Finance Asia*, September, 31–33.

Abu Daud Al-Sijistani (1996). *Sunan Abī Dā'ūd*, 1st Ed. Beirut: Dār al-Kutub al-'Ilmīyah.

Abu Ghuddah, AS n.d. Ijarah (Lease).

Al-Alwani, TJ (2005). *Issues in Contemporary Islamic Thought*. Herndon, VA: International Institute of Islamic Thought.

Al-Amine, M-BM (2008). *Risk Management in Islamic Finance: An Analysis of Derivatives Instruments in Commodity Markets*. Leiden: Brill.

Al-Islāmbūlī, AMK (2005). Lā tabī mā laysa ʿindaka: Muḥāwalah li-qirā'at al-naṣṣ.

Al-Masri, RY (2002). The binding unilateral promise (Wad) in Islamic banking operations: Is it permissible for a unilateral promise (Wad) to be binding as an alternative to a proscribed contract? *Journal of King Abdulaziz University: Islamic Economics*, 15, 29–33.

Al-Shāfiī, MI (1940). *Al-Risālah*, AM Shākir (ed.). Cairo: Muṣṭafá Al-Bābī Al-Ḥalabī.

Archer, S and RAA Karim (2002). *Islamic Finance: Innovation and Growth*. London: Euromoney Books and AAOIFI.

Ayub, M (2007). *Understanding Islamic Finance*. Hoboken, NJ: John Wiley & Sons.

Bank Negara Malaysia (2009). Draft of Shariah Parameter Reference 2: Ijarah Contract (SPR2).

Billah, MM (2003). *Islamic Law of Trade and Finance: A Selection of Issues*, 2nd Ed. Petaling Jaya, Selangor, Malaysia: Ilmiah Publishers.

Bris, A, WN Goetzmann and N Zhu (2004). Efficiency and the bear: Short sales and markets around the world. *Yale ICF Working Paper No. 02–45; EFA 2003 Annual Conference; AFA 2004 San Diego Meetings; 14th Annual Conference on Financial Economics & Accounting*.

Clunie, J and T Ying (2006). *Developing Short-Selling on the Mainland Chinese Equity Markets*. Edinburgh: Centre for Financial Markets Research, The Management School, University of Edinburgh.

Cuno, KM (2006). Contrat salam et transformations agricoles en basse Égypte à l'époque ottomane. *Annales*, 61, 925–940.

Davidson, R (2008). Meeting all tastes. *Risk*, September 1.

De Marchi, N and P Harrison (1994). Trading "in the wind" and with guile: The troublesome matter of the short selling of shares in seventeenth-century Holland. In *Higgling: Transactors and Their Markets in the History of Economics*, N De Marchi and MS Morgan (eds.), pp. 47–65. Durham, NC: Duke University Press.

DeLorenzo, YT (2008). A Shariah compliant alternative to selling short with borrowed securities. http://zulkiflihasan.wordpress.com/2008/12/29/a-shariah-compliant-alternative-to-selling-short-with-borrowed-securities-by-shaiykh-yusuf-talal-de-lorenzo/ [Accessed 8 October 2009].

DeLorenzo, YT (2007). The total returns swap and the Shariah Conversion Technology stratagem. http://www.dinarstandard.com/finance/DeLorenzo.pdf [Accessed 8 October 2009].

Doumani, B (2006). Le contrat salam et les relations ville-campagne dans la Palestine ottomane. *Annales*, 61, 901–924.

Dusuki, AWD (2008). *Islamic Finance: An Old Skeleton in a Modern Dress*. Kuala Lumpur: International Shari'ah Research Academy for Islamic Finance.

El-Gamal, MA (2006a). *Islamic Finance: Law, Economics, and Practice*. Cambridge, UK: Cambridge University Press.

El-Gamal, MA (2006b). Short Selling and the Travesty of Islamic Finance. *Islam and Economics*. http://elgamal.blogspot.com/2006/09/short-selling-and-travesty-of-islamic.html [Accessed 8 October 2009].

Farrell, D, S Lund, E Gerlemann and P Seeburger (2007). *The New Power Brokers: How Oil, Asia, Hedge Funds, and Private Equity are Shaping Global Capital Markets*. McKinsey Global Institute. http://www.mckinsey.com/MGI/.

Ferguson, N (2008). *The Ascent of Money: A Financial History of the World*. New York: Penguin.

Figlewski, S (1981). The informational effects of restrictions on short sales: Some empirical evidence. *The Journal of Financial and Quantitative Analysis* 16, 463–476.

Fung, JKW and AKW Fung (1997). Mispricing of index futures contracts: A study of index futures versus index options. *The Journal of Derivatives*, 5, 37–45.

Habil, A (2007). The tension between legal values and formalism in contemporary Islamic finance. In *Integrating Islamic Finance into the Mainstream: Regulation, Standardization and Transparency*. Cambridge, MA: Harvard Law School.

Hassan, K and M Lewis (2007). *Handbook of Islamic Banking*. Cheltenham: Edward Elgar.

Hedgeweek (2008). Shariah compliance poses challenge to Middle East managers. January 30.

Ibn Mājah, MY (1998). S*unan Ibn Mājah*, 1st Ed. Beirut: Dār al-Jīl.

Iqbal, Z and A Mirakhor (2007). A*n Introduction to Islamic Finance*. Singapore: John Wiley & Sons (Asia).

Johansen, B (2006). Le contrat salam: Droit et formation du capital dans l'Empire abbasside. A*nnales*, 61, 863–899.

Jones, CM and OA Lamont (2002). Short-sale constraints and stock returns. *Journal of Financial Economics*, 66, 207–239.

Kahf, M (2004). Islamic banks: The rise of a new power alliance of wealth and shari'a scholarship. In *The Politics of Islamic Finance* pp. 17–36. Edinburgh: Edinburgh University Press.

Kamali, MH (2000). *Islamic Commercial Law: An Analysis of Futures and Options*. Petaling Jaya, Malaysia: Ilmiah Publishers.

Kennedy, D (1976). Form and substance in private law adjudication. *Harvard Law Review*, 89, 1685–1778.

Khan, MA (1983). *Issues in Islamic Economics*. Lahore: Islamic Publications.

Liau, Y-S (2009). Islamic short-selling can develop market: Bourse. *Reuters,* April 16.

Lo, AW and AC MacKinlay (2001). A *Non-Random Walk Down Wall Street*. Princeton, NJ: Princeton University Press.

Majis Majma Al-Fiqh Al-Islami Al-Duwali (1993). Qirār raqm: 72 (3/8) bi-sha'n baÿ al-ᶜarbūn. *Majallat Al-Majmaᶜ (Journal of the OIC Fiqh Academy)*, 1, 641.

Mālik A (1986). A*l-Muwaṭṭa'*. Cairo: Dār Iḥyā' Al-Kutub Al-ᶜArabīyah.

Meyer, E (2006). The other side of the coin: Pioneer of the structuring of Islamic hedge funds Eric Meyer, president and CEO of Shariah Capital, responds. *Banker Middle East*, October, 41.

Muhyiddin, Y (2009). Speech on "Malaysia's policy on the liberalization of the services sector and its impact on the economy" at the IFN 2009 Issuers and Investors Asia Forum, 3 August 2009, Kuala Lumpur.

Ryding, KC (2005). A *Reference Grammar of Modern Standard Arabic*. Cambridge, UK: Cambridge University Press.

Schoon, N (2009). *Islamic Banking and Finance*. London: Spiramus Press.

Securities Commission Malaysia (2007). *Resolutions of the Securities Commission Shariah Advisory Council*, 2nd ed. Kuala Lumpur: Securities Commission Malaysia.

Securities Commission Malaysia (2009). Islamic alternative to short selling. *Malaysian ICM: Quarterly Bulletin of Malaysian Islamic Capital Market by the Securities Commission,* 4, 2–5.

Shah, BP (2009). Interview with author.

Siddiqi, MN (2007). Shari'a, economics, and the progress of Islamic finance: The role of shari'a experts. In *Integrating Islamic Finance into the Mainstream: Regulation, Standardization and Transparency.* Cambridge, MA: Harvard Law School.

Thani, NN and MH Hassan (2009). Interview by author.

Thomas, A, B Kraty, M Hussain and S Cox (2005). Salam. In *Structuring Islamic Finance Transactions,* pp. 93–101. London: Euromoney Books.

Uberoi, P, R Chatterji and D Bidar (2009a). Promises on the Horizon: An Introduction to the Wa'ad. www.allenovery.com/AOWeb/binaries/52774.PDF [Accessed 8 October 2009].

Uberoi, P, R Chatterji and D Bidar (2009b). The wa'ad on the Street. *Risk,* August 1.

United States Code of Federal Regulations (2009). Title 17: Commodity and Securities Exchanges. Regulation SHO — Regulation of Short Sales. § 242.200: Definition of "short sale" and marking requirements. (69 FR 48029, Aug. 6, 2004, as amended at 72 FR 36359, July 3, 2007; 72 FR 45557, Aug. 14, 2007.)

Usmani, MT (2007). Sukuk and their Contemporary Applications. Manama, Bahrain: Accounting and Auditing Organization for Islamic Financial Institutions http://www.alqalam.org.uk/UserFiles/File/Mufti%20Taqi%20sukuk%20paper.pdf [Accessed 8 October 2009].

Venardos, AM (2006). *Islamic Banking & Finance in South-East Asia: Its Development & Future,* 2nd Ed. Hackensack, NJ: World Scientific.

Warde, I (2010). *Islamic Finance in the Global Economy,* 2nd Ed.

Zaher, TS. and MK Hassan (2001). A comparative literature survey of Islamic finance and banking. *Financial Markets, Institutions & Instruments,* 10, 155–199.

Zaky, NZDY (1992). *An Islamic Perspective of Stock Market: An Introduction.* SG Abod (ed.). Kota Bharu: Dian Darulnaim.